GITANJALI REBORN

Some Books from Social Science Press and Aurum Books

Gandhi: Anti-biography of a Great Soul (HB)
MICHAEL DE SAINT-CHERON

Shades of Difference: Selected Writings of Rabindranath Tagore wth Audio Visual Material, *Tagore and His World* (HB)
Edited by RADHA CHAKRAVARTY

Calcutta: The Stormy Decades (HB)
Edited by TANIKA SARKAR AND SEKHAR BANDYOPADHYAY

Dalit Women: Honour and Patriarchy in South India (HB)
CLARINDA STILL

Tamil Brahmans: The Creation of a Middle-Class Caste (HB)
CJ FULLER AND HARIPRIYA NARASIMHAN

Persistence of Poverty in India (HB)
Edited by NANDINI GOOPTU AND JONATHAN PARRY

Savage Attack: Tribal Insurgency in India (HB)
Edited by CRISPIN BATES AND ALPA SHAH

The Year of Blood: Essays on the Revolt of 1857 (HB)
RUDRANGSHU MUKHERJEE

The Autobiography of a Revolutionary in British India (HB)
KALI GHOSH

4 Victoria Terrace: Memoirs of a Surgeon (HB)
SUBIR K. CHATTERJEE

The Many Worlds of Sarala Devi: A Diary
Translated by SUKHENDU RAY and
The Tagores and Sartorial Styles: A Photo Essay (HB)
MALAVIKA KARLEKAR

Viramma: Life of a Dalit (PB)
VIRAMMA, JOSIANE RACINE, AND JEAN-LUC RACINE

Everyday Nationalism: Women of the Hindu Right (HB)
KALYANI DEVAKI MENON

Marriage, Love, Caste & Kinship Support (HB)
Lived Experiences of the Urban Poor in India
SHALINI GROVER

Religious Division and Social Conflict: The Emergence of Hindu Nationalism in Rural India (PB)
PEGGY FROERER

Literature and Nationalist Ideology: Writing Histories of Indian Languages(PB)
HANS HARDER

The Everyday State and Society in Modern India (PB)
Edited by CJ FULLER AND VERONIQUE BENEI

Economics and Its Stories (HB)
AMAL SANYAL

Telecommunications Industry in India: State Business and Labour in a Global Economy(HB)
DILIP SUBRAMANIAM

Cultural History of Modern India (PB)
Edited by MEENAKSHI KHANNA

Delhi: Ancient History (PB)
Edited by UPINDER SINGH

Income Poverty and Beyond Human Development in India
Edited by RAJA J CHELLIAH AND R SUDERSHAN

The Politics of the Pharmaceutical Industry and Access to Medicines: World Pharmacy and India (HB)
Edited by HANS LOGREN

SERIES: EVERYDAY LIFE OF POLITICAL STRUGGLES

Windows into a Revolution: Ethnographies of Maoism in India and Nepal (HB)
Edited by ALPA SHAH AND JUDITH PETTIGREW

Rebels from the Mud Houses: Dalits and the Making of the Maoist Revolution in Bihar (HB)
GEORGE KUNNATH

Unruly Hills: Nature and Nation in India's North-East (HB)
BENGT G. KARLSSON

SERIES: GERMAN WRITINGS ON INDIA AND SOUTH ASIA

'When the war began we heard of several kings': South Asian Prisoners in World War I Germany (HB)
Edited by FRANSIZKA ROY, HEIKE LIEBAU AND RAVI AHUJA

Cultural Encounters in India The Local Co-Workers of the Tranquebar Mission, 18th-19th centuries (HB)
HEIKE LIEBAU

'Everwhere is Becoming the Same'? Regulating IT-work between India and Germany (HB)
NICOLE MAYER-AHUJA

SERIES: FRENCH WRITINGS ON INDIA AND SOUTH ASIA

Scholars and Prophets: Sociology of India from France in the 19th and 20th Centuries (HB)
ROLAND LARDINOIS

Tocqueville in India (HB)
JEAN ALPHONSE BERNARD

AURUM BOOKS

Sabotage (PB)
ANITA AGNIHOTRI
Translated by ARUNAVA SINHA

Opium Poppy (PB)
HUBERT HADDAD
Translated by RENUKA GEORGE

Forthcoming SSP

Much Ado Over Coffee: The Indian Coffee House Then and Now (HB)
BHASWATI BHATTACHARYA

Forthcoming Aurum Books

Revolutionary Passions (HB)
HAMIT BOZARSLAN, GILLES BATAILLON AND CHRISTOPHE JAFFRELOT
Translated by SOMA DATTA GUPTA

Why Me? (HB)
Edited by DUBET ET AL

GITANJALI REBORN

William Radice's Writings on Rabindranath Tagore

Edited by

MARTIN KÄMPCHEN

SOCIAL SCIENCE PRESS

Published by

Esha Béteille
Social Science Press
69 Jor Bagh, New Delhi 110003

ISBN 978-93-83166-15-2

Set in Adobe Garamond Pro
Typeset by Manmohan Kumar, Delhi 110035
Printed by Sumit Advertising,
2, DLF (part) Industrial Area, Moti Nagar,
New Delhi-110 015

To my dear wife Elizabeth, truest of guides.

William Radice

Contents

Preface

In the years 2011 to 2014, Rabindranath Tagore celebrated a global presence not seen since his lifetime while his popularity was at its peak. The reason was three major anniversaries which followed each other in quick succession: Tagore's 150th birth anniversary in 2011, the 100th anniversary of the publication of the English *Gitanjali* in 2012, and the 100th anniversary of the Nobel Prize in 2013. India and all countries connected with India globally felt obliged to make the best of this auspicious coincidence. Indeed, a multitude of conferences, seminars, festivals, performances were lined up. Rabindranath's books were republished, translated, films produced and exhibitions of his paintings held all over the world. There were a few people—experts and lovers of Rabindranath Tagore—who were riding the crest of such enormous activity. One of them was William Radice.

From 2010 to the later part of 2013 his presence in Tagore events became almost obligatory. He travelled through three continents tirelessly—Asia, Europe and America—to talk about his poet whom he had studied, translated, and lectured about, since four decades. Clearly, he became the western face of Tagore scholarship and of Tagore values. Like Rabindranath went around the world to spread the message of peace and international understanding in the years between the two World Wars, so William Radice travelled tirelessly to spread his love and fascination for Tagore. The same missionary enthusiasm! I believe, William did not refuse a single invitation if the dates did not clash.

He is singularly equipped for such discipleship. He had learnt Bengali as a young man in London and started to read Rabindranath's poems soon after being able to read Bengali at all. Being a poet himself, he succumbed to the urge of translating Rabindranath almost immediately. With translating Tagore's poetry, William found his true fulfillment as a poet and creative person, although he has produced not less than ten volumes of his own poetry to date. William Radice became Lecturer of Bengali at London University which gave him the opportunity to share his knowledge and love for the poet with his students. The watershed event was however the publication of his *Selected Poems* of Rabindranath Tagore by Penguin Books UK in 1985.

All of a sudden Tagore rose from the proverbial ashes like a phoenix. Besides Rabindranath's own well-known prose versions of his Bengali poetry, there had been other translations in English, mostly by well-meaning and scholarly followers and associates. They were in prose, many inaccurate, rather condensed versions of the originals and not reflecting their literary greatness. Now here was a man, a poet himself, who transformed Rabindranath's poems into English poems and still was philologically accurate. William told the world that poetic magic can be translated.

Ever since the *Selected Poems* went into several editions, from 1995, including in India, it became the object of discussion, praise, criticism and gave rise to other, similarly worthy, translations by others. Just as Tagore appeared on the global scene with one single book, *Gitanjali*, so he was resurrected, for non-Bengali readers, by one single book, the *Selected Poems*. William Radice later translated a selection of Tagore's short stories, his short, aphoristic poems, two plays, and finally his Bengali *Gitanjali*. We will read a great deal about William's elaborate *tour de force* in this collection.

William Radice's *Gitanjali* translation appeared in 2011, in time for the birth-anniversary celebrations. William rightly felt that he was successful in analysing and exposing the poet W. B. Yeats' considerable flaws in the editing of the English *Gitanjali*. He was able to prove that Yeats had revised Tagore's *Gitanjali* manuscript in such a way that it, to a considerable extent, falsified Tagore's deeper inspirations and intentions.

In the years 2011 to 2013, William Radice travelled from event to event to declare the damage caused by Yeats' revision of the English *Gitanjali* and to explain how he, in his new book, has been able to demonstrate the true greatness of the Indian poet by reconstructing the original manuscript and offering his own modern verse translation. In our collection of lectures we will see him returning to this book in almost every text.

Radice's translation of *Gitanjali* is without doubt a great contribution to literature, to Tagore literature in particular. Yet it remains conspicuous by the silence which still surrounds it.

In this collection we witness William Radice at his best. He transcends his scholarship and dares to become personal and emotional. His oratorical powers are used to declare his love and admiration for Rabindranath, especially his poems and songs. We have the William Radice who speaks up, gives evidence, tries to convince and collect fellow admirers. Observe how his fertile mind throws up new ideas on Rabindranath, new perspectives and points to ponder on in every single lecture! Self-possessed as poets tend to be, he reveals how Rabindranath Tagore has possessed him all along. In 2011, William Radice turned 60 years, and appropriately these lectures were an opportunity for him to take stock, to look back at what he had accomplished.

In May 2013, he met with an accident from which he has recovered admirably. But he has chosen, for the time being, to lead a retired and somewhat reclusive life with his family in England.

When I offered to William Radice to edit his lectures he readily agreed and sent me a mass of files. Sifting through them, I have selected and edited the nineteen lectures and essays presented in this book. William Radice and I have known each other since the mid-1980s. He was the major inspiration for my own translations of Rabindranath from Bengali into German. We have been friends, have travelled together, been present together in meetings in India, Germany, England and Scotland. Almost every year we met, corresponding and collaborating all the time. It was only natural that I would take up the editing of this volume. Many lectures have been abridged to avoid repetitions. Sometimes they could not be eclipsed totally for fear of destroying the context and the flow. In most cases, I have been able to ascertain where each lecture was delivered or where an essay was published. This has been noted at the end of the text. We thank the publishers of already printed essays for their permission to reprint them.

I thank the publisher, Esha Béteille, for her competent and enthusiastic participation in preparing this book. And my gratitude to Chandana Dey for her reassuring support towards the end. We are grateful to Somnath Ghosh for his imaginative cover design.

Martin Kämpchen, Santiniketan

Bibliographical note

The following books have been mentioned and quoted from frequently. Hence we use only short titles:

Selected Poems
Rabindranath Tagore: *Selected Poems*. Translated by William Radice. Penguin Books UK, London 1985; Penguin Books India, New Delhi 1995.

Selected Short Stories
Rabindranath Tagore: *Selected Short Stories*. Translated by William Radice, Penguin Books UK, London 1991; revised edition 1994.

English Writings
The English Writings of Rabindranath Tagore. Edited by Sisir Kumar Das. Sahitya Akademi, New Delhi Vol. 1 1994; Vol. 2 1996; Vol. 3 1996; Vol. 4, edited by Nityapriya Ghosh, 2007.

Gitanjali
Rabindranath Tagore: *Gitanjali: Song Offerings*. Translated from the Bengali by William Radice, Accompanied by a new text of Tagore's translation based on the original manuscript. Penguin Books UK / India, London/New Delhi 2011.

Bringing in the Harvest

Bengalis who know my translations and have compared them to the original are well aware of the problems which every line poses, the often agonizing dilemmas that confront a translator in every sentence that he translates. They are perhaps less aware of the daunting, overall challenge. Rabindranath is their writer: they can plunge into the ocean of his works, and bask and swim with ease. The foreign translator lacks that confident familiarity. He often feels lost and adrift in that vast *Rabīndra-rachanābali*, and is in danger of drowning.

Consider the audacity of what I have attempted, given my totally un-Bengali upbringing and background. An English boy of 18, between finishing his privileged school education and going up to Oxford to read English, comes to India for a few months. He is generously accommodated at the Lawrence School, Sanawar, teaches a bit, writes lots of poems, has lessons in playing the *sarod*, and is paid a small stipend. He uses that money to travel round India, and of all the places that he visits, Calcutta fascinates him the most. He returns to England with some awareness of Bengal as a distinct region, and of the complex culture of 19th century Bengal. The films of Satyajit Ray, which he has seen in his mid-teens, begin to take a place in his mind as Bengali films, not just as Indian films.

He starts his English degree at Magdalen College, Oxford, but his interest in India remains, and sometimes distracts him from his studies. The sufferings of Bangladesh, whose liberation struggle of 1971 now leaps on to the pages of British newspapers, intensifies and expands his awareness of Bengal. Having won the Newdigate Prize for poetry in 1970, he is beginning to think of himself as a poet, and he spends most of his second year at Oxford writing a whole book of poems.[1] But how, as a poet, will he earn his living? He does not feel committed enough to English literary criticism to become a school or university teacher of English. He wonders about branching out into something quite different. Bengali has a rich literature: hardly any non-Bengalis have studied it. He mentions this idea to his mother, Betty Radice, whose classical scholarship and editorship of the Penguin Classics series has brought him into contact with the world of literary translation. She is enthusiastic: she rings up a professor she knows at the School of Oriental and African Studies (SOAS) in London. He confirms that Bengali can be studied there. The young man applies, and is given (against nil competition) a scholarship for a two-year Diploma in Bengali. His teacher, Dr Tarapada Mukherjee, is surprised to find, on returning to SOAS from India for the start of the academic year, that he has a new student. The student tells him that, as well as wanting to read Bengali literature, he would like to learn to speak the language. "What do you want to learn to speak Bengali for?" asks Dr Mukherjee. "There are millions of Bengalis who can do that already."He decides, however, that maybe I—his student—am worth being taught, and for two years gives me many hours of one-to-one attention. The language is hard: all those different kinds of 't' and 'd' that do not exist in any European language; a script that is beautiful—especially in Dr Mukherjee's elegant handwriting—but which obliges the learner to tease out every new word letter by letter; a vast vocabulary, almost every word of which is new and unrelated to anything in English. The linguistics that I studied as part of my English degree has given me an interest in grammar; but I do not have a good track record in languages. I gave up French after O Level, and for Latin A level I got the abysmal grade of D.

The biggest and most basic challenge that I faced—and still face nearly forty years later—is that I started to learn Bengali too late. Even by the time we enter our teens, our natural language learning capacity has gone. We can learn new languages as adults, and if we work hard we can learn them quite well. I certainly worked very hard during my

[1] *Eight Sections*. Secker & Warburg, London 1975.

two years as a postgraduate student at SOAS; I have continued to work hard all my life; and people tell me that I speak Bengali accurately. But in my heart of hearts I know that I shall never know it as even a young child who is a native speaker knows it. I cannot go to a Bengali play and follow and enjoy it as the audience does; I cannot 'skim' a book or newspaper as I can in English; I sometimes do not catch what people say to me on the telephone or in conversation. So the largest obstacle for me or any foreign translator of Rabindranath who has not started to learn Bengali till his adult years is the sheer difficulty of the language. One remains reliant on dictionaries, or on help from native speakers, and it is always possible to make mistakes of a sort that a native speaker would never make.

Nevertheless, the foreign translator has some advantages over the translator who can read the original in his mother-tongue. Native speakers can 'swim' in Rabindranath's writings like a fish, but on the 'dry land' of a second or acquired language they may not feel so at home. The foreign translator, by contrast, may be helpless in the water without a life-jacket or a boat, but can walk on land with confidence. The land—the place where we want to arrive or come ashore in a translation—is his natural element. I may never—to my frustration—know Bengali as well as I would like. But I do know English. It is my mother-tongue.

In India, many people are as familiar with English as they are with any South Asian language, and this is why many excellent native-speaking translators of Rabindranath have emerged in recent decades—translators particularly of his prose. But for very few Indians is English actually the 'mother-tongue', the language they learn on their mother's knees, the very first language that they hear when they are born. This is a crucial difference, and it is what has encouraged me to persevere in my career as a translator of Tagore, despite all the difficulties and setbacks.

Now that I have three grandchildren, and can observe their language development with more detachment than was possible when my wife and I were anxiously bringing up our own two daughters, it is very clear to me that language starts with sound and rhythm. When we learn languages as adults, we have no option but to pronounce—as best we can—words as complete, written entities. Infants, however, charmingly come out with approximations of words, based not on script but on the sounds they hear. All parents delight in these efforts, and happily explain to others what their children mean by sounds that are intelligible only to those who hear them every day.

The rhythms and sounds of poetry are rooted in these infant experiences. They are enhanced by the nursery rhymes and songs that parents recite and sing to their children. Tagore famously wrote about how his poetry was rooted in that very early exposure. Indians, very rightly and properly, experience that early enchantment in the mother-tongue, not in English. This is why the translation of poetry—as opposed to prose—presents such a major challenge to translators who are translating out of, not into, their mother-tongue.

When I started in 1973–74 to read Rabindranath's poetry, guided by Tarapada Mukherjee, I had to struggle hard with grammar and with the meanings of words just as any foreign learner has to do. But as a poet myself, and one for whom the sounds and rhythm of poetry have always been immensely important ever since I had delighted as a child in the poetry of Lewis Carroll, Edward Lear, Hilaire Belloc and Walter de la Mare, I found myself responding to the sounds of Rabindranath's poems in an instinctive and intuitive way.

I cannot claim, even now, that I hear the poems in quite the same way as a native speaker would hear them, but they immediately get 'translated', from the very first reading, into sounds and rhythms that are natural to me in my mother-tongue. I have often spoken of the impact that Tagore's poem *Āgaman* ('Arrival') from *Kheyā* had on me when I first read it in Bengali. I didn't fully understand it, its imagery and symbolism were unfamiliar to me, but I responded to its sound, and almost immediately set about trying to translate it. In 1977, the Oxford poet and classical scholar Peter Levi wrote a book called *The Noise Made by Poems*. The 'noise' of my translation, which I later revised and included in my *Selected Poems* of Tagore (1985), may be only an approximate equivalent to the 'noise' of the Bengali, but it has its own life and music, and seems to convince readers that this is a great poem.

The aspect of translation that, for the translator out of the mother-tongue, is the hardest, is therefore for me the easiest. The range of verse techniques, using metre, rhyme and phrasing, that I have employed in order to translate Rabindranath's poetry have not, of course, been given to me on a plate. Like any poet, I have gradually built them up over the years, and many of them have been acquired through the challenge of trying to find equivalents in English to Tagore's techniques in Bengali. But they have become natural to me, as natural as technique is to a musician, even though he or she has worked long and hard to acquire it. When I read a new poem by Rabindranath, instantly its form and sound and rhythm start to grow in my mind like a seed.

In some ways, the act of creative translation requires a relaxation of the mind, rather than a conscious act of will. As in the writing of a poem of one's own, one has to sit back and let the seed grow in a natural and spontaneous way, so that it emerges as a complete and convincing poem. The relative ease of this process brings dangers of its own. When I make mistakes in my translations—and I have made many mistakes over the years, though I have tried to correct them in reprints—these are not merely because of ignorance and the limitations I have as a translator who did not start learning Bengali till he was an adult. The mistakes can also arise because my own creative energy takes over: the poem, if it appeals to me, it implants itself so strongly in my mind that my imaginative conception of it, even though it may be wrong-headed, takes over. Yes, I am sailing a boat, not swimming naturally like a Bengali; but a wind can fill the sails of a boat so forcefully that it becomes quite hard to control. The mood in which I have translated many of Tagore's poems is not so different from that evoked by the song at the beginning of his play *Tāser Desh*, which in my translation reads:

Sharp winds blow,
Clouds rush across the skies—
    Boatman, let's go

Boatman, let's go!
Hold the rudder in your grip,
I'll haul the mainsail up,
Heave-ho
Heave-ho!
Mooring chains clink and clatter,
Boat feels no grief or terror,
Can't now endure its tether,
So eager
For the flow—
Heave-ho!
Day after day counted,
Heart and mind so agitated,
Don't say
Can't go!
Sea of doubts inside
Will be crossed—
Don't look aside
Don't backslide!
If mighty Shiva,
Dreadlocks stormy,
Goes crazy,
Wave-tossed
In the frenzy,
Don't look askance,
Keep up the dance,
Sing of victory—
Heave-ho
Let's go
Heave-ho![2]

[2] Rabindranath Tagore: *Card Country*. Translated by William Radice. Visva-Bharati, Kolkata 2008, p.13.

Bengali readers and critics, unaware of the creative *furor* with which I have worked, naturally enough look for discrepancies between the words of my translation and the words of the Bengali original. The comments that they then make, in reviews or in private correspondence, are certainly one of the challenges that I have had to face as a translator of Tagore. This close attention by native speakers, generally appreciative and encouraging, but also quite merciless in exposing my errors, is probably a rather unusual phenomenon in the world of literary translation. Vast amounts of English literature are translated into other languages, but native-speaking readers very rarely take any interest at all in those translations. I, as a translator of Bengali into English, am not let off so lightly. Martin Kämpchen, who has been a close friend throughout my career as a Tagore translator, sometimes says wistfully that he wishes more people in India (where he lives for much of the year) could read his German translations of Tagore. I tell him in turn that he is lucky not to be subjected to the scrutiny that I have to face. I don't know which fate is preferable!

But taking note of the reactions of native speakers is only a part—and over the years has become a smaller and less demanding part—of the arduous process by which I try to 'steady the boat' of my translations. This process is not unique to translations: in my own poems too the process of polishing and revising in order to make them as 'sea-worthy' and 'watertight' as possible can be equally arduous and painstaking. But with translations, one is not as free as one is in one's own writing. To perfect the work and make it publishable and lasting one has to take a whole host of factors into account.

My mother warned me of the demands and restrictions that translation could impose on me if I also wanted to be a poet. In a letter to me of October 1974, she wrote: 'I don't want you to be under any delusions about translation being more creative than critical writing—in the sense that nothing in my experience involves so much drudgery, minute application, exasperation at being tied to another's thought processes. Great self-discipline is needed if one is to be a faithful interpreter and not fall into the temptation of "improving" one's original. For me there is satisfaction in a job well done and in a reasonably well-phrased sentence, but every time I start on a new translation I have to push myself to get down to it and wonder why I thought I could...You can only learn if you can translate by working on something fairly substantial. Be prepared to find that like some poet-translators I know, you find the process too limiting and demanding.'[3]

As an English poet-translator, based in the West but widely published and read in India, I have had to face two ways. On the one hand I've had to try to put Tagore's writings across to a readership that is largely ignorant of his cultural and historical background. On the other, I have had to make my work acceptable in a context in which Tagore is well known and where a great deal of scholarship has accumulated. This is an enormous double challenge.

When I started working on my *Selected Poems* of Tagore, it quickly became clear to me that the book would have to be far more than a translation. If I was to give a new and credible impression of Tagore's range and power as a poet, I would have to select poems from the whole span of his output, I would have to annotate them carefully, and I would have to write an extensive introduction. The wind in my sails would have to be carefully and meticulously directed and controlled by scholarly effort. This is not an easy thing for a poet. It was something that frightened me away from a career as an academic specialist in literature, for I felt that I was by nature a practitioner, not a critic or scholar. Yet how could I explain where Tagore's poems had come from without this effort? How could I explain his Bengal Renaissance heritage, his debt to Kalidasa or the Upanishads, his relationship to the Bengali Vaishnava tradition, or his love of folk poetry or the songs of the Bauls without reading, research and scholarship?

Recently, Penguin India have brought out a selection of my translations of Tagore's short stories in an elegant but low-priced

[3] William Radice and Barbara Reynolds (eds.): *The Translator's Art: Essays in Honour of Betty Radice*. Penguin UK, London 1987, p.29.

edition for their new 'Evergreen' series. When the book arrived at my home in Northumberland my first reaction on opening the packet was of joy and relief at seeing my translations completely shorn of Introduction and notes. Really, great literature should not require that kind of apparatus. But in order to put Tagore across to a Western world that had largely forgotten what they knew about him (and whose knowledge during his lifetime was in any case based on many misconceptions), I had no choice but to present him quite elaborately.

In the Indian context, the challenge of making my work acceptable to well-informed readers and to scholars of Tagore has been particularly acute in my new book, commissioned by Penguin India for the 150th birth-anniversary. This book is a re-translation of all the poems that are in Tagore's English *Gitanjali* of 1912. But it also confronts head-on the iconic status that Tagore's own translation has in India. You cannot translate *Gītāñjali* anew without taking on board the fact that it contains some of modern India's most famous and influential utterances. How should I translate a poem as famous as *Chitta yethā bhay-shunya* ('Where the mind is without fear'), or the song translated by Tagore as 'When the heart is hard and parched up, come upon me with a shower of mercy', which he sang in Bengali to Mahatma Gandhi when he broke his fast at Yerwada Prison in 1932? In the end, and quite unexpectedly, I tackled this challenge by looking afresh at Tagore's own translation as well as doing a new one of my own.

In talking about the translations in this new book—or indeed about any of my translations of Tagore—I could of course focus on the 'line-by-line' problems, on the difficulties there can be in finding precise equivalents for Bengali words, or in dealing with images and references that may be 'culturally bound', and therefore difficult to convey in English. There are also special challenges in translating poems that are songs. But when the work is done, even if it has been long drawn out and painful—as it was, for example, in my *Selected Short Stories* of Tagore—those difficulties tend to fade quite rapidly from my memory. I know that there are many differences between the first edition of *Selected Short Stories* in 1991, which was faulty, with even the gender wrong for the two male cousins in *Byabadhān* ('The Divide'), but it would take me a long time to excavate them, and it does not seem to be necessary now. The bigger, global challenges are what loom largest in my mind as I reflect on my translations today, and that is why I have focussed on them in this essay.[4]

A question that I do find myself asking quite often is: would my work on Rabindranath have been easier if I had concentrated entirely on him, to the exclusion of everything else? He alone is so huge, one of the most prolific writers the world has known, and also one of the most diverse and complex. To translate Tagore is a sufficient life work for anyone, and yet I have stubbornly and recklessly combined it with all sorts of other work. My doctorate at Oxford in the 1980s was not on Tagore but on Michael Madhusudan Dutt; I have doggedly gone on writing poems of my own, publishing ten books of them, even though I have not been as successful as a poet than I have been as a translator; I have taught Bengali and supervised research students at SOAS; I have dabbled in journalism, broadcasting and opera; and I have always been busy on the domestic front too, sharing in housework and the raising of our talented daughters because my wife has had an equally demanding career as a teacher and headmistress. Was it necessary to do quite so much, and would my work on Tagore have been easier if I had not spread my wings so widely?

Looking back now at the age of 60, I do not see how my career could really have been otherwise. To translate Rabindranath at all, I have had to build a house. All the elements in the house—the foundations, the floor, the walls, the windows, the roof, the decorations and furnishings—have been necessary. How could I have translated his poems if I was not, in another room of the house, a poet myself? How could I have acquired the necessary command of the language

[4] It was my friend Arun Deb of Konnagar who, with unstinting care and generosity, went through every sentence of the first edition of *Selected Short Stories*, and helped me to make many corrections and improvements for the revised edition of 1994. I shall always be grateful to him and to his whole family and circle of friends in Konnagar, for their hospitality and support.

and cultural background if I had not also professionally taught Bengali language and literature at SOAS for 23 years? How could I have understood the Bengal Renaissance from which Tagore sprang without studying, through my work on Madhusudan, one of the great formative figures of the Renaissance? How could I have found my way into the songs of *Gītāñjali* without being a musician myself? Playing the piano—a pastime that has entered my professional life through my work with opera composers—belongs to another very important room in the house, which if I did not enter every day I would not be able to approach a poet such as Tagore, for whom poetry and music were always—in Milton's famous words—'Blest pair of Sirens, pledges of Heav'ns joy, / Sphear-born harmonious Sisters…'

The road I have followed as a translator of Tagore has never been easy, and has often taxed my physical and mental health to the limit. But the rewards have been many. It has enabled me to earn my living as a lecturer at SOAS; it has given me many warm and long-lasting friendships; and it has above all brought me into close contact with one of the greatest creative imaginations the world has ever known. The road is, perhaps, not quite as arduous as it once was, and for that I am devoutly grateful.

When I worked on my translations of *Gītāñjali* at Santiniketan in the last quarter of 2010, I felt a greater *ānanda* and *moksha* in the work than I had ever felt before, and a greater ease and confidence. This was in spite of the fact that, soon after my arrival as a Visiting Professor at Rabindra-Bhavan (Visva-Bharati), I fell and broke my right wrist. The physical challenge of completing the book using dictation and my left hand was considerable, but what I remember now is the ease and the flow of it, not the trial and the pain. I suppose this is because I have learnt something over the years, and know my way round in the house that I have laboriously constructed.

The overall challenge, though, will remain, and if I want to continue with my work, it may in some respects become harder because of the handicaps of advanced age. But in this birth-anniversary year, and in my 60th year, I can allow myself the pleasure of bringing in the harvest.

But just as Rabindranath himself found that it was impossible for him ever to rest from his labours, so also I suspect my future years will continue to be like what he expressed in his great poem *Shankha* ('The Conch', 1916). I cannot claim to partake in its call for moral or political action, but as a poet I resonate with the energy and sound of this poem. I end with the last three stanzas (from *Selected Poems*), for they express better than any words of my own why the challenge of translating Rabindranath has been immense and exhausting yet perpetually exciting—always worth rising to.

O change me, touch me with youth, alchemize me! Let fiery melody
Blaze and twirl in my breast, life-fire leap into ecstasy!
    Let night's ribs crack; let skies,
    As they fill with dawning enlightenment, raise
    Terror in remotest dark. From today
I shall fight to seize and carry aloft your conch of victory.

Now I know I can no more close my eyes in slumber.
Now I know that monsoon showers of arrows must batter
    My heart. Some people will rush to my side;
    Others will weep and sigh in dread;
    Horrifying nightmares will rock the beds
Of sleeping hearers: but today your conch will joyously thunder.

When I looked to you for rest I received nothing but shame;
But dress me for battle now, let armour cover each limb.
    Let new obstructions chafe and challenge me;
    I shall take all blows and hurts unflinchingly;
    My heart shall drum redress for your injuries;
I shall give all my strength, win back your conch and make it
    BOOM.[5]

[5] *Selected Poems* (1985), p. 77.

The Genius of the Poet Tagore

I started learning Bengali in 1972, by doing a Postgraduate Diploma in the language at the School of Oriental and African Studies, University of London. Within a year I was beginning to read poems and stories by Rabindranath Tagore. I have been reading, translating and working on Tagore ever since. Forty years is a long time, and when I started to think about my lecture here today, I found myself recalling the very first poems by Tagore that I read and which I attempted to translate. To my delight I found those early translations among my papers, and it was interesting and instructive to look at them again. I have got four of them here. Two of them I went on to revise and include in my *Selected Poems* of Tagore (1985). The other two have remained unpublished. I am interested now not so much in the strengths or weaknesses in the translations, but in my choice of these four poems. What was it about them that appealed to me, and why did I immediately feel when I first struggled to read them and understand them in Bengali, that they were the work of a poet of genius?

The first of the four was a poem whose title has always had personal significance for me. It was called *Āgaman*, which means 'Arrival'. It was first included in a book called *Kheyā*, 'The Ferry', which Tagore published in 1906. I remember how when I first read this poem I felt that I had myself arrived somewhere, because although I was still struggling with the language and the grammar, and could only half understand the meaning of the poem, I could appreciate its power and energy as a poet. The rhythm of this was so powerful that I immediately felt impelled to attempt a translation that would capture the rhythm and rhyme scheme, so I came out with this:

> And when our work was fully done, the light was turning grey we told our weary selves,
> 'be sure, no one will come today.' Every village home a fastness,
> Every door in grip of darkness—
> Someone stood apart and said, 'the King is on his way.'
> We just laughed and said, 'no no, no one will come today.'

When I came to revise the translation I changed the full rhymes to half rhymes, because I found that although the first verse was accurate, later on inaccuracies crept in because of the pressure, the need to find full rhymes in English. Usually half rhymes gave me more scope. But the basic form and rhythmic impulse of the translation survived in the revised version. I cannot imagine translating this particular poem without using a metre and a rhyme scheme that matched the original, though Tagore himself did a prose translation of this poem for his book *Gītāñjali*.

The rhythmic power of the poem operates on several levels, and is closely linked to its dramatic structure. There are six stanzas and in the first four the people who are tired and trying to sleep are reluctant to believe that a King is about to arrive and visit their humble home. But one or two of them know that the King is on his way and in the climactic fifth stanza they are proved right when the King arrives and the people who have been sleeping find they are completely unprepared to receive him. So in this poem we have the rhythm of the words, the rhythm of the phrases, the rhythm of the lines, the rhythm of the stanzas, but also the rhythm and structure of the whole poem. To get to that climactic fifth stanza is always electrifying. In my English translation in its revised form this reads like this:

> Where is the throne? The King has come, we made no preparation!

Alas what shame, what destiny,
No court, no robes, no finery—
Somebody cried in our ears, 'O vain, O vain this lamentation:
With empty hands, in barren rooms, offer your celebration.'[1]

The last stanza of the poem stresses that the King has arrived with the storm, with thunder and lightning. This idea of some kind of transcendent experience emerging from darkness and storm and even violence is an important idea in Tagore's writings particularly of the so called *Gītāñjali* phase.

So here was a poet who could do amazing things with his language, with words and with rhythm, but also had a profound dramatic sense! It was those two aspects, the rhythmic and the dramatic, that attracted me to this poem.

When I first read this poem, I was also reading Tagore's famous play, *Dākghar* ('The Post-Office', 1914), in which a boy who is dying of a fatal illness is waiting eagerly for a letter from the King. The King arrives at the end of the play, at night and in darkness—not in a storm, but nevertheless the connections between the poem and the play are immediately apparent.

Another poem that attracted me was revealing of Tagore's narrative gifts, his mastery of the art of story-telling as well as lyric poetry and drama. This was a famous poem called *Dui Bighā Jami*, which means 'Two bighas of land', roughly equivalent to half an acre. Tagore included it in a book called *Chitrā* ('The Multi-coloured', 1896), which belongs to the same decade as his finest short stories. This poem, many stories and magnificent letters stem from his experience of managing the estates that the Tagore family owned along the Padma river which is now the north-west region of Bangladesh. It was an experience that was crucial and informative for Tagore because it brought him into close contact with the rural people. *Dui Bighā Jami* is about a poor tenant farmer who is thrown off his land by a landlord who simply wants to

[1] *Selected Poems* (1985), p. 72.

appropriate the land so that he can extend a garden attached to his house. The poem is a dramatic monologue by Upen, a poor farmer. Like *Āgaman* it is written in six stanzas, though the stanzas and the lines are longer than in *Āgaman*. The first two stanzas tell how Upen is evicted from his land and forced to become a wandering *sādhu*, or ascetic, who nevertheless keeps pining for his ancestral plot of land. In the end, he feels compelled to return to it. In the third stanza we have famous and beautiful lines that express not only Upen's close relationship with his motherland, but also the profound feeling that Tagore developed for the land and the people of Bengal, a feeling that all Bengalis can share when they read this poem. Let me just read you this stanza in my translation:

> I bow, I bow to my beautiful motherland Bengal!
> To your river-banks, to your winds that cool and console;
> Your plains, whose dust the sky bends down to kiss;
> Your shrouded villages, that are nests of shade and peace;
> Your leafy mango-woods, where the herd boys play;
> Your deep ponds, loving and cool as the midnight sky;
> Your sweet-hearted women returning home with water;
> I tremble in my soul and weep when I call you Mother.
> Two days later at noon I entered my native village:
> The pottery to the right, to the left the festival carriage;
> Past temple, market-place, granary, on I came
> Till thirsty and tired, at last I arrived at my home.[2]

That stanza is deeply emotional, but the next one is even more so for in it he expresses his distress on seeing how his humble plot of land, which supplied food for him and his family, has been prostituted, has been turned into a kind of shameless seducer for being made into a luxuriant garden. The last two stanzas of the poem complete what is really, like many of Tagore's short stories of the period, a very sad

[2] *Selected Poems* (1985), p. 56.

story, for Upen sits there under his favourite mango-tree in the garden, thinking about the past, and when two ripe mangos suddenly fall to the ground nearby he takes them to be some kind of message from the land, from the tree that 'my mother still knows her son, maybe.'

In the last stanza the gardener appears, tells the landlord that Upen has returned, and the landlord appears with his retainers and they violently drive Upen away and he is forced to flee, never to return.

It is a simple, heart-rending story, beautifully told in superbly crafted rhymed stanzas. The verse technique impressed me, the story moved me, and I think above all I was struck by the poem's combination of emotional and descriptive richness with a touching directness and simplicity. Here was a poet who might have been difficult for me to read, and who still even after all these years often presents huge challenges because of the complexity and sophistication of his language, but who could nevertheless achieve such simple effects of clarity, simplicity and lucidity.

Maybe this inherent simplicity is what attracted me to another poem, a shorter one. It is a sonnet, in fact, though at the time I am not sure I really recognised it as a sonnet. The translation of it that I found was not done as a sonnet, though I did use metre and rhyme, or sometimes half rhyme. The poem is from another book that Tagore published in the 1890s, *Chaitāli* (1896), whose title means much the same as *Chitrā*. The poem was called *Durlabh Janma* ('Precious Life'). Like *Āgaman*, this poem was ultimately included in *Gitanjali*, where none of the poems are given titles. Let me read you the poem in my early version, and then in my version for my new translation of *Gitanjali*. I did the new translation in sonnet form, because I wanted all the sonnets in *Gitanjali* to appear as sonnets in my translation—something that Tagore was not able to do in his own prose translation.

When I did the new translation I did not have the old one to hand, and indeed I think I had forgotten that I had ever done it. Both the translations are equally valid, and I read them both to you now in order to make the point that a poet of Tagore's stature can survive a variety of translations. As with *Āgaman* and *Dui Bighā Jami*, the power of the poem lies perhaps more deeply in its essential conception, in its motivating ideas and feelings, what in Bengali would be called the poem's *bhāb*, which Tagore himself tellingly translated as 'emotional idea.' The language and form used to express that idea effectively is of huge importance too, but translation—which cannot after all capture all aspects of the language, rhythm and style of the original—can show that if the basic idea behind the poem is strong, then the poem will work almost regardless of the strength of the translation. Here are the two versions:

One day the end of sight will come,
Eyelids fall across my eyes for the last time.
Next day as always night will fade,
And over the waking world the dawn will wake.
Life will play on, with its noise,
And time flow on, through human joys and woes.
As I think of this today, I gaze
At the universe with eager eyes.
Nothing is worthless, everything I see
Seems precious to me today.
The humblest places on earth
Are precious, the slightest lives of the world.
Of what I desired or gained, keep all—
Give me what I ignored because it was small.

The second version is:

One day this precious gift of sight will cease—
My last blink will forever seal my eyes.
The following day will dawn the same as this,
The world will wake to see the same sunrise.
The noisy play of the world will carry on—
In homes, the time will gladly, sadly pass.
Thinking of this, towards this world I turn

And look at it with new-found eagerness.
The simple things that didn't seem to count
All now take on a value beyond price:
Places or lives of which the least amount
Of note was taken will now more than suffice.
Away with all I've got or didn't get!
Give me what's humble: things that I forget.[3]

The short poem 'Precious Life' is partly about death, or about facing up to the reality that death will come to us. Death is a major and recurrent theme in Tagore's poetry throughout his long life. Of course death is one of the two great themes that occur in all poetry the world over, the other thing being love. But in Tagore's case death took on a very special importance, because he was mercilessly exposed to it through loss and bereavement. The poem *Chhabi* ('Picture') is generally taken to be written in memory of Tagore's sister in law Kadambari, to whom he was devoted and who gave him a great deal of support and encouragement when he was emerging as a poet in his teens. She committed suicide in 1884 when Tagore was 23 years, and arguably he never really got over that loss. It was the first of many more bereavements to come, the worst time being the early 1900s, when he lost his wife, his middle daughter, his father, and his youngest son all within the period of six years. But when Tagore writes about death, he usually uses the subject as an opportunity to write about life too. The fourth poem is no exception. It is a much longer one, and is written in a quite different style and form. It is a famous poem called *Chhabi* from a book called *Balākā* ('Wild Geese', 1916), which is regarded as one of Tagore's greatest books of poems. In the poem, Rabindranath looks at a picture of someone he loved and lost—presumably Kadambari. Readers of the poem can identify it with anyone that they have loved and lost. First of all Tagore concludes that the picture is nothing but a picture because it has nothing of the qualities of life that he sees in

[3] *Gitanjali* (2011), p. 117.

the natural world around him. But then, half-way through the poem, in a kind of *volte-face* that is characteristic of a number of poems in *Balākā,* he writes:

Has the poet gone out of his mind?
Are you a picture?
No, no, you are not a picture only!
Who says you are confined
By the pencils stricture,
To frozen melancholy?
If your joy had truly died
This river
Would have dried;
The golden tracery of the clouds
Would have been rubbed out forever.
If the shadow of your shining hair
Were no longer here,
Then where
In all of nature could I find
The shadow play of wind and sunbeam
Through restless, rustling myrtle-shrouds?
It would all be a dream.
Have I forgotten you?
You have made your home at the ground of my being—
Hence my forgetting.
Walking distractedly along the path,
Do I not forget the flowers?
Do I not forget the stars?
Yet these
Are the very sweetness of my life-breath,
The very music of my pondering.
It would be wrong
Not to have forgotten:
How can the heart that has taken you into its rhythm,

The blood that has absorbed you
Remember you?
You are not before my eyes,
You are inside them;
You are the blueness in blue,
The greenness in this spring days greenery.
In you my universe has the centre of its harmony.
I do not know how,
I cannot explain,
But your music plays in my song;
You are the poet at the poets core,
You are not just a picture, no, you are more!
You came to me one sunrise,
Then at night I lost you.
And now
I have crept through the dark to find you once again.
You are not a picture, you are more.

That was from the old translation that I did many years ago, which I never published and which I haven't actually ever used or quoted. Reading it again now, I wonder why I didn't publish it. It may have been partly because a close Bengali friend of mine pointed out certain details that perhaps were not fully accurate, but which I did not feel I could successfully revise. It may also be that the poem had too deep a personal significance for me, because I myself suffered a bereavement at a vulnerable age, when my sister died in 1969 aged twenty of lupus erythematosus when I was sixteen years.

I was attracted to this poem, as so many readers of the Bengali, by its poignant subject, but also by an extraordinary richness and flexibility in its language and form.

The Bengali original varies in its line lengths, and it also moves to and fro across the page in a strangely expressive and beautiful way. A budding poet myself when I translated this, I was fascinated by this visual shape, and I tried—and I have continued to try in all translations of poems of this sort—to arrive at a layout in my English translations that is similar in its effect. This poem and others in the book *Balākā* represent a trend in Tagore's poetry towards greater and greater formal flexibility and freedom. In this poem he uses rhyme, and most of the rhymes come in couplets, in consecutive lines, though interestingly at the end of each section of the poem he varies the rhyme pattern so that the last three lines are rhymed ABA instead of AA. In my translation I placed the rhymes more flexibly, but I generally used full rhyme, and these rhymes are very important to the effect of the translation.

So we have now, added to the qualities that have already emerged—qualities of rhythm, drama, narrative, character, description and simplicity—we have quality of flexibility, almost an improvisatory quality in the way in which the lines vary in length and in their position on the page, and also in the *volte-face* in the middle of the poem: as though the poem was going in one direction, and then suddenly, on the spur of the moment, Tagore takes it off onto another.

The four poems that I have just shared with you came my way, all those years ago in the 1970s, serendipitously, by good chance, in that they were among those that my teacher at SOAS, Dr Tarapada Mukherjee directed me to. But I homed in on them because, unconsciously probably, I felt they were great poems, even though consciously I remember being quite resistant to an acceptance of Tagore's greatness at that time, partly because I had been rather put off by his own translations. That caution is reflected in a pencil note that I find on my typed copy of my translation of 'Precious Life'. The typed copy has the poem written out below by hand, with a literal translation of each word, and at the top of the page I have written 'not a particularly remarkable poem—I did this as a lecture illustration'. Actually I think I was being far too cautious: I now think it is a remarkable and beautiful poem, deceptive in its simplicity.

The variety in these poems was what particularly appealed to me because in Tagore's own translations there seems to be a certain sameness. As the years have gone by, I have become more and more impressed by the variety and diversity in Tagore's writing—not only in his poetry but in his writing in all the genres. But I have also become more aware of the unity. Defining the unity is harder than demonstrating the variety. I have come to feel very strongly that there is a characteristic Tagorean rhythm running through everything he wrote or created, whether they are poems, songs, prose works or even paintings. Defining that rhythm would take long, but Tagore's own brilliant and technical essays on rhythm and metre provide us with the key. A point that he stresses in the essay called *Chander Artha* ('The Meaning of Metre', 1916) is that combined or double consonants in the Bengali language have a different weight from single consonants and it is crucial to understand the difference if one is to hear the rhythms and metres of Tagore's writings properly. As I only recently discovered, Tagore makes the same point in a short preface to his book *Mānasī* ('The Lady of the Mind', 1890), a book regarded as showing Tagore's emergence as a fully mature poet, In this preface he says that words like *nimne* or *svaccha* or *urdhve* which sound like two syllables in fact should each be regarded as having the weight of three syllables. Take any piece of writing by Tagore, whether in verse or prose, and you will find the interplay between single consonants and combined or double consonants is crucial to its rhythmic effect. Two lines of *Chhabi* I translated as 'Who says you are confined/by the pencils stricture, /to frozen melancholy?' I was trying to capture that kind of sonic effect by the combined consonants in my English translation, 'Pencils stricture'. The constant sense of stopping and starting that you get because of these combined consonants is something that may have been in Tagore's mind when he wrote a short poem, which in my translation of his three collections of brief poems I translated as:

Music is made
From blocks in the road,
Frustration, confusion,
    Stop, start.

The rhythm of sadness
Creates transcendent delightfulness
Through musical art.[4]

As with Tagore's sense of rhythm, so for his general aesthetic sense and his own understanding of what great poetry can achieve, we can turn to his own discursive writings for many insights. For example, there is a remarkable essay called *Bikār-Shaṅkā* ('Fear of Imbalance'), which was delivered as one of the weekly sermons that Tagore gave at prayer meetings in the glass temple at Santiniketan. It is about how to achieve balance in religion and in human relations and in love. But it also has some fascinating things to say about how to achieve balance and completeness in poetry, which Tagore says needs to combine three things: technical control or a perfectly achieved *kabyer kalebar* or 'Poetic body'; *jñān*, knowledge or understanding; and *bhāb*, or feeling. In all four of the poems that I have presented to you, those three qualities can be found, and that is why, in Tagore's own terms, they are all fully achieved poems.

Chicago Institute of Art at the opening of the Exhibition: *The Last Harvest*—Paintings of Rabindranath Tagore. 27 March 2012.

[4] Rabindranath Tagore: *The Jewel That Is Best: Collected Brief Poems*. Translated by William Radice, Penguin Books India New Delhi 2011, p. 127 (*Sphulinga* no. 55).

Globetrotting with Rabindranath

Kolkata, Santiniketan, Hyderabad, Mumbai, Delhi and Ahmedabad; Marbach, Copenhagen, Lund, Zagreb and Rijeka; London, Dartington, Cambridge and Birmingham; Stockholm, Leiden, Salamanca, Barcelona and Valladolid; Washington and Chicago; Kuala Lumpur and Singapore… Who would have thought when I started learning Bengali in 1972 that Bengali and particularly Rabindranath Tagore would eventually take me all over the world? His 150th birth-anniversary has kept me and other Tagore specialists exceptionally busy this year, but it seems that conferences, seminars, celebrations and lecture invitations are likely to go on for at least the next two years, culminating in the centenary of Tagore's Nobel Prize in 1913.

This interest worldwide is both unsurprising and surprising. It is unsurprising, given that after winning the Nobel Prize Tagore became, in the 1920s and 30s just about the most famous poet in the world. Fame brought him many opportunities to travel, and he ceased them eagerly, globetrotting in a way that was unprecedented before the age of air travel. Through his English translations and secondary translations of those translations, through his lecture appearances and his extraordinary personal charisma, he left behind pieces of his legacy wherever he went, and it is not surprising that many of the events that I have attended have been linked to Tagore's own visits and travels. But the international spread of these events (extending far beyond those that I have managed to attend, whether in Beijing, Berlin or Costa Rica) is surprising, given that

Tagore—except perhaps in Bengal—is hardly a household name. He is not Shakespeare, or Mozart, or the Beatles! Many people have never heard of him. All of us who specialise in Tagore know that if we are invited to speak about him in a secondary school outside India, say, we can safely assume that we will have to give the pupils absolutely basic information about who he was and what he achieved. Moreover, many of the events that I have attended have not attracted large audiences. Tagore alone is not a crowd puller, and organisers of commemorative events have had to be ingenious in finding other ways in filling halls or seminar rooms.

Nevertheless, I do not think that Tagore's 150th birth-anniversary has been a waste of time. I and all the other regular participants (quite a small group, so we keep on meeting each other) have been delighted to accept all the invitations we have received, and I have never doubted for a minute that Tagore was a great man whose astonishing achievements in so many fields deserve to be discussed, explored and commemorated.

What has been gained? Perhaps it is too early to say. The events are still going on. I already have Kolkata, Dhaka, Chittagong, Edinburgh, and Budapest in my diary for next year, and many of the publications arising from anniversary events will not appear for another few months. But I think it is possible to draw some conclusions about Tagore's standing today compared to how it was when I began my own work, and what trends and challenges relating to Tagore can be expected in the future.

Tagore has attracted a good number of quips and sneers over the years, which are routinely trotted out by those who wish to make fun of him (or make fun of Bengalis for their devotion to Tagore). They also now circulate widely over the internet. One of these is Jorge Luis Borges' comment—referring to the Nobel Prize—that Tagore was a 'hoaxer of good faith, or, if you prefer, a Swedish invention'. Another is less well known: I remember an uncle of mine who was in the ICS quoting this Clerihew—

If only Tagore
Wouldn't draw!
His literary stuff
Is tedious enough.

If those lines have not appeared in print before, they will no doubt be useful ammunition for those wishing to pour their scorn on the roving exhibition of Tagore's paintings that have just opened in the Victoria and Albert Museum in London. I myself enjoy these quips when I am in the mood, and am happy to quote them sometimes, because I feel that Tagore would have found them amusing himself. But quips of this sort—unimaginable with a figure such as Shakespeare—do reveal a fundamental problem that those of us who care about Tagore have had to grapple with. To put it bluntly, *there is, with Tagore, a credibility gap*. Those attending anniversary events or contributing to commemorative volumes are all convinced of his greatness. But there is a harsh, cold world outside full of people who are not so convinced.

Maybe as an Englishman I have been more acutely aware of this credibility gap than admirers of Tagore from other cultures and countries. The British literary establishment (for want of a better term) has always been extremely resistant to Tagore. Read Bikash Chakravarty's introduction to his collection of letters to Tagore from literary figures (*Poets to a Poet*, 1912–1940), and you will learn that even at the height of Tagore's success with *Gitanjali* (1912), his circle of literary admirers in Britain was small, eccentric and not really representative of the mainstream. Mainstream figures such as W. B. Yeats and Ezra Pound who were enthusiastic to begin with, quite rapidly lost interest. Despite all the work done by me, Ketaki Kushari Dyson and others since the 1980s to put Tagore's reputation as a poet on a new basis, there are entrenched views going on a century, that have proved extremely hard to shift. Tagore is vaguely remembered for *Gitanjali* and other English translations that enjoyed an initial vogue, but which failed in the end to convince most British readers and critics that he was a great and significant poet.

The resilience of this attitude was perfectly demonstrated by an article in the *Guardian* (London) on the 7 May 2011 by the veteran journalist Ian Jack (who has a long standing interest in India). The article was published with a quotation in bold: 'Is his poetry any good? The answer for anyone who can't read Bengali must be: don't know. No translation is up to the job'. The article concluded that 'perhaps the time has come for us to forget Tagore was ever a poet, and think of his more intelligible achievements. These are many. He was a fine essayist, and educationist who founded a university; an opponent of the terrorism that then plagued Bengal…'. Perhaps Jack was being deliberately provocative, and the flurry of comment and protest that his article provoked was not a bad thing: it did at least get Tagore into the pages of one of our major newspapers. But unfortunately his article will come to be seen, I believe, as representing a new orthodoxy that is only marginally an improvement on the old. It appeared the day after Jack had chaired a lecture by Amartya Sen at the British Museum which essentially argued the same: that Tagore the poet was inaccessible to non-Bengalis and the best thing to do was to focus on his other achievements. Sen in his lecture placed the emphasis on Tagore's discursive writings on nationalism, universalism and history, Tagore's credibility as an intellectual has certainly risen a few notches as a result of this and other lectures and essays by Sen, a Nobel Laureate himself. Ian Jack in his article accepted that it was agnostic about Tagore the poet, but accepting of his status as a thinker and historical figure, and willing therefore to raise '2 cheers at least' for the 150th birth-anniversary.

The establishment of Tagore's credibility as an intellectual and thinker will not of course satisfy those who, as I do, passionately care about his poetry, his songs, his plays, his fiction, or his paintings. I myself have argued in lectures and articles that to focus on Tagore's thought and discursive writings can not only be a distraction from his profound achievements as a creative artist but can also be misleading.

Take any of his creative works, from a single song to a great poem such as *Tapobhañga* ('The Wakening of Shiva'), or a novel like *Gorā* and you will find the complexity, many sidedness, paradox and ambiguity that we expect to find in any great work of art. Nevertheless, the very real gain in credibility and intellectual respectability that has been won for Tagore in his anniversary year is a real advance.

His own translations in *Gitanjali* and other books dissatisfied me because they seemed to lack any kind of intellectual backbone, whereas when I read him in Bengali I felt the backbone was always there—even in his most romantic, rhapsodic and visionary poems. The backbone lay partly in his sheer virtuosity: his extraordinary mastery of metre and verse form. That was why I tried in my translations to find English metres and forms that would convey something of that same intellectual control. I also tried in my introduction and my notes to the poems to show how closely his poetry was linked to his thought—particularly his religious ideas.

Ian Jack's article indicates that there is still a long way to go in terms of making Tagore the poet as credible as Tagore the thinker. But a number of publications and conference papers this year have given me hope that this new-found appreciation of Tagore as a thinker will in the long run enhance the international understanding of his creative achievements. Particularly significant is Michael Collins' new book *Empire, Nationalism and the Postcolonial World: Tagore's Writings on History, Politics and Society.*[1]

Michael Collins is a historian teaching at the University College London. His book derives from his Oxford DPhil thesis. It is a highly academic work, and will not be read much outside academic circles. But works of scholarship can spread ripples, and I foresee a considerable ripple effect from Collins' painstaking pursuit of unity amidst the often baffling contradictions of Tagore's discursive writings. Was Tagore pro or anti the West? Was he pro or anti modern? Scholars at Tagore conferences argue endlessly about such issues. Through

[1] Routlege UK, London 2011.

carefully reading Tagore's discursive writings in English, Michael Collins has arrived at a conception very similar to my own view based on his poetry, that in everything he did he strove for *purnatā*, wholeness or completeness. He could be deeply critical of imperialism or the nation's state or the dehumanising effects of capitalism and industry. But his belief in history as an unfolding revelation—and in his own creative work as an expression of a unifying *jīban-devatā* made him also see the 'spirit of the age' that spawned imperialist expansion or scientific advance as tending towards unity, internationalism and freedom. He believed this because, in Collins' words, his 'monistic spiritual perspective—derived largely from the *upanishadic* insistence on the essential oneness of the universe—provided the basis for his philosophy of history'.

The marginalisation of Tagore is also the fragmentation of Tagore. If we can successfully move even one aspect of Tagore into the centre, as Collins has successfully done with Tagore's discursive writings in English, then we will begin to see his creative achievements taking a much more central position too. This will not, in my view, in any way diminish Tagore's radicalism, his often subversive challenge to orthodoxy, whether in education, economic development, or man-woman relations. Rather the reverse. When really great writers or thinkers occupy the centre of the stage, as Shakespeare has done for so long, then they have a tendency to seem more and more radical, not tame or respectable.

What other shifts have started to occur during this birth-anniversary year? In every case they imply a shift to a position that is both more central, but also more radical. The first area where I detect a significant shift with real potential for the future, is in perception of the environmentalist or activist Tagore.

One of the biggest triumphs of the anniversary year was the Tagore Festival held in Dartington in Devon from 1 to 7 May, inspired and masterminded by Satish Kumar. At least three different venues at Dartington Hall (founded by Leonard K Elmhurst, who worked with Tagore at Sriniketan with money from his American wife

Dorothy) were filled with extremely well attended events: lectures, recitals, dance performances, and poetry readings. Satish Kumar commands a considerable following in Britain through his editorship of the ecological magazine *Resurgence.* He is also the guiding light behind Schumacher College at Dartington and the Small School at Heartlands, and he acknowledges Tagore as a major influence on his life as an environmental activist and educationist. Through his vast network of international contacts, he was able to attract as speakers big names in environmentalism and leading conservationist such as Jane Goodall, leading British poets such as Benjamin Zephaniah and Simon Armitage, new age gurus such as Deepak Chopra, environmentalists such as Jonathon Porritt, and many talented dancers and musicians. Many people who spoke or attended the Festival did not know that much about Tagore, but were all deeply committed to what they perceived to be his values. With our world now facing unprecedented existential challenges because of over population, global warming and environmental degradation, Tagore whose works are full of prophetic warnings about the dangers we now face, is likely to seem an increasingly powerful and relevant voice.

I thought of Dartington at the ICCR conference on 'Tagore's vision of the contemporary world' at Azad Bhavan, in New Delhi, 10 to 12 October 2011 when I heard Ananda Lal, saying dryly about the exploitative dam in *Mukta-Dhārā* or the digging for gold in *Raktakarabī*, 'if that is not topical, what is?'. I also thought of Dartington when I heard, at the same conference Eiko Ohira speaking so movingly about the devastating earthquake and tsunami in Japan on 21 April this year*—telling us how cherry blossoms continued to bloom despite the heaps of rubble, giving new meaning to T. S. Eliot's famous line 'April is the cruelest month'. Listening to my friend Martin Kämpchen, speaking both in Delhi and at the seminar 'My Tagore; Why Tagore' at Ahmedabad on 15 October 2011 which we both also attended, and hearing about his own Tagore-inspired work as a community activist

* 2011. Editor

in Santal villages close to Santiniketan, I again reflected on how vital it is always to keep this aspect of Tagore's vision in mind. It is a major reason for remembering him, and it attracts many people worldwide to him who are not especially interested in poetry or literature at all.

A second major area where there has been a real shift—one which is particularly close to my heart because I am myself a keen amateur musician—is *Rabīndrasangīt*, the unique and marvellous songs of Tagore. For Bengalis, and for Tagore himself, the songs are central, but for non-Bengalis worldwide, Tagore's songs have remained his least known, least understood and appreciated aspect of his creative genius. The reasons for this have nothing to do with the songs themselves or the fact that they are composed in a language that very few non-Bengalis know. The reason for the inaccessibility of the songs has much more to do with their domestication, their—dare I say it—'ghettoisation'. The conventional way of performing them, with harmonium, metronomic rhythm, excessive amplification, and the addition of all sorts of inappropriate instruments, and the ubiquity of Rabindrasangit and every kind of Bengali celebration or social occasion, has made them as alien to non-Bengalis as British Christmas pantomime is to non-Brits, or Spanish bullfights are to non-Spaniards. In my experience, even in India outside Bengal, Rabindrasangit has had the effect of separating Tagore from others, not bringing him closer to them.

For me, Tagore's songs are unique and wonderful combinations of melody and poetry that are very frequently ruined in performance. It has long been a dream of mine to persuade singers of Rabindrasangit to perform without all the clutter of harmonium, *tablā* and other instruments. At Dartington, my friend Debashish Raychaudhuri and his daughter Rohini gave a simply wonderful performance of Rabindrasangit, set free, so to speak, from performance conventions, through a dialogue with me on the stage, and explanations of the structure of the songs and the meanings of the words from them and me. The songs were immediately made as fully accessible to an international audience as the songs of Schubert are accessible to all, whether they know German or not.

In Ahmedabad, we repeated the experiment, to a Gujarati audience, who, because of a long standing interest in Tagore and his songs, are normally quite content to listen to Rabindrasangit sung in a conventional way. But for them too, when they heard the songs sung with this new directness and simplicity, with such total concentration on the meaning and mood of the words of the song, the experience was revelatory. The ovations that Debashish and Rohini received in both Dartington and Ahmedabad will remain with me as one of the greatest triumphs of the anniversary year.

I do believe that this new way of performing Rabindrasangit, which is largely a matter of bringing it up to global standards of performance, where one would expect full respect for the composer's original intentions, carefully planned programmes, and translations of the texts, represents a revolution, a sea-change in the perception of Tagore's genius that will have an increasingly global effect. Another highly significant manifestation of that sea-change is the fact that the distinguished Rabindrasangit singer Swagatalakashmi Dasgupta has recently recorded the complete *Gītabitān* (Collected Songs of Tagore) in Kolkata with only a *tānpurā* accompaniment.

The effect of hearing Rabindransangit sung in this way is like seeing layers of grime and varnish being removed from an old master painting that is being cleaned. Alongside this revolution in performance, comes crucial scholarly work by musicologists such as Lars-Christian Koch in Berlin, who gave a brilliant presentation at the Tagore conference held at the University of Chicago (27 to 28 October 2011). Koch has recently completed a major study in German of the songs of Tagore.[2] I gathered from his presentation that he argues in his book that problems in the performance of Rabindrasangit set in very early on because the writing down of the songs in *Ākārmātrik*, and the control of their performance by the Visva-Bharati Music Board, led to a monotonous

[2] Lars-Christian Koch: *My Heart Sings. Die Lieder Rabindranath Tagores zwischen Tradition und Moderne*. Series: *Klang Kultur Studien / Sound Culture Studies*. Vol. 5, LIT-Verlag, Berlin etc. 2012.

rhythmic rigidity that was absent in recordings of the songs by Tagore himself, or by contemporaries such as Sahana Devi.

Once it is better understood what Tagore's songs actually are, then the door is wide open for all sorts of fascinating and creative fusion experiments. When I hear the best of his experiments, I often feel that they are taking us closer to the real spirit of the songs than the conventional way of performing them. In Ahmedabad, Partha Ghose, whose understanding of Tagore's songs is as profound as his appreciation of Tagore's scientific interests, played us the fascinating arrangements of Rabindrasangit that he recorded in Kolkata with a very fine string quartet. Recently, in the town in Hexham near where I live in Northumberland, two fine local musicians performed arrangements of Tagore songs by the musicologist Alain Daniélou (1907–1994), whose subtle piano accompaniments bring out the 'latent harmonies' in Rabindrasangit as perceptively and powerfully as Partha Ghose's string quartet arrangements. What matters above all in Rabindrasangit, as in any great music is quality, insight and feeling. This can be achieved in any number of ways, so long as one starting point is the original song as conceived and imagined by Tagore himself.

Rabindrasangit brings me to my third broad area where I feel exciting changes are afoot and where there is real potential for the future. Many of the most exciting events that I have been taking part in this year have been performance events involving actors, dancers and musicians. 'Flying Man (*Pākshi-Mānab*): Poems for the 21st century by Rabindranath Tagore' at the British Library on 17 May was a great event. Some of the greatest poems of Tagore, with a special relevance to the anxieties and concerns of the 21st century, were read by me and two Bengali readers, in my translation and in the original Bengali. Music was provided by Zoe Rahman (piano) and her brother Idris Rahman (clarinet), two of Britain's finest young jazz musicians. They showed that deeply felt jazz improvisations, combining with recitation, can give extraordinary new life and power to Tagore's poetry. On 5 to 6 August, Akademi, the Centre for South Asian

Dance, staged an amazing and innovative dance production based on Tagore. The choreographer was Ash Mukherjee, who is trained in both Bharatiya Natyam and western ballet. The musical score combined Rabindrasangit, recitation of my translation of Tagore's poem *Nagar-Sangīt* (*Song of the City* is the title of the production), and improvisations by another outstanding British jazz clarinettist, Arun Ghosh. In Valledolid in Spain on 4 October, the three-city 'Tagore En España'-Festival, co-ordinated by Indranil Chakravarty, reached a stunning climax—it was an inspiring and memorable experience of my life—with my presentation of a complex programme in Spanish to a large and enthusiastic audience in a spirit of freedom, creativity and international cooperation that went absolutely to the heart of what Rabindranath Tagore was all about. I should add that Paramita Biswas was the third Tagore singer whom I have had so far managed to persuade to sing without accompaniment. I hope there will be many more.

There are areas such as the appreciation of Tagore's paintings, where the work of Raman Siva Kumar, curator of the Tagore paintings exhibition, 'The Last Harvest', that opened in Berlin, has been particularly important. There are the insights into Tagore fiction that were provided by Sanjukta Dasgupta at the Delhi conference, and by Supriya Chaudhuri in Chicago, with the special importance that his stories and novels have for women as 'resistance narratives'. There has not been a single paper or event from which I have not learnt something, and which has not given me ever more hope that Tagore's reputation and stature can only grow.

I feel I should end with Tagore's own voice. It is not difficult to find on the internet Tagore's own extraordinary rendering of his song *Tabu Mone Rekho*. The recording was played at a number of the events this year: in Rijeka in Croatia on 21 May, in Chicago on 28 October, and in Hexham, Northumberland on 27 November. Everyone—absolutely everyone—is moved by this recording as soon as they understand the words. Among the things that I hope that my own work in this birth-anniversary year, especially in my new translation of *Gitanjali*, has achieved is this new and *transferable* way in translating Tagore's songs. What I do—and it took me many years to arrive at this very simple technique—is to preserve the repetitions of the lines which occur when the song is sung. I also indicate the four sections of the songs with line breaks.

In Spain, my translation of *Tabu Mone Rekho* was readily translated into Spanish and I think it will not be long before Spanish musicians turn this into a song of their own. Tagore actually wrote the song in 1895, and may not have been thinking of himself or his future at all. But it is impossible to hear it now without thinking of the song as prophetic, and when I hear Tagore sing it himself, with the rhythmic flexibility that is such a feature of his poetry and prose, and with an astonishing catch in his voice in the last line which suggests that he had a lump in his throat and was scarcely able to complete the song, I know to the depths of my heart that Tagore was one of those creative geniuses that simply make one proud and privileged to be human. He will be remembered, and all of us who have participated in the commemorations this year, and have spent so many hours in his globetrotting footsteps, can take pride in what we have done to ensure that he will indeed always be remembered.

Remember me, still remember me,
    if I go far away,
        still remember me
If old love gets covered by the mesh of new love,
        remember me
        still remember me

If I stay close by,
    yet you cannot see whether, like a shadow,
        I am present or not,
        remember me
        still remember me

If tears comes to your eyelids
If tears come to your eyelids
If play ceases one day, one spring night,
        still remember me
If work is stopped one day, one autumn dawn,
        remember me

If I come to your mind,
    yet heavy tears no longer brim
        in the corners of your eyes
        still remember me
Remember me, still remember me[3]

[3] *Gītabitān: Prem* 151.

Gitanjali Reborn, One Hundred Years Later
The Story of a Discovery

The international reception of Tagore has three phases. The first phase, during his lifetime, I call the 'prophetic phase'. The second phase, beginning in the mid-1980s, I call the 'literary phase', in which respect for his Bengali writings was spread through a wave of new translations. The third phase is the one we are in now, and I call it the 'anniversary phase'. It may be too early to say what defines this phase, but I myself see a resurgence of interest in Tagore in the performing arts, a new appreciation of his paintings, and a new and close attention being paid to his ideas, including his ideas about education.

I want to drive home the point that, in whatever aspect in which we are considering Tagore, he was always fundamentally a poet. He himself stressed this time and time again, and we will not understand his thinking and his activity in any field unless we remember this. Moreover, a candid and objective history of his experiments with education needs to take into account the tension that he often felt between his poetic vocation and the organisational demands that his school—and even more his university, Visva-Bharati,—imposed. I noticed recently some very frank passages in his letters to C.F. Andrews. Writing wistfully of his 'first great sweetheart—my muse', he continues in a letter written on the voyage back from the USA to Europe in 1921:

> But where is this sweetheart of mine, who was almost the only companion of my boyhood, and with whom I spent my idle days of youth exploring the mysteries of dreamland? She, my Queen, has died;

> and my world has shut against me the door of that inner apartment of beauty which gives the real taste of freedom. I feel like Shah-Jehan when his beloved Mumtaz was dead. Now I have left to me my own progeny—a magnificent plan of an International University. But it will be like Aurangzeb, who will keep me imprisoned and become my lord and master to the end of my days. Every day my fear and distrust against it are growing in strength. For it has been acquiring power from outside my own resources, and it is material power.
>
> Santiniketan has been the playground of my own spirit. What I created on its soil was made of my own dream-stuff. Its materials are few; its regulations are elastic; its freedom has the inner restraint of beauty. But the International University will be stupendous in weight and rigid in construction; and if we try to move it, it will crack. It will grow up into a bully of a brother, and browbeat its sweet elder sister into a cowering state of subjection. Beware of organization, my friend! They say organization is necessary in order to give a thing its permanence, but it may be the permanence of a tomb-stone.[1]

This tension was part of a deeper conflict he felt between the creative and moral sides of his nature:

> In this modern age of the philosophy of relativity I suppose I cannot claim for myself the quality of absolute poetdom. It is evident that the poet in me changes its features and spontaneously assumes the character of the preacher with the change of its position. I have evolved in me a certain philosophy of life which has in it a strong emotional element, and therefore it can sing as well as speak. It is like a cloud that can break out in a shower of rain, or merely tinge itself in colours and offer decorations to the festival of the sky. For this reason I give rise to expectations which are almost of a contrary character—I am asked to give gladness, and I am asked to give help.
>
> To give gladness requires inspiration; to give help requires organization—the one depends principally upon myself, and the other upon means and materials that are outside me. Here come in

[1] Rabindranath Tagore: *Letters to a Friend*, edited with two introductory essays by C. F. Andrews, George Allen & Unwin, London 1928, p. 148.

> difficulties which make me pause. Poesy creates its own solitude for the poet. The consequent detachment of mind which is necessary for creative life is lost or broken when the poet has to choose a constructive programme. The work of construction requires continuous employment of attention and energy—it cannot afford to grant leave to the poet to retire and come to himself.
>
> This creates conflict within my nature and very often makes me think that the guidance of the Good is not always for the Best. And yet, its call being natural to me, I cannot ignore it altogether. But what constantly hurts me is the fact that, in a work of organization, I have to deal with and make use of men who have more faith in the material part than in the creative ideal.[2]

Tagore won the Nobel Prize for Literature in 1913 for his poetry, and especially for his own English translation of *Gitanjali*. We are celebrating the centenary of *Gitanjali* this year (2012), the middle one of three consecutive anniversaries: the 150th anniversary last year of Tagore's birth in 1861, the centenary of *Gitanjali* this year, and the centenary next year of Tagore's Nobel Prize. Nobel Prizes are not everything, and there were times when Tagore felt that his Prize had been a 'poisoned chalice'. *Gitanjali* is not everything either, and for a long time, in my own work on Tagore, I tended to avoid it. It was linked so strongly to the 'prophetic phase' in the appreciation of Tagore—linked to the feeling worldwide that he was more a sage or even a saint than he was a poet—that I wanted to get right away from it, and re-establish his reputation on the basis of a wider and deeper appreciation of his achievements as a Bengali poet. My *Selected Poems* of Tagore which I suppose did inaugurate the new, 'literary phase' in Tagore's reception, included only one poem included in the English *Gitanjali*, a poem which was originally called *Āgaman*, 'Arrival', and was first published in a book called *Kheyā* ('The Ferry', 1906). It certainly belongs to *Gītāñjali*, but it is rather different in style from most of the other poems and songs in the book.

[2] Ibid., pp. 177–78.

Gradually, I have worked round to *Gītāñjali*, and I have come to realize that, like it or not, Tagore's international reputation as a poet does stand or fall on this book. It made an extraordinary impact at the time, leading directly to his Nobel Prize. It continues to move and inspire people in many countries and many languages; and it does, I now firmly believe, contain many truly great poems.

Penguin India last year (2011) published my new translation of *Gītāñjali*. It was not a book that I had earlier planned to do. I did not want to translate the earlier, Bengali, book called *Gītāñjali* (1910), because two English translations of that book had appeared in recent years, one by Brother James Talarovic, and the other by Joe Winter. Full of riches though the Bengali book is, it does not have quite the range and diversity of form and style that is such a remarkable feature of Tagore as a poet in Bengali and which I myself have always wanted to convey. On the other hand, how could I retranslate a book that was already such an established classic in Tagore's own version? Yet as a poet myself, knowing *Gītāñjali* mainly through Tagore's translation, I had never really responded to it.

I think my reservations about this book were shared by many other readers in Britain and the English-speaking world—even in India. If it was indeed flawed and weak, would this not remain a serious stumbling-block, an obstacle to the international acceptance of Tagore as a truly great poet? But audaciously, when Penguin India asked me if I would consider doing a new translation for Tagore's 150th birth-anniversary, I decided to tackle it, hoping that if I gave it the deep attention that translation requires, I would find qualities in it that had eluded me before.

I started the translation in 2009, and immediately felt with the very first poem that I was indeed on to something. You know how it begins in Tagore's English version: 'Thou hast made me endless, such is thy pleasure. This frail vessel thou emptiest again and again, and fillest it ever with fresh life.' The original Bengali is extraordinarily simple, and the words have an open-endedness which means that interpretations can go in different directions according to one's mood and one's sense of the poem's feelings. In my own new version, it came out with an edge to it, almost an irony.

> You've made me limitless,
>   It amuses you so to do
> You exhaust me, then fill me up again with new life
> You've made me limitless,
>   it amuses you so to do.[3]

I found that by preserving the poem's song structure, it took on a new kind of rhythmic life. For many years I didn't know what to do with Tagore's songs. Only gradually, as I came to understand the structure of the songs when they are sung—their repeated refrains and other repeated lines, and a basic division into four parts—did I realise that a translation could, by preserving those features, instantly indicate that this is a song text, not just a poem to be read on the page. This technique, which you will find throughout my new *Gitanjali* in the translations of the poems that are actually songs, has already aroused some controversy.[4] But I firmly believe that once a poem is a song it is as difficult to imagine it as not being a song, as it is to imagine someone who is married as being unmarried again.

So I had a method for translating the songs. I also discovered that the simplicity of language in many of these poems gave me rich opportunities for ambiguity and for new implications that some people might feel are impositions on the original, but which in my view are simply bringing out some of the many possibilities that are there in the original, just as the performance of a piece of great music will bring out the inherent possibilities that are there in the notes of the score.

In the beginning of my translation effort I was groping towards ideas that have now become much clearer. I was suggesting, for

[3] *Gītāñjali* 3 in *Gitanjali* (2011), p. 6.

[4] It was criticised by Nityapriya Ghosh, in a review of my book in the Bengali journal *Desh*, on the grounds that Tagore also published many of his songs as poems and intended them to be read as poems, not just sung and heard as songs.

example, that we should become much more attuned to the *sequence* of poems in *Gītāñjali*, and should read the whole book as a *sādhanā*, a spiritual endeavour or unfolding. It should not be read as an expression of *rishi*-like calm or Vedantic self-mastery, which is how W. B. Yeats and other Western admirers tended to read it when it first came out in 1912. *Sādhanā* in Indian tradition always suggests a process, rather than a finished state of self-realization. It is thus full of the pain, suffering and uncertainty that are inevitable in the evolution of the soul and of mankind as a whole from 'darkness to light'. To appreciate the *sādhanā* of *Gītāñjali*, we need to look carefully at the way one poem follows another, at the striking and sometimes quite violent juxtapositions and changes of direction that occur.

A year later, reading the English *Gitanjali* this was—in its familiar, standard form as published first by the India Society in London, and then very soon afterwards by Macmillan—seems to me both right and wrong. It is right in that I am now convinced—having carefully researched the process by which the manuscript of *Gitanjali* was converted into its published form—that the ordering of the poems was a very important part of Tagore's original conception. It is wrong in that in the published text, profound changes were made in the number and order of the poems, and many aspects of their style and expression. The published *Gitanjali* does not now seem to me the coherent unfolding or *sādhanā* that it was when Tagore first did his translations. These differences between the manuscript and the published text—the way in which a creative work that was originally coherent and balanced became, in its published form, incoherent and arbitrary—are the subject of my talk today.

The conclusions I have reached on this have arisen from research that I did in the last quarter of 2010 in Rabindra-Bhavan, Santiniketan. I arrived there as a Visiting Professor at the end of August, and my main objective was to finish the translation of *Gītāñjali* that I had started about a year previously. I had only drafted translations of 40 of the 103 poems, so my work was cut out simply to complete the translations and write a short Introduction. I thought the book would be a slim poetry book, similar in size to *Gitanjali* as originally published in 1912. Little did I know how radically the book would change and expand. It has turned into far more than a new translation. It also contains an investigation of Tagore's own translation, more thorough and detailed than has been attempted before.

Knowing when I arrived in Santiniketan that to complete the book I would have to do at least one translation a day, I decided that I had better get on with writing the Introduction without waiting until I had finished the translations themselves. So I went into Rabindra-Bhavan and ordered some standard books on Tagore from the library. Reading the pages on the English *Gitanjali* in Prasanta Kumar Paul's multi-volume biography *Rabijībanī*, I learnt that the manuscript of Tagore's translation had been preserved among the William Rothenstein's papers in the Houghton Library at Harvard. I learnt, too, that Rabindra-Bhavan possessed a microfilm copy of this manuscript, so I went along to the archive section to look at it. The microfilm copy has been replaced with a digital copy, which like most of Rabindra-Bhavan's archival holdings can be conveniently read on a screen.

As I started to look at the pages of the manuscript, I rapidly became astonished. There were massive and extensive differences between the manuscript and the published text. Firstly, the number of poems was different. There were 83 poems in the manuscript, compared to 103 in the published text. Secondly, there was a total change in the order of the poems. When I later started to compare and analyse the order carefully, I found that only one poem—no. 57, *Ālo, āmār ālo, ogo/ālo bhuban-bharā* in the original, a song from Tagore's play *Achalāyatan*—is identified by the same number in the manuscript as in the published text. Thirdly, there were extensive alterations in the paragraphing. Famous poems such as 'Where the mind is without fear', which in the published text are printed in short, bible-like verses, in the manuscript appear as pieces of continuous prose. These differences in the paragraphing may not initially seem significant, but to me they had an immediate and major effect on the rhythm and 'speed' of the poems. (A prose poem that is a single piece of prose without paragraph divisions moves much faster than one that has been chopped up into short paragraphs.) Fourthly—and this is something that only became fully clear when I started to compare every line of the manuscript with the published text—there are many more commas in the text than in the manuscript. Commas, like paragraph divisions, can slow a text down and affect its rhythmic and emotional energy. Finally, it did not take long for me to see that there were many differences in vocabulary and phrasing.

When I left the archive section to go back to my office and read more of what critics and biographers had written about *Gitanjali*, I found that two Bengali critics had addressed in detail the differences between the manuscript and the text. Shyamal Kumar Sarkar, of the English Department at Visva-Bharati, published two articles on the manuscript of *Gitanjali* in the *Visva-Bharati Quarterly*.[5] Saurindra Mitra, in his Bengali book *Khyāti-akhyātir nepathye*,[6] devoted some sixty pages to an analysis of the differences. But I found that both these writers focus on variations of vocabulary and phrasing, and had almost nothing to say about the other, more fundamental differences. Both these writers assume that the differences are largely attributable to the editorial intervention of W. B. Yeats. Shyamal Kumar Sarkar is on the whole supportive of Yeats, and regards most of the changes as an improvement. Saurindra Mitra, by contrast, wants to protect Tagore from the slander, that much of the success of *Gitanjali* (when it first came out), was due to Yeats. He is particularly infuriated by a letter that Yeats wrote to the publisher George Macmillan on 28 January 1917, in which he claimed that his revision of *Gitanjali* had been 'exhaustive' and that Tagore's later books of translations were inferior largely because they had not been so thoroughly revised.

[5] Shyamal Kumar Sarkar: On the autograph manuscript of *Gitanjali (Song Offering)*, *Visva-Bharati Quarterly*, vol. 43, nos. 3 and 4 (Nov. 1977–April 1978), pp. 234–62; The manuscript of *Gitanjali*: a supplementary note, *Visva-Bharati Quarterly* vol. 3 and 4, (Nov. 1978–April 1979) pp. 150–75.

[6] Ananda Publishers, Kolkata 1977.

Having now researched the matter myself, I too have no doubt that the differences between the manuscript and the text are largely attributable to Yeats. I differ from Shyamal Kumar Sarkar in finding many of these changes inferior to what Tagore himself wrote in the manuscript. I differ from Saurindra Mitra in concluding that Yeats' own description of his editing as 'exhaustive' was not incorrect. Saurindra Mitra's argument that the changes that Yeats made were relatively trivial and that some of them could have been made by Tagore himself, becomes much less convincing when those changes are placed longside the more thoroughgoing alterations to the number, sequence, paragraphing and punctuation.

My question, was: should we regard the standard text of *Gitanjali* as set in stone? Might it be possible to create a new text and arrangement for the book that would be closer to the manuscript and therefore to Tagore's original conception and intention? My book arrives at the radical conclusion that we should, nearly a century after the publication of *Gitanjali*, look again at this most famous of Tagore's books. We should not assume that, just because it came out with Yeats' *imprimatur*, won Tagore the Nobel Prize for Literature in 1913, and was translated into all the major languages of the world, that the text that became standard is necessarily the best text of Tagore's translation that we could have.

My book offers an alternative: not only does it contain an entirely new translations of all the poems that are in the English *Gitanjali* (including three in the manuscript that were omitted), it also has—alternating with my translations—a new text of Tagore's translation, based on his manuscript. This text contains some editorial adjustments by me (all of them referenced in footnotes that give the actual manuscript reading), but far fewer than those that were made by Yeats. In the tables that I have provided in appendices to my book, I calculate that there are more than 300 changes between the manuscript and the text that are attributable to Yeats. In my own new text, there are only about 80 changes, most of them very small. Moreover, my text follows the manuscript number and sequence. Since the manuscript has 83 poems, the remaining poems I put in a section called 'Additional Poems'. I have arranged these in the chronological order of their Bengali originals. Unlike the main sequence of 83 poems, we do not have manuscripts for all these additional poems. Three of them were written on spare pages at the end of the main *Gītāñjali* manuscript; 12 of them can be found in a bundle of miscellaneous manuscripts in the Houghton library that is known as the 'Crescent Moon Sheaf'; for the remaining eight we do not have any manuscripts at all.

The second of Shyamal Kumar Sarkar's articles for the *Visva-Bharati Quarterly* focuses on the 'Crescent Moon Sheaf'. He suggests that the 12 poems that were used for *Gitanjali* may be what has survived of a second notebook that Tagore filled with additional translations on the voyage to England, and which he handed over to William Rothenstein on his arrival in London. This second notebook, however, is lost. So we do not know if the manuscripts in the Crescent Moon Sheaf are pages from this notebook or separate manuscript copies. The typed copy of *Gitanjali* on which Yeats is said to have made his corrections has also been lost, so it is always necessary to say that we cannot finally *prove* that the changes were Yeats's work, though all the information that we have points to that likelihood.

The easiest way to demonstrate that *Gitanjali* as conceived and executed by Tagore in his manuscript has a shape and coherence that the published text lacks is to look at the sources for the poems. In Appendix A of my book I have given a table which shows in two columns the books from which the poems are taken: the manuscript on the left and the published text on the right. The 83 poems in the *Gitanjali* manuscript are of three types. There are the songs or song-like poems form the Bengali *Gītāñjali* (published in 1910) and from its follow-up volume *Gītimālya* (1914); there are poems from the earlier book *Naibedya* (1901), most of which are sonnets; and there are ballad-like poems from *Kheyā* (1906). The only exception to these three groups is the song from *Achalāyatan*, which I mentioned earlier. All the poems except that song from *Achalāyatan* (which comes at no. 57) are from *Gītāñjali* and *Gītimālya*, and therefore have an obvious unity of style. No. 58 is another song from *Gītimālya* which was dropped from the published *Gitanjali.* It is not clear why. Maybe this one and the other two that were omitted were left out by mistake. It is a very fine song and translation, it introduces a note of pain—preparing the way for the sequence of sonnets from *Naibedya*, many of which are austere and painful in tone. The *Naibedya* poems continue until no. 73, and are followed by a group from *Kheyā*. The last four poems in *Gitanjali* as originally conceived by Tagore in his manuscript are once again from the Bengali book *Gītāñjali* itself. They round off the sequence, and confirm that whatever else the book may contain it is essentially a book of 'song offerings'.

The sequence in the published text, by contrast, has nothing of that balance or coherence. The three types of poems—the *Gītāñjali*/*Gītimālya* poems, the *Naibedya* poems, as well as the *Kheyā* poems—are mixed up from the beginning, not presented in groups, and they are further mixed by the 23 additional poems. These poems come from a very diverse group of books. They include, for example, 'On the seashore of endless worlds children meet' and two other poems from *Shishu* (1903), which Tagore wrote on the spare pages at the end of the *Gitanjali* notebook and which he was also to include in his later collection, *The Crescent Moon* (1913). They are fine poems, but they are extraneous to *Gitanjali* as originally conceived. This is also true of other poems that were added, such as the one from *Smaran* (1903; Tagore's book of poems in memory of his wife), the poem from *Kalpanā* (1900), which Tagore translated as 'Deity of the ruined temple', and a poem from *Utsarga* (1914), which is witty and brilliant but which really has nothing to do with the rest of *Gitanjali.*

How did this jumble come about? It seems to me that Yeats and Tagore's other friends in England, on seeing that he had a second notebook of translations in addition to the main *Gitanjali* notebook, suggested that these additional poems be included, and then simply shuffled the poems together to produce an arrangement that made sense to them, but which had nothing to do with the *sādhanā* of *Gitanjali* itself.

When I look at the order of poems in the published *Gitanjali* now, having seen how coherent Tagore's conception of it was in the manuscript, I find that the only thing that can be said about it is that the poems about death are grouped towards the end. This itself shows a misconception: for it is a very un-Indian thing to do, to put death at the end of a *sādhanā*, rather than light, truth, and immortality.

As regards the changes that were made to individual poems, here are two examples, both of them very famous poems indeed. Most of you will know the first one by heart. Here it is in the standard published text:

Where the mind is without fear and the head is held high;
Where knowledge is free;
Where the world has not been broken up into fragments by narrow domestic walls;
Where words come out from the depth of truth;
Where tireless striving stretches its arms towards perfection;
Where the clear stream of reason has not lost its way into the dreary desert sand of dead habit;
Where the mind is led forward by thee into ever-widening thought and action—
Into that heaven of freedom, my Father, let my country awake.

Gitanjali 35

In the manuscript, Tagore's translation of this sonnet from *Naibedya* reads like this:

> Where the mind is without fear and the head is held high; where knowledge is free; where the world has not been frittered into fragments by narrow domestic walls; where words come out from the depth of truth; where sleepless striving stretches its strenuous arms towards perfection; where the clear stream of reason has not lost its way into the dreary desert sand of dead habit, and where the mind is led forward by thee into ever-widening thought and action—there waken up my country into that heaven of freedom, my father![7]

[7] *Gitanjali* (2011), p. 95.

There are several things to observe about these two versions. Firstly, the standard version has been broken up into short paragraphs. This may not seem so significant if you take this poem on its own, but the overall effect of introducing such short paragraphing throughout *Gitanjali* is considerable, and changes the whole energy and flow of the book. The short paragraphs are one of the things that have made many readers describe the language of Tagore's *Gitanjali* as 'biblical'. In my view, the biblical effect derives more from the paragraphing and the punctuation than it does from the language as such.

Secondly the concluding phrases of the poem have been swapped round in a way that I consider unnecessary. There is nothing actually wrong with what Tagore wrote, except perhaps for 'waken up'. It is more natural in English to say either 'wake up' or 'wake' or 'awaken'. In my version of the text I have changed 'waken' to 'wake', preserving the colloquial vigour of 'up'. Thirdly there is, I think, an English mistake in the standard text that should have been corrected. (I have counted at least 20 examples of mistakes in English in *Gitanjali* that Yeats should have corrected, but missed.) In 'where the clear stream of reason has not lost its way into the dreary desert sand of dead habit', 'into' does not express what Tagore actually means here. The original Bengali speaks of the desert sands soaking up the stream of reason. 'Into' suggests that the stream of reason actually wants to get to the dreary desert sand, just as if I say 'I lost my way into the centre of town' I mean that I wanted to get to the centre of town but I lost my way and didn't get there. 'Into' implies purpose and motion towards, and is perfectly appropriate in the last clause of the poem, '...into that heaven of freedom...' In my own new text of Tagore's translation, I have changed the misleading 'into' to 'in', and other native English speakers (and some Indian speakers of English too) agree with me that this correction is justified.

My second example is almost equally famous, for this is the song that Tagore sang in Bengali to Mahatma Gandhi when he broke his fast at Yerwada Prison in 1932. It was one of Gandhi's favourite songs; when Tagore was asked to sing it, he found he could not remember the tune, so he made up a new tune on the spot. Here is the standard text:

> When the heart is hard and parched up, come upon me with a shower of mercy.
> When grace is lost from life, come with a burst of song.
> When tumultuous work raises its din on all sides shutting me out from beyond, come to me, my lord of silence, with thy peace and rest.
> When my beggarly heart sits crouched, shut up in a corner, break open the door, my king, and come with the ceremony of a king.
> When desire blinds the mind with delusion and dust, O thou holy one, thou wakeful, come with thy light and thy thunder.
>
> *Gitanjali 39*

In the manuscript the translation reads like this:

> When the heart is hard and parched up come upon me with a shower of mercy. When grace is lost from life come with a burst of song. When tumultuous work raises its din on all sides shutting me out from beyond come to me, my lord of silence, with thy peace and rest. When my beggarly heart sits crouched, shut up in a corner, break open the door, my king, and come in with thy regal splendour. When desire blinds the mind with delusion and dust, Oh thou holy one, thou wakeful, come with thy light of thunder.[8]

In this too we note that short paragraph divisions have been introduced. But more than that, several commas have been inserted. Again, if we look at this superficially and take this poem in isolation, the insertion of the commas may seem justifiable and not a significant departure from the manuscript. But try reading it aloud, and you will immediately sense the difference. Tagore in his manuscript uses

[8] *Gitanjali* (2011), pp. 27–28.

commas when they are absolutely necessary, but is otherwise sparing in his use of them. This may be partly because Bengali sentences with their frequent use of participles do not require commas in the way that English sub-clauses often do. But I think he was also sparing in his use of commas because his highly sensitive ear told him that his translations would move faster and with more energy if there were not many commas. Notice how the first three sentences in his translation build up and grow in length. The absence of a comma before 'come' in each case creates a sense of urgency, and this is particularly strong in the third, long sentence, where the use of commas round 'my lord of silence' also gives special emphasis to that phrase.

As regards changes of language, there are two that seem to me highly significant. 'Come in with thy regal splendour' has been changed in the published text to 'come with the ceremony of the king'. Saurindra Mitra rightly says that 'ceremony' is a typically Yeatsian word (it reminds us of 'The ceremony of innocence is drowned' in his poem 'The Second Coming'), and is not as good a translation of the Bengali word *samāroha* as 'regal splendour'. I agree, and I am also struck by the weakness of the repetition of 'king', which Tagore in the manuscript has avoided by his use of the powerful adjective 'regal'. At the end of the poem, Tagore's interesting phrase 'come with thy light of thunder' has been changed to the much more obvious and less interesting 'come with thy light and thy thunder'. For the thunder actually to contain the light (or *vice versa*) is a typically Tagorean idea. It reminds me of one of the aphorisms in his late book of paintings combined with verses, *Chitralipi* (1940). Opposite a painting of a black bird, Tagore puts a Bengali verse which he also gives in his English translation: 'The dark takes form/ in the heart of the white/ and reveals it.'

Time and time again as I went through the manuscript comparing it closely with the published text, I found that what Tagore originally wrote made better sense and there was no need to change it. There are some things that needed correction, but they are mostly small errors to do with prepositions, articles, and verb endings. Often Yeats has changed more than was necessary, perhaps because he worked from the assumption that Tagore as an Indian did not know English well enough and therefore if his work was to be published it would need substantial revision.

The full effect of reverting in my book to the number and sequence of poems that we find in the original manuscript is, at present, still quite hard for me to judge. My hope is that as readers get used to the new sequence and read Tagore's translations alongside my own, they will find the *sādhanā*, the spiritual unfolding that I believe was his original motive in selecting and arranging the poems for his English *Gitanjali*. From poem no. 5, the *sādhanā* that was *Gitanjali* was now firmly underway, and would continue until he reached no. 83, which reads in the manuscript:

> Let all the strains of joy mingle in my last song—the joy that makes the earth flow over in riotous excesses of verdure, the joy that sets the twin brothers—life and death—into mad capers over the whole world, the joy that sweeps in with the tempest shaking and waking all life with wild laughter, the joy that sits still with its tears on the open red lotus of pain, and the joy that throws everything it has upon the dust and knows not a word.[9]

The completeness of this poem, the *purnatā* that combines both life and death into a spirit of *ānanda* or joy, brings the *sādhanā* of *Gitanjali* to its proper conclusion. Maybe in the context on 1912, Yeats was right: *Gitanjali* did need to be a bit longer, the fine additional poems that were in the second notebook deserved to be added, and the grouping of poems about death at the end made the book appealing and accessible to Edwardian taste. Maybe without Yeats' intervention and this re-arrangement, Tagore would not have won the Nobel Prize in 1913. But a century later, the 'real *Gitanjali*' seems more important to focus on than any prize, even a Nobel. In fact, the more one goes into the history of *Gitanjali*, the more painful and problematic that

[9] *Gitanjali* (2011), p. 113.

history becomes, despite the stunning initial success of the book. These painful aspects are what made Tagore increasingly ambivalent about his translations as time went on, and increasingly ready to express in letters to friends regret that he had done them at all.

My hope is that my book will offer a kind of closure to this painful, one hundred year old history, and also a new beginning. Poem no. 83 was placed at no. 58 in the published *Gitanjali*, but the more I look at it now, in the original Bengali, in Tagore's manuscript translation, and in my own new translation, the more convinced I am that this is the poem with which *Gitanjali* should have ended. Let this poem also take us forward to a better understanding of what this great poet intended. I end with my own translation of it:

As if with all *rāginīs* my last song is filled—
As if its tune can all my joys unfold:
The joy with which the soil of the earth smiles.
That in the restless trees and leaves uncurls;
The joy with which those close companions, life and death
Wander insanely all across the earth—
These are the joys which in my closing song unfold.

The joy that comes in clothes of raucous storms,
Whose laughter shakes awake life's sleeping limbs;
The joy that waits to shine in sorrow's tears
Or blooms in the blood-red lotus-gifts that pain confers;
The joy that scatters all things in the dust,
Which no last word has ever quite expressed—
These are the joys which in my closing song unfold.[10]

Asiatic Society of Mumbai 4 December 2010.

[10] Ibid.

Painting the Dust and the Sunlight Rabindranath Tagore and the Two *Gitanjalis*

Was Rabindranath Tagore—in terms that have been so important in the long history of Indian philosophy and spirituality—essentially *dvaitavādi* or *advaitvādi*, a dualist or a non-dualist? If one reads Tagore's writings on his religious and poetic philosophy, whether in English or Bengali, one can easily reach the conclusion that he was a dualist. In *The Religion of Man*, the Hibbert Lectures given in Oxford in May 1930 on which his Bengali book of 1933, *Mānuser Dharma* was based, Tagore carefully defines the *advaitavādi* tradition, but only in order to distinguish himself from it. In Chapter XIII, 'Spiritual freedom', he writes, 'as in the world of art, so in the spiritual world, our soul waits for its freedom from the ego to reach that disinterested joy which is the source and goal of creation. It cries for *mukti*, its freedom in the unity of truth.'[1] Finding that longing at the popular as well as the sophisticated level, he writes of 'the poet saint Kabir' and other such singers that 'truth is unity, and therefore freedom is in its realization. The texts of our daily worship and meditation are for training our mind to overcome the barrier of separateness from the rest of existence and to realize *advaitam*, the Supreme Unity which is *anantam*, infinitude.'[2] Yet in his fourteenth and final chapter, he writes—giving this statement the emphasis of his final paragraph:

[1] *English Writings* (1996), vol. 3, p. 162.
[2] Ibid., p. 163.

> But such an ideal of the utter extinction of the individual separateness has not a universal sanction in India. There are many of us whose prayer is for dualism so that for them the bond of devotion with God may continue forever. For them religion is a truth which is ultimate and they refuse to envy those who are ready to sail for the further shore of existence across humanity. They know that human imperfection is the cause of our sorrow but there is a fulfillment in love within the range of our limitation which accepts all sufferings and yet rises above them.[3]

In Bengali, one of the clearest and best expressions of Tagore's dualism that I have found recently is in his essay 'Manus', (Man), included in the first volume of *Sāntiniketan*, his collected religious addresses delivered at Santiniketan.[4] Beginning with a description of the hubbub of the *Paus-melā* at Santiniketan, he writes of how if one wants to commune with Nature in all her glory, one has to get right away from human beings. Why? Because 'God has deliberately destroyed to some extent Man's harmony (*sāmanjasya*) with Nature—that is his *jeu d'esprit* (*ei tār ānander kautuk*).'[5] Most of the endeavours of art and religion—as well as human efforts in the field of government and law-making—are an attempt to recover the order and harmony that we have lost, to bridge the gulf between Man and the rest of the universe. 'At the heart of all yearning (*chāoyā*) is the yearning to cross to the other side (*pār hate chāoyā*), This separateness keeps saying, "Oh, let me cross this gulf."'[6] But he goes on to argue that if this gulf didn't exist we wouldn't be able to cross it. How can we cross it? By 'extinction of the self'? 'Never!' (*kakhano-i nay*). If that were the case, then we would get consolation from all kinds of loss. But human experience is quite otherwise. Loss of possessions or of people dear to us causes us intense distress. 'If there is anything that human beings

[3] Ibid., p. 171.

[4] The essay is dated 8 Paus, 1315 (1909), in Rabindranath Tagore: *Santiniketan* I.2 Visva-Bharati, Kolkata 1934–35.

[5] Ibid., p. 75.

[6] Ibid., p. 77.

ultimately do *not* want it is extinction.' Do we then want *dis*harmony? We don't want that either, because we don't want all the sorrow and sinfulness that comes from such *bicched* ('separateness'). What we actually want is love. When do we find love? 'When there is a balance of separateness and unity (*milan*); when separateness does not destroy unity, and unity does not swallow up separateness; when two come together, yet there is no opposition between them but instead there is mutual support (*parasparer sahāy*).'[7]

In numerous essays and sermons Tagore emphasizes that love and poetry and all creative expression come from relationship, from an interplay or *līlā* between Man and God, World and Spirit, this side and that side, finite and infinite, real and ideal, and so on. In *My Reminiscences* (1917), the English translation by Surendranath Tagore of *Jībansmriti* (1912), he defines 'the subject on which all my writings have dwelt' as 'the joy of finding the infinite in the finite and [the?] finite in the infinite'. The case for Tagore as *dvaitavādi*, a dualist, seems unassailable.

Yet if we turn to one of the most famous passages in *Jībansmriti*—and I have looked carefully at the Bengali original, not the English translation—we find a vivid description of a life-changing experience that was distinctly *advaitavādi* or non-dualist.

It happened to him as a young man in the early 1880s, when he was staying with his brother Jyotirindranath and sister-in-law Kadambari—muse, mentor and an inspiration to Rabindranath both before and after her tragic suicide in 1884—at their house at no. 10 Sudder Street, Kolkata. He describes how he had increasingly been making a habit of going out on to the roof of the main Tagore residence at Jorasanko to watch the sunset. Was the transcendental mood it instilled in him merely a magic effect of light? 'Not at all. I came to see clearly, that the actual reason [for my mood] was that the evening entered me, and I lost sight of myself.' (*sandhyā āmār-i madhye āsiyache—āmi-i dhākā pariyāchi*) He began to realize that he

[7] Ibid., pp. 78–79.

could escape from the ego this way, 'and see the world as it should be seen'. He tried to communicate this revelation to others, but 'I know I was not at all successful'.[8]

Then on one, never-to-be-forgotten morning he had a much more powerful experience. He was standing on the verandah of the Sudder Street house, looking at the trees in the garden of the Free School at the end of the street. 'The rising sun could be seen through the leaves of the trees. As I watched, it suddenly seemed as if a curtain had been removed from my eyes. I saw the whole universe suffused with an extraordinary grandeur (*aparup mahimāy*)—with waves of joy and beauty all around. Layers of sorrow (*bisād*) in my heart were penetrated in a trice, and the light of the universe flooded my entire inner being. That very day my poem *Nirjharer svapnabhanga* ('The Awakening of the Stream') poured out in a flood of inspiration.'[9]

This event seems to have remained for Tagore the supreme religious experience of his life. It was his 'Road to Damascus'-moment, his discovery of the same vision of love and beauty and unity and joy with which Dante ended the *Paradiso* of his *Divine Comedy*. But his ecstatic mood didn't last long. He recalls rather wryly how for a few days he was able to tolerate a gentleman who had previously irritated him with the question, 'Have you ever seen God with your own eyes?' and who, when Rabindranath told him he had not, then described how God was constantly 'swarming' before his eyes (*chokher sammukhe bij-bij karite thāken*). But when Rabindranath went with Jyotirindranath and Kadambari to Darjeeling, and expected the mountains to raise his ecstasy to an even higher level, he found to his surprise that 'the humble Sudder Street house had won'. It seemed that the vision, exalted though it was, had required a humdrum, human, urban context that in the Himalayas was lacking. He ends the passage with the stark declaration: 'I had seen a jewel; it was suddenly shut off and I saw a

[8] *Rabīndra-rachanābali* vol. 17. Visva-Bharati, Kolkata 1943, p. 396. (My translation).

[9] *Rabindra-rachanābali*, Ibid., p. 396.

box. But however beautifully the box might be decorated, there was no danger of mistaking that it was only an empty box.'[10]

Is this *advaitavādi* experience—crucial though it was in Tagore's religious, emotional and poetic development—sufficient in itself to cast doubt on his predominantly *dvaitavādi* position? In terms of his philosophy (though he often denied that he was a philosopher), the answer is 'probably not'. But philosophy is not the only way in which a poet—and musician—might express his *advaitavādi* tendencies, and I want to consider—by examining the poems and songs of 'the two *Gitanjalis*'—whether *dvaitavād*, dualism, is actually sufficient as an underpinning for everything that is going on in them.

As a translator and reader of Tagore, it has taken me a long time to work round to *Gitanjali*. Why has it taken me so long? The main reason was that in my *Selected Poems* I wanted to get right away from 'the English Tagore'. My aim instead was to establish his reputation and credibility as a great poet in Bengali, with an output far more complex and variegated than one could tell from his own English translations. My selection included only one poem from the English *Gitanjali*, 'Arrival' (*Āgaman*), which was actually the very first poem by Tagore I translated, though I didn't at the time realize it was in *Gītāñjali* (no. 51), because it comes not from the Bengali book of that name but from *Kheyā* ('The Ferry-boat', 1906). Another reason was that many of the poems in *Gītāñjali* are actually songs, and it was my policy in the book not to include songs.[11]

If I am paying more attention to *Gītāñjali* now,[12] this is not just because I have come to accept that in terms of the totality of Tagore's career, both Eastern and Western, *Gitanjali* has to be accorded a central place. It is also because I have been working more and more on *Rabīndrasangīt*, Tagore's songs—their words, their music and their

[10] *Rabīndra-rachanābali*, ibid., pp. 397–98.

[11] *Selected Poems* (1985). pp. 31–32 (Introduction), for the rationale for excluding songs.

[12] The author here alludes to his translation of *Gitanjali* which he had begun when writing this paper. It resulted in his book published in 2011 (editor).

interpretation by performers past and present. Not only does *Gītāñjali* contain many profound and beautiful songs; it also represents a phase in Tagore's output in which the distinction between poetry and song virtually disappeared. As an attempt to express the character of these song-poems in English prose-poetry, Tagore's own translations have become more interesting and attractive to me than they were before. They vary, I think, in literary quality, but at their best they are a considerable creative achievement, an expression of real imagination and inventiveness in a language that was not primarily his own. I have discovered how well they can work when read aloud: the sensitive ear of a *mahākabi* is ever active in them, in their rhythms and cadences and word-painting. It is also fascinating to look at the differences between his English versions and the Bengali originals: there are often good and understandable reasons for the subtle changes or cuts or additions he has made.[13]

I have referred to 'the two *Gitanjalis*'. There are two *Gitanjalis* because the Bengali book of that name (1910) is not the same in its content as the English *Gitanjali* (1912). The former is a collection of 157 lyric poems in Bengali, many of which are also songs. It was followed by *Gītimālya* (1914) and *Gītāli* (1914). The three books together are often referred to by Bengali critics as 'the *Gitanjali* phase', to which also belonged the plays *Rājā* (1910) and *Dākghar* (translated as 'The Post-Office', 1914). The phase stemmed from a period of grief and introspection that arose from a shattering series of bereavements: the deaths of Tagore's wife Mrinalini Devi in 1902, his daughter Renuka (Rani) in 1903, and his son Samindranath in 1907. The phase also reflects his disillusionment with the violent turn taken by

[13] A close comparison between Tagore's translations and his Bengali originals can be found in Chanchal Kumar Brahma's *Englander Dikprante Rabir Uday O Rabir Asta* (Kolkata 2000), a chapter of which is reproduced in Subhankar Bhattacharyay and Mayukh Chakraborty, eds., *Gitanjali: Song Offerings,* Kolkata: Parul Prakashani 2007, pp. 349–61. This volume, by the way, is a very useful compilation, containing as it does the English *Gitanjali*, the Bengali poems/songs and the sources of Tagore's English versions, and a rich array of critical essays on *Gitanjali* in England, Germany, France and the Netherlands.

the Swadeshi campaign against Lord Curzon's partition of Bengal in 1905. In terms of poetic technique, *Gītāñjali* and its two successors brought a complete intermingling of poetry and song. Even those poems for which Tagore did not compose melodies are song-like in their structure and rhythm, and they are full of the imagery of music.

The other *Gitanjali* is the English *Gitanjali*, Tagore's famous book of prose-poems, published first by the India Society in London in November 1912 and by Macmillan in March 1913. With an Introduction by W. B. Yeats, the book achieved such sudden and rapturous acclaim that Thomas Sturge Moore recommended Tagore to the Swedish Academy for the 1913 Nobel Prize for Literature. Even though the Royal Society of Literature in London had backed Thomas Hardy for the Prize, the Nobel Committee voted 12 out of 13 in favour of Tagore. The news reached him at Santiniketan on 16 November 1913, and utterly transformed his life, making him the 'first intercontinental literary superstar'.

The English *Gitanjali* overlaps with the Bengali *Gītāñjali* by just over half: 53 of its 103 poems are from the Bengali *Gītāñjali*. The remaining poems come from ten other books, not all of which belong to the '*Gitanjali* phase'. I would say there are essentially three types of poems—though Tagore's style of translating them disguised the differences between them. There are the song-like poems of the *Gitanjali* phase proper; then there are stern, nationalistic poems in sonnet form that he published in *Naibedya* (1901), including what in India has become Tagore's most famous poem of all—'Where the mind is without fear and the head is held high' (no. 35), and almost, after the *Jana gana mana* (also by Tagore) a second 'national anthem'; thirdly, there are the symbolic poems of the sort he published in *Kheyā* (1906), of which *Āgaman* is a typical example.[14]

[14] The only Westerner who realized that *Gitanjali* was actually quite a miscellaneous collection was its French translator, André Gide. See his introduction, translated by Chinmoy Guha, in *Gitanjali: Song Offerings*. UBSPD, New Delhi in association with Visva-Bharati, Kolkata 2003, pp. 268–84. Gide writes: 'Since I have nothing but praise for the book, I would like to begin

My focus here is on the song-poems, the poems of the *Gitanjali* phase proper, and I want to illustrate my points by referring to the twelve songs that, in 2008, came out on a CD, masterminded and performed by the Kolkata-based singer and theatre-director Debashish Raychaudhuri. I have known Debashish for a long time, and he asked me if I would write Notes for this CD, translate those songs in his selection for which translations by Rabindranath himself do not exist, and also record recitations.[15]

I found this a most stimulating challenge, not least because I finally arrived at a way of translating Rabindrasangit that satisfies me and which I hope will encourage non-Bengali readers to see Tagore's song-poems in a new light.

At a lecture in 2008 to students and staff in the English Department of Jahangirnagar University, Bangladesh[16] I played them one of Debashish's recordings, and followed it with a recording of my English translation, read not by me but by Louise Coigley, a British specialist in verse recitation with a background in the Rudolf Steiner movement.[17]

---

by pointing out a serious flaw in it. The book may be slender, but it is badly assembled. By that I do not mean that it does not match with our western rhythms, our metres, our measures. No, but we come to know from a short note printed at the end of the book that *Gitanjali* is made out of disparate bits and pieces originally published in Bengali in three volumes: *Naibedya, Kheya* and *Gitanjali*—which lends its title to this garland. Other poems, too, scattered here and there, which appeared in various magazines, merrily divert our minds.' (p. 268)

[15] *The Dust and the Sunlight*, songs and recitations from Rabindranath Tagore's *Gitanjali*, 2 CDs compiled, edited and directed by Debashish Raychaudhuri, Hindusthan Musical Products Ltd., IP 6173/74. The songs are sung by Debashish himself, his daughter Rohini Raychaudhuri, Rano Guhathakurata and Sharmila Roy.

[16] 'Translation Challenges in *Meghnadbadh-kabya and Rabindrasangit*', Jahangirnagar University, Bangladesh, 20 March, 2008. Delivered from notes, not from a written text.

[17] Rudolf Steiner and his successors have always laid a lot of emphasis on solo and choric poetry recitation, and at the Speech School at East Grinstead, West Sussex, intensive courses and diplomas in verse recitation are taught. Louise Coigley shares the recitation with me on Debashish Raychaudhuri's CD-set.

She was later to join me in making recordings for Debashish's CD. I challenged them to detect what was new about my way of translating a song-text of this sort, the main difference between my method and Tagore's. I first played them Debashish's recording of *Dhāy yena mor sakal bhālobāsā,* then read out my translation.

Let all my love rush
Lord, towards you, towards you, towards you
Let all my deepest hopes run
Lord, to your ears, to your ears, to your ears
Let all my love rush
Lord, towards you, towards you, towards you

Wherever my thoughts are, let them respond to your call
Wherever my thoughts are, let them respond to your call
Whatever my fetters, let them all snap
O Lord, at your pull, your pull, your pull
Let all my love rush
Lord, towards you, towards you, towards you

This beggar's bag outside me, let it be emptied endlessly
And let my heart be secretly filled
Lord, by your gifts, your gifts, your gifts
This beggar's bag outside me, let it be emptied endlessly
And let my heart be secretly filled
Lord, by your gifts, your gifts, your gifts

O inmost friend, let all that is lovely in this life
O inmost friend, let all that is lovely in this life
Let it burst out today
Lord, with your songs, your songs, your songs
Let all my love rush
Lord, towards you, towards you, towards you[18]

[18] The song is in the Bengali *Gītāñjali* but not in the English one; that is why there is no translation by Tagore himself.

The difference was obvious. The simple step that I had taken is to preserve in my English the repetition of words and phrases that is normal and indispensable when a song by Tagore is sung. I feel there are a number of advantages in this. Firstly, it becomes immediately apparent to the reader that this is a song, not a poem, as repetitions are a feature of songs in all languages the world over. Secondly, in reciting the translation, the reader has the opportunity to vary the tone and pace and emotional effect of each recurrence just as a singer will vary such repetitions in his or her sung interpretation. Thirdly, and most importantly, by introducing line-breaks in the translation, the four sections or *tukkas* of the vast majority of Tagore's songs—the *āsthāyi, antarā, sanchārī* and *ābhog*—can be clearly demarcated.

From no translations of Rabindrasangit that I have seen can one gain any awareness of the structure of the song, though Chanchal Kumar Brahma argues that Tagore's translation decisions are influenced in places by his own awareness of the four *tukkas*.[19] Yet, this incomparable form, derived, I gather, from Dhrupad, but used over and over again by Tagore with wonderful resourcefulness and variety, is vital to the beauty, mystery and profundity of the songs. What words are there to express the way in which the recurrent *āsthāyi* grounds the song, the *antarā* rising into a higher octave takes it up to a higher plane, the meandering *sanchārī* descending into a lower octave explores new depths, and finally—and most magically of all—the *ābhog*, repeating the melody of the *antarā* but with new words, gives the melody an entirely fresh emotional nuance?

The only parallel in Western music that I can think of is the way, in sonata form, the recapitulation of the first subject, but in a different key, gives a new meaning to the music, transformed not only by the key-change but by all that has happened in the development section.

[19] According to Haricharan Bandyopadhyay's two-volume Bengali dictionary (third edition, 1988), *tukka* is the original form of this technical term. I gather, however, from Chanchal Kumar Brahma's study of Tagore's translations (see note 13 above) that the Hindi form *tuk* is also now current in Bengali.

Without the melody, the full effect of this form in a song by Tagore cannot, of course, be registered. But I believe that by preserving repetitions and demarcating the four sections clearly, a sensitive reader can perceive the subtle shifts that take place, especially if alongside the silent or spoken reading of the text the song itself can be heard.

Is the song I have just cited *dvaitavādi* or *advaitavādi*? In its words, there is plenty of dualism in it. There is a clear distinction between 'I' (the poet, or the human soul) and 'You' (God, or the divine spirit). It is full of the yearning, the longing, the *chāoyā* that Tagore defined in the essay *Mānus* referred to earlier. 'Deepest hopes', 'fetters', and 'beggar's bag', all express unrealizable desires, the inevitability of *bicched*, the impossibility of *milan*. Yet love, and the songs that are both 'yours' and the poet's own songs combined, supplies a way of bridging the gulf.[20] In other words, from the depths of *dvaitavād*, *advaitavād* can emerge, but only through the agency of music, which is by definition beyond words, and therefore beyond all *bicched*.

This is the fundamental point that I want to make. As a poet and religious thinker, Tagore was certainly a dualist. But as a musician—and as a poet whose identity often converged with his identity as a musician and a composer/singer of songs, he tended towards non-dualism. This was a logical consequence of the inherent nature of music as an art that goes beyond words. In all cultural traditions, music has been the art by which human beings have reached out towards the transcendental, and the living reality of the transcendental has been expressed through music more completely than through any other art form.

Poetry of course, in its sound and rhythm, has a musical dimension, which is why we are better able to find and express the transcendental in poetry than we can in prose, though prose itself—and particularly

[20] Just before writing this paper I received from Professor Tarapada Bhattacharyaya a translation he has published of 75 songs by Tagore: *Songs that Bridge the Gulf* (Sri Sri Omkarnath Samskrita Siksha Samsad, Kolkata 2007). I was interested by his selection and approach, and I particularly liked the title of his book—hence my echo of it here and elsewhere in this paper.

prose as written by a poet/musician such as Rabindranath—can itself be poetic in its effect.

In his discursive and philosophic writings, Tagore often reached for musical metaphors as a way of expressing Man's highest spiritual aspirations and expressions. In *The Religion of Man*, Chapter VIII is called 'The Music Maker', and he writes in this chapter:

> While these races pass away one after another they leave great accomplishments behind them carrying their claim to recognition as dreamers not so much as conquerors of earthly kingdoms, but as the designers of paradise. The poet gives us the best definition of man when he says:
>
> We are the music-makers,
> We are the dreamers of dreams. [21]

He goes on:

> No doubt it is wonderful that music contains a fact which has been analysed and measured, and which music shares in common with the braying of an ass or of a motor-car horn. But it is still more wonderful that music has a truth, which cannot be analysed into fractions; and there the difference between it and the bellowing impertinence of a motor-car horn is infinite.[22]

In the *advaitavādi* passage in *Jībansmriti* that I have examined, he writes of how after his vision from the verandah of the Sudder Street house all the scenes of common life that he observed took on an extraordinary purposefulness, grace and beauty: 'The porters and labourers and other people who were walking along the street seemed amazing to me in their movements, the structure of their bodies, the grace of their faces; they all seemed to flow like the play (*līlā*) of waves on the ocean of the universe (*nikhil*).' He goes on: 'In the limbs of

[21] Rabindranath Tagore: *The Religion of Man*, Macmillan, New York 1931, p. 120. [*English Writings* (1996), vol. 3, p. 135. The quotation is from the Ode: 'We are the Music Makers' by Arthur William Edgar O'Shaughnessy (1844–81).]

[22] Ibid., p. 121.

people as they carried out some ordinary task a miraculous quality of movement (*gati-baicitrya*) was expressed that I had never noticed before—*a music at every moment in the movement of the whole human body enchanted me*.' (my italics)[23]

The musical metaphor here is highly significant, and the association of music with movement; for movement and rhythm are as crucial to music as pitch. Most of Tagore's songs use metre, *chhanda*, and rhyme, *mil*, in the words, but this is concealed and overridden by the rhythm and phrasing of the music, a rhythm and phrasing that I believe can be represented in English translation by the use of repetition and line-breaks, though Tagore undoubtedly did his best to reflect it too in the musicality of his Bible-influenced prose-poetry.[24]

In the words of many songs by Tagore, dualistic elements can be found: from the 'solitary wayfarer' whom the lover asks not to pass by the open gates of his house 'like a dream' in no. 1; to the 'sorrow that is absolutely mine own' in no. 2; the friend who wanders 'abroad on this stormy night on thy journey of love' in no. 4; the 'perils of overmuch desire' and the 'perils of weak, uncertain desire' in no. 8; and the burdens of 'people and possessions' in no. 9. But there are also non-dualist tendencies. One can point to them without necessarily bringing the music into the equation, though the music always immeasurably enhances their effect. This is partly because the *imagery* of music is so widespread in Tagore's song-poems of the *Gitanjali* phase. See, for example, no. 3, which I have translated as follows:

[23] *Rabīndra-rachanābali*, vol. 17, p. 397.

[24] One might well ask, why Tagore did not think of using repetitions in his own translations, or in the printed versions of the Bengali texts of his songs. I think the answer to that is that the repetitions were so deeply embedded in his mind—just as they are embedded in the minds of Bengalis when they read the songs as texts—that he took them for granted. This is rather like how, in the traditional way of reciting Urdu *ghazals*, the repetitions of lines for rhetorical effect are taken for granted by readers, who do not therefore feel any need to see them reproduced in the text.

When the universe is sunk in sleep, and the sky is dark
Who is it who plucks the strings of my veena so?
When the sky is dark
When the universe is sunk in sleep, and the sky is dark

Somebody has snatched sleep from my eyes, I sit up upon my bed
Somebody has snatched sleep from my eyes, I sit up upon my bed
I open my eyes and look, but I do not see who it is
When the sky is dark
When the universe is sunk in sleep, and the sky is dark

My soul is alert and humming and full
I do not know what mighty message yearningly sounds in the music
My soul is alert and humming and full
I do not know what mighty message yearningly sounds in the music

I do not understand with what pain my heart is so tearfully full
Or to whom I wish to give the garland from my own neck
When the sky is dark
When the universe is sunk in sleep, and the sky is dark

In an earlier draft of this translation, I wrote 'yearningly sounds in my music'. Debashish Raychaudhuri corrected this to 'the music'. At first I wasn't sure about this, thinking that 'my veena' earlier on (*āmār bīnā*) justified the insertion of 'my' before *sur* ('music') in the third, *sanchārī* section of the song. But on reflection, I realized that music unites both the poet's own veena and the divine musician who is mysteriously plucking the poet's veena for him. In other words, music is 'bridging the gulf' between Man and God, world and spirit, pain and joy. Similarly in no. 11, the poet recalls carefree childhood days when 'I never cared to know the meaning of the songs thou sangest to me. Only my voice took up the tunes, and my heart danced in their cadence.' Music here is a metaphor for the way in which children, in their innocence, seem less separated from God than adults are, with their burden of pain and loss and experience: a notion of childhood that can be found in many of Tagore's songs and poems, especially those he put into his English collection *The Crescent Moon* (1913).

This last observation takes me into territory I do not explore here: the ways—other than through music—by which Tagore expresses his *advaitavādi* tendencies. Despite what he says about the difference between Man and the rest of Nature in his essay, *Mānus*, there are plenty of poems in which Tagore finds in Nature an all-embracing, non-dualistic harmony. Children, with their ability to engage directly with the world without any 'shadow' intervening, are another manifestation of it. Also, Tagore's famous concept of the *jīban-debatā*, the mysterious deity guiding and uniting and harmonising all his diverse creative activities, whether they were joyous or painful, can in quite a few poems take on a monistic character.[25]

Another favourite image of 'the ineffable', with its roots in the Upanishads, is 'the sun'. In his celebrated—and highly influential—Introduction to the English *Gitanjali*, W. B. Yeats, in stressing how Tagore's spirituality embraces and never rejects the world, wrote: 'This is no longer the sanctity of the cell and the scourge; being but a lifting up, as it were, into a greater intensity of the mood of the painter, painting the dust and the sunlight.' I would like to end with the following thought. 'Dust'—another very important image in Tagore, and expressive, just as it is in Christian tradition, of mortality, the world, sin, human limitation—can be found in the 12 songs on which I have focussed, and especially in no. 6, whose second, *antarā* section in my translation reads:

[25] In my Notes to my translation of 'Last Tryst' (*Shes abhisār* from *Sānāi*, 1940) of *Selected Poems*, I wrote: 'I do not believe it is possible in the last analysis to separate the *jīban-debatā* from God or Brahman himself what the concept stands for is the mystery of the way in which God reveals himself in human life and experience. In 1.19 the word which I have translated as 'indescribably lovely' is *anirbacanīya*, 'inexpressible.' In *RM* (*The Religion of Man*) 186 Tagore uses it to describe the Supreme Unity, or God, and translates it as 'ineffable'.' (*Selected Poems*, p. 171).

When I give you the *pūjā*-basket all my grime is revealed
When I give you the *pūjā*-basket all my grime is revealed
So I cannot place my life at your feet
Through your kindness, your kindness
Through your kindness my life must be cleansed
Otherwise how will I ever be able to touch your feet?

The dualism here is clear; but the melody of the song reaches out to and embodies a bridging of the gulf, a reconciliation of the dust and the sunlight. It seems to me that ultimately, as poet, Tagore is *advāitavādī* not in the traditional Indian sense but in the way that all great poets are. All great poets, I would say, reach out for and achieve a vision in which dust and sunlight are combined and reconciled. The spirit is real, but the world is real too, and poets—whose medium, unlike the pure, non-verbal medium of music, is language, and therefore bound up with the world—have to pay tribute to both. This was Tagore's great achievement. He succeeded, in poem after poem and song after song, in 'painting the dust and the sunlight', in Yeats' eloquent phrase.[26] So my final answer to the question I posed at the beginning, 'Was Tagore *dvāitavādi* or *advāitavādī*?' is that he was both, and this was because he was primarily neither a seer nor a prophet nor a mystic; nor indeed was he a pure, non-verbal musician or composer. He was a poet, a *kabi*, and that is why we honour him with reading, study, translations and papers such as this.

Based on a lecture delivered by invitation of Rabindra Bhavan, Ahmedabad at the Gujarat Law Society Auditorium, 2 April, 2008.

This is a shortened version of the essay published in Amalendu Biswas, Christine Marsh and Kalyan Kundu (eds.) *Rabindranath Tagore: A Timeless Mind,* The Tagore Centre UK in collaboration with Indian Council for Cultural Relations, London 2011.

[26] Hence our use of it as the title of Debashish Raychaudhuri's CD-set.

Transplanting the Songs of Tagore

What is a Tagore song? The answer to that question might seem relatively simple. A *Rabīndrasangīt* a song by Tagore—is a poetic text in metre and rhyme, some to a melody and rhythm that Tagore composed himself. Usually the melodies were composed simultaneously with the writing of the words, though sometimes Tagore wrote poems which he later then turned into songs. Tagore would sing the song himself, and the melody would be written down in traditional Indian notation by other people. They needed to be written down straight away, because Tagore himself often forgot the melody, so ceaseless was his creation of new songs.

In 1932, when Mahatma Gandhi—in jail for the seventh time in his life—fasted in protest at the governments 'Communal Award' (separate electorates for untouchables that he thought would be decisive), Tagore rushed to Yerwada Central Jail to be at the Mahatma's bedside. Gandhi was particularly fond of song no. 39 of the English *Gitanjali* that Tagore had translated as 'When the heart is hard and parched up, come upon me with a shower of mercy.' When Gandhi asked Tagore to sing the song, he had to make up a new tune on the spot, because he had forgotten the original melody.

Nevertheless, the songs of Tagore, unlike many of the other musical traditions of the Indian sub-continent—are a composed tradition. The melodies have been preserved in the many volumes of the *Swaralipi*, published by Visva-Bharati, and the texts of the songs are preserved in the collection *Gītabitān*. There are textual issues in the accurate notation of the songs which the scholars of the future will no doubt wrestle with, just as European scholars have worked over generations to establish the correct *Urtext* (original or authentic text) of the works of the great European composers. Sometimes details such as which lines to repeat when the song is sung have not been accurately recorded in the *Swaralipi*, and instead performance traditions have developed. There are also edited versions of the *Swaralipi* that have been left behind by great singers of Tagore's own generation, such as Sahana Devi, and these will also have to be taken into account. But by and large one can point to the text of a Tagore song and to the melody written down in the *Swaralipi*, and say with self-confidence that this *is* the song.

But is it actually as simple as that? Search for any popular Tagore song on the internet, and you will find performances on YouTube and other websites that vary greatly in style, tempo and instrumental accompaniment. Contemporary recordings on CD are likely to have all kinds of electronic and instrumental enhancements that would astonish Tagore were he able to hear them today. Whether these additions are enhancements or corruptions is a matter for debate. But whatever one's personal taste, this is clearly a rapidly expanding tradition that allows for far more latitude and variation in performance than would be acceptable in the songs of, for example, the European composers Schubert or Debussy.

Some of this latitude can be attributed to imprecision in the Indian system of notation. The basic melody and *tāla* (rhythmic cycle) can be indicated, but the *Swaralipi* lacks the detailed dynamic markings that are possible with western musical notation—markings that were used more and more by composers from the 18th century onwards to indicate precisely the tempo, mood, loudness, softness, crescendo, diminuendo, and so forth. In western notation we also normally expect precise scoring in terms of instrumentation, but this is lacking in the Rabindrasangit tradition. It is known that Tagore himself disliked the harmonium, and preferred instrumental accompaniments to be limited to *tānpurā*, *esrāj*, flute sometimes, and *tablā* in the more rhythmic songs. But none of these instruments were specified precisely, which is why performers today feel free to add any instruments that they like.

If the identity of a song is found as much in its performance as in its written form, then the identity of Rabindrasangit has today become very varied indeed, though paradoxically a kind of 'sameness' in the mood of their performance has crept in which often seems at odds with what the words of the song are saying. A mood of romantic longing is what seems to appeal most to singers of Rabindrasangit and their audiences. At a typical performance of Rabindrasangit in public, the same instrumental forces are used throughout the concert, and this diminishes the huge variety of mood and imagery in the songs, and can become wearisome to listeners who cannot understand the words. But like it or not, and however remote this may have become from Tagore's own intentions, the performance styles that prevail today have become part of what Rabindrasangit is all about, and have to be incorporated into any answer that can be given to the question: 'What is a Tagore song?'

The answer becomes even more complicated when we include, as we must, translations of Tagore's songs into English and other languages, and musical settings of those translations. Take, for example, Tagore's famous and haunting song *āmi chanchala he*. Tagore himself translated this song in *The Gardener* (no. 5; 1913). This book was published on the crest of the wave that was sent surging through the world of literature by the stunning success of *Gitanjali* in 1912. So all those people in many countries who were thrilled by *Gitanjali*, rushed to read *The Gardener* as well and the book was mentioned in Tagore's Nobel Prize citation in November 1913, as well as *Gitanjali*. I suspect that the many western composers who started to set Tagore's own translations to music were attracted to *The Gardener* even more than to *Gitanjali*. One of them was the Austrian composer Alexander Zemlinsky (1871 in Vienna to 1942 in the USA). In his day, Zemlinsky was a successful composer of operas, though these are rarely performed today. He was also a distinguished conductor, and a friend of the composers Gustav Mahler and Arnold Schönberg. His massive *Lyrische Symphonie* (1922)—really the only work by Zemlinsky that is well-known today—was modelled on

Mahler's *Song of the Earth*, being a 'song-symphony' for solo singers and a massive orchestra, written throughout in a lush and romantic style, and using texts by Tagore that to audiences of the time must have seemed as exotic as the Chinese poems that Mahler used for *Song of the Earth*. Seven of Tagore's translations are used (in a German translation from Tagore's English rendering), connected by orchestral interludes, and the work begins with *āmi chanchala he*. But what a long way this has travelled from its Bengali original! No use is made of Tagore's own melody—and it is most unlikely that Zemlinsky knew of its existence—and the setting depends therefore on Tagore's own rendering in poetic prose:

I am restless. I am athirst for faraway things.
My soul goes out in a longing to touch the skirt of the dim distance.
O Great Beyond, O the keen call of thy flute!
I forget, I ever forget, that I have no wings to fly, that I am bound in this spot evermore.

I am eager and wakeful, I am a stranger in a strange land.
Thy breath comes to me whispering and impossible hope.
Thy tongue is known to my heart as its very own.
O Far-to-seek, O the keen call of thy flute!
I forget, I ever forget, that I know not the way, that I have not the winged horse.

I am listless, I am a wanderer in my heart.
In the sunny haze of the languid hours, what vast vision of thine takes shape in the blue
of the sky!
O Farthest end, O the keen call of thy flute!
I forget, I ever forget, that the gates are shut everywhere in the house where I dwell
alone!

Tagore's way of translating his poems and songs into poetic prose (he was a Bengali poet, not an English poet, and therefore wisely did not attempt English metre or rhyme) has suited western composers right up to the present day, because the setting of strophic form with repeated lines and refrains has largely fallen out of favour. With classical or 'serious' composers this is so: with musicals and pop songs, of course, metres, rhymes and refrains have remained very popular indeed. Whereas Tagore's own song *āmi chanchala he* is full of repeated lines and phrases, and the words of the song are rich in rhythm and rhyme, in Zemlinsky's setting there are no repetitions except at the end, where the line 'O farthest end, O the keen call of thy flute!' (*O fernstes Ende, o ungestümes Rufen deiner Flöte!* in the German) is repeated with haunting, lingering effect. Zemlinsky *Lyrische Symphonie* is a masterpiece of its kind, and the long orchestral introduction that leads into the first song is particularly beautiful. It is reprised at the end of the symphony, and probably it is this opening and closing music that makes the strongest impression at a first hearing of the work.

Listening to the setting of the first song more than once, I am struck by the way the melodic and emotional emphasis falls on words such as *fern* ('faraway'), *Sehnsucht* ('longing') and *Weite* ('distance'), and clearly the poem appealed to Zemlinsky as an expression of longing for the 'Great Beyond', for a world of transcendent perfection that is forever unattainable. That is certainly central to the poem, whether in its original Bengali or in Tagore's English translation, and the various performances of it by Rabindrasangit singers that I have heard also emphasise that same mood. In some cases a long instrumental introduction is added, though I am pretty sure those that have done this are as ignorant of Zemlinsky's setting as he would have been of the original song by Tagore.

Āmi chanchala he is among several songs by Tagore that I was recently asked to translate for a dance production that is being planned by the Akademi of South Asian Dance UK (London). For years I was reluctant to translate Tagore's songs, because I felt that they needed the melody: a translation of the words alone would be insufficient. In the introduction to my *Selected Poems* I quoted from a comment that Tagore made in *Creative Unity* (1922) about his first encounter with Baul singers who came to influence his own songs so deeply. He wrote:

> The first Baul song, which I chanced to hear with any attention, profoundly stirred my mind. Its words are so simple that it makes me hesitate to render them in a foreign tongue, and set them forward for critical observation. Besides, the best part of a song is missed when the tune is absent; for thereby its movement and its colour are lost, and it becomes like a butterfly whose wings have been plucked.[1]

In recent years, however, I have developed a technique for translating Tagore's songs that works for me in literary terms, and which also conveys to the reader something of their rhythmic, formal and musical structure. The technique is really very simple, though as with many simple discoveries it took me a long time to reach it. Unlike my translations of Tagore's poems, I do not try to reflect the metre and rhymes of the original, because in my view (and Rabindrasangit singers that I have spoken to agree with this) when the song is sung we are not particularly aware of the metre or the rhymes. Instead, a different kind of pattern takes over based on the four part structure that most Tagore songs have, and the repetition of lines.

When I translate a Tagore song—and many of the poems in my new translation of *Gitanjali* are songs—I listen to recordings of the song before I start, and carefully note which lines are repeated. This is laid down by the *Swaralipi* or by performance tradition, but the extent of the repetition varies from song to song. In some songs the whole of the opening *sthāyi* (or refrain) is repeated at the end of the second section or *antarā*, and again at the end of the *ābhog*, the fourth and final section. In other songs maybe only one or two lines are repeated. These repetitions are not arbitrary. When I discussed them with Professor Indrani Mukhopadhyay, Head of Sangit-Bhavan at Visva-Bharati, Santiniketan,

[1] 'An Indian Folk Religion', in: *English Writings* (1996), vol. 2, p. 523.

she confirmed that in this matter of repetition *āmrā sādhin nai* ('We are not free.'). There is a deep connection between the repetitions and the *bhāb* or mood of the song. *Āmi chanchala he* is unusual for having a large number of repetitions at the beginning and at the end.

I'm restless, ah!
  thirsting for the distant
I'm restless, ah!
  thirsting for the distant
I'm restless, ah!
  thirsting for the distant
I'm restless, ah!
  thirsting for the distant

The day goes by, I wait at my window in hope of it
The day goes by, I wait at my window in hope of it
Longing with all my heart and soul for its touch
  I'm thirsting for the distant

O distant, O hugely distant, you play a demented flute
I forget that I have no wings, that I'm stuck here indoors

I'm restless, ah!
  thirsting for the distant

I'm crazed O distant, I'm adrift
In the lazy sun-drenched noon, in the play of shady trees
In the lazy sun-drenched noon, in the play of shady trees
What is this image I sense of you in the blue sky,
rising in my eyes?
O distant, I'm adrift

O distant, O hugely distant, you play a demented flute
I forget that the door of my house is closed

I'm restless, ah!
    thirsting for the distant
I'm restless, ah!
    thirsting for the distant
I'm restless, ah!
    thirsting for the distant
I'm restless, ah!
    thirsting for the distant

These repetitions seem to me to give the song a kind of nervous, almost phonetic energy that is central to its meaning. Zemlinsky's setting, or performances of the song by Rabindrasangit singers such as Kalim Sarafi, Maya Sen, Sadi Mohammad or Debabrata Biswas emphasized the *Sehnsucht* or 'longing' in the song. The repetitions, when I put them into my translation, seemed to shift the emphasis more to the restlessness, to the *chanchala* aspects of the song. They guided me towards an interpretation of *byākul bāñsarī* as 'demented flute', which some may say takes a liberty with the meaning but which for me is in keeping with what I take to be the essential meaning and mood of the song.

It seems to me that with Tagore's global reach, and the proliferation of settings and performances that the internet now facilitates, each song by Tagore is like a plant of a particular species that can be transplanted or grown in many different places. It grows differently according to local soil or weather conditions, and its size and shape and appearance will vary accordingly to the taste of the gardener who cultivates it. It can be crossed with other plants, and bred into new styles and shapes. When I listen to a fusion experiment such as the wonderful version of *ānanda-dhārā bahiche bhubane*[2] by the young British jazz musicians Zoe and Idris Rahman (available on their CD *Where Rivers Meet*), I encounter a song that has definitely been transplanted, crossed or fused with a quite different tradition—in this case with jazz, as opposed to

[2] *Gītabitān*: Pūjā 326 ('A stream of bliss moves the world')

the romanticism of Alexander Zemlinsky. But it is still the same song, still the same species of plant.

In lectures that I gave recently in Copenhagen and Lund about Tagore's relevance today, I mentioned 'adaptability' as one of his greatest strengths and qualities. The poems, songs, stories, plays, novels, even paintings of Tagore are proving to be an incredibly rich resource. With Asian literary and cultural traditions rapidly catching up with European traditions in terms of their influence worldwide, I am convinced that we will see Tagore's works being used in ways that at present we cannot even imagine. I know this from my own collaborations over the years—for example—with the Indian-born composer Param Vir whose opera *Snatched by the Gods* (based on Tagore's electrifying narrative poem *Debatār Grās*), with a libretto by me based on my own translation of the poem, is in my view one of the most significant and powerful adaptations of Tagore that have so far been made.[3]

When people talk about Tagore's relevance today, they often have his social or educational ideas in mind, and these are very important. But I do not believe that his ideas and ideals alone make him relevant. It is the power of his art that will make him live on, and indeed make his legacy continue to expand and mutate. Maybe the ultimate identity of *āmi chanchala he* or of any song or creative work by Tagore is as elusive as the *sudūr* ('distant') that he longs for in his famous song. All performances of it whether good or bad, all translations, all musical settings of those translations are attempts to reach out to something that we can never hold. Anyone listening to the song does so in a specific local context, but the song can transport the listener away from that context, so that in the words of the song itself he or she forgets 'that I have no wings to fly, that I am bound in this spot evermore'. I am reminded of Tagore's famous poem *Bāñsi*, which I translated as 'Flute-music' in my *Selected*

[3] It was commissioned by the German composer Hans Werner Henze for his Munich Biennale of 1992, and has thereafter been performed in many European cities in several different productions.

Poems. This translation has been much anthologised, most recently in the *Oxford Anthology of Bengali Literature*.[4] The appeal of this poem seems to lie in precisely this kind of disjunction between the local and the universal. When the humble clerk Haripada, who missed his opportunity to get happily married, sits alone in his squalid room in Calcutta, and listens to music being played not even on a flute but on a 'cornet' (Tagore may possibly have meant clarinet), he is transported or translated or transplanted away from his surroundings:

At the corner of the alley lives Kāntabābu—
Long hair, carefully parted,
Large eyes,
Cultivated tastes.
He fancies himself on the cornet:
The sound of it comes in gusts
On the foul breeze of the alley—
Sometimes in the middle of the night,
Sometimes in the early morning twilight,
Sometimes in the afternoon
When sun and shadows glitter.
Suddenly this evening
He starts to play runs in Sindhu-Bāroyā rāg,
And the whole sky rings
With eternal pangs of separation.
At once the alley is a lie,
False and vile as the ravings of a drunkard,
And I feel that nothing distinguishes Haripada the clerk
From the Emperor Akbar.
Torn umbrella and royal parasol merge,
Rise on the sad music of a flute
Towards one heaven.[5]

[4] OUP, Delhi, 2010.

[5] *Selected Poems* (1985), pp. 97–98.

If we could ask Haripada for his reply to the question 'What is a song?' he would probably answer that it is precisely this: it is something that carries us away, which can 'translate' us. That probably is, when all is said and done, why we are celebrating Tagore's achievements with such fervour hundred-and-fifty years after his birth. His greatest creative works make us think about the world we are in with all its problems, but they also carry us right away from it, and sometimes we are all badly in need of release of that kind.

First published in: *Indian Horizons* (New Delhi) vol. 58, no. 1 (January–March 2011), pp. 55–63.

Master of Empathy
Probing the Genius of Rabindranath

Back in the 1970s when I had no job and was trying to find one in the United States, I exchanged several letters with Edward C. Dimock, the famous scholar of medieval Bengali and professor of Bengali at Chicago University. I remember one of his letters particularly, and I was very pleased when I searched through my files and was able to find it. I had sent Professor Dimock one of my early translations of Tagore's poetry, and he replied:

> The translation you sent me is very nice indeed, and bodes well for a complete book of translations from Tagore. Which, I might add, is in my opinion very much needed. It is well past time for new work on Tagore, and for a re-assessment of his poetry from a truly critical point of view. I would be delighted to review the scheme. Ramonujan and I have had in mind for some time new translations of the *Gitanjali* poems, but cannot seem quite to get down to it. I have a student currently working on *Chitrā*, and the more the merrier. The man was undoubtedly a genius, but nobody seems to worry about how or why. (20.10.76)

The last sentence of that paragraph, 'The man was undoubtedly a genius, but nobody seems to worry about how or why' should perhaps be blazened as a motto for all the many symposia and conferences and celebrations of Tagore in this anniversary year. Or perhaps it should be our motto for work on Tagore over the coming decades. At Tagore events we get a lot of discussion of his ideas and ideals—his educational ideas and practice, his internationalism, his religious thinking, his concern for rural development and the environment, and so forth. All these are important, and it is excellent if people are attracted to Tagore because they find his ideas and ideals resonate with many of our contemporary concerns and anxieties.

But I often feel frustrated that his creative work—and the qualities in it that make it so varied and great—are rather left out of the discussion. It seems that there is a very real need for more practical literary appreciation. Whether we are looking at Tagore's poems, or his stories, or his novels, or his plays, or listening to his songs, or looking at his paintings, we need to think more deeply about what makes these works important and great. What are their qualities? What made him a creative genius? Ideas and ideals alone do not make a creative artist. And furthermore, it is my conviction that to read Tagore through the lens of his ideals, and to see his creative works as essentially vehicles for ideals and ideas, is the wrong approach.

Tagore defined art as 'the response of man's creative soul to the call of the Real.'[1] Reality in all its aspects is exceedingly complex. Great literary works, whether by Tagore or by anyone else express that complexity. I constantly find, when I read Tagore's poems and other literary works, that they are full of paradoxes and counter-currents. They say many things at once, and one can keep on finding new meanings in them. You cannot reduce them to a set of ideals, anymore than you can reduce life itself in that way.

Today I want to focus on the quality of empathy—of sympathy and understanding for other people whatever their age or gender or background—that is, in my view, a major quality in Tagore. We find empathy *par excellence* in his short stories. But I want to range more widely and try to understand how empathy fits into his genius and outlook as a whole.

Let me begin with a poem, the second poem in Tagore's book *Punashcha* ('The Post-Script', 1932). Tagore wrote more than sixty

[1] *The Religion of Man,* Allen & Unwin, London 1931, p. 139.

books of poetry, and many of them can be regarded as turning points, because he was constantly changing and turning and breaking new ground as a creative artist. *Punashcha* is especially significant as a turning point because in it he announced in a preface that he was embarking on a new experiment, a new kind of poetry. Here is my translation of this preface:

> I translated the songs of *Gitanjali* into English prose. This translation was regarded as poetic. Since then the question has been in my mind: might it be possible to give to Bengali prose—free of rhyme and metre's explicit sound effects—a similarly poetic flavour [*rasa*]? I remember I asked Satyendranath to attempt this, but he never did. Then I myself had a go, in a few compositions in *Lipikā*. When they were printed they were not, however, broken up into lines—probably through timidity on my part.
>
> Later, at my request, Abanindranath undertook the same experiment. In my view, these writings fell within the definition of poetry, but were let down by their linguistic excess. I decided to try again myself.
>
> Let me make one thing clear. In prose poetry [*gadya-kābya*], it is not enough simply to dispense with fixed metre; its movement into the free world of prose becomes natural only if one discards the ornate and over-modest coverings that pertain to the language and expression of poetry. I believe it is possible greatly to extend the claims of poetry to the frankness of prose, and I have written the poems published in this book with this aim in view. There are some unrhymed poems among them that still have metre, but I have tried to get away from special poetic diction. Thus *tare* [for *janya*], *sane* [for *sange*], *mor* [for *āmār*] and other words that are not used in prose have been avoided in all these poems.

This new adventure, that of bringing poetry and prose into a new and fertile relationship is further announced in the second poem in the book, called *Nātak*, which means play or drama. This is the poem that made a special impression on me when I read it recently.

I immediately found myself reading the poem aloud. It seems to me a special and fascinating feature of Tagore's *gadya-kābya*, or free verse poem, that you really do have to read them aloud to hear and feel their subtle rhythms. His poems and songs that are in more formal verse, with metre and rhyme, of course can gain hugely from being read aloud too, but one can also read them silently and hear the rhythms and appreciate the form in one's head. That's not so with the *gadya-kābya*. If you don't read them aloud, you read them as one would read prose, focussing perhaps more on the content than on the form or sound or rhythm. The poem is written in the informal, colloquial style of a letter. It is not clear who the letter is to or why he is writing it. The verse letter became for Tagore a form that he used quite often in his free verse poems, just as he used it in his famous short story, *Strīr patra* ('The Wife's Letter'). He begins by saying that he has written a play, and then summarises the story of the play. It is about the hero Arjuna paying a visit to heaven as a guest of Indra, the king of the gods. The dancing nymph Urvashi appears with a garland for him. Arjuna says, 'You shouldn't be giving the garland to me, you should give it to one of the gods.' Urvashi replies that the gods have no need of garlands from her, they are well provided with such things already. She wants to give it to him, because he is a human being, and she wants to form a connection with human beings.

Tagore then goes into a section which he wryly reflects on whether what he has just written is good or not. He seems to be on the point of abandoning the poem, but then decides that having started it he had better plough on. He goes back to mentioning the play that he has just written, and says that his friends have asked him to write it in blank verse, but he chose to write it in prose. He then goes into the last and most important part of the poem, in which he writes about the differences between poetry and prose and how he wants his poetry to take on the qualities that prose can have. Here is a translation of this last section of the poem:

Let me speak of my play.
My friends asked for it to be in blank verse.
I've written it in prose.
Poetry is the sea –
the creation of literature's first age.
Its qualities are in the ebb and flow of metre,
in undulations of rhythm.
Prose came much later –
it seated itself outside the fixities of metre.
Beauty and ugliness, good and evil came jostling into its courtyard.
Tattered patchwork quilts and the finest of shawls
were combined in it,
Harmony and disharmony jingling and jangling together.
Prose's great continent rose into the sky
in roaring and song, in dance-steps both wild and measured.
It sometimes breathed fire,
sometimes hurled torrents.
In some places the ground was flat, in others it was rugged;
impenetrable forest here, parched desert there.
To master it you need imperial powers –
you have to learn to survive overthrow,
learn various ploys and stratagems.
Its rhythm does not come floating on a stream from outside –
it must be found within,
in ways both light and heavy.
I've written my play in that kind of prose –
in which there is the stillness of eternity,
but also the turbulence of time.

The style of this poem is improvisatory, almost casual: its manner is what makes *Punashcha* so strikingly fresh and new. At first it seems as if the three parts of the poem do not have much to do with each other but the more one goes into it the more one sees that the poem is in fact most cleverly and cunningly constructed and contrived. The point about the story of Arjuna meeting Urvashi in heaven is that it expresses the idea of a meeting or union between heaven and earth. The second section, in which the poet asks himself whether what he is doing is any good or not, raises issues about what is durable and what is fleeting or what is impermanent in art, and whether those two things can somehow be combined. The third part raises further paradoxes: can one create an art in which roaring (*garjan*) is combined with song (*gān*), in which disharmony can be combined with harmony?

What, you may ask, has this got to do with my announced topic for this lecture: empathy? To explain the connection, I need to go back to the short stories that I mentioned earlier and to the sensitive qualities of empathy and sympathy that they contain. The first thing that needs to be said about Tagore's short stories, and his novels too, is that it is extraordinary that he could have excelled as a writer of prose fiction as well as being a poet and a song writer. Can one think of any other great writer, in any language, in which this is so? There are of course in English literature great novelists like Thomas Hardy and D. H. Lawrence who also wrote poems. Many great poets from Milton to Coleridge to T. S. Eliot have also been fine writers of essays. But I know of no other writer for whom poetry and prose are of equal importance and status: they are in fact two sides of the same coin. That equivalence, that equal relationship, that complementarity is what Tagore is focusing on in that poem, and he sets out to explore these qualities further in other poems in *Punashcha* and in subsequent books where he uses free verse-forms.

Tagore's versatility, his mastery of so many genres, is of course something that is constantly celebrated at Tagore festivals and symposia. But have we thought enough about why he is as great a prose writer as he is a poet? I think there is a fundamental reason for this desire to write poetry and prose, and to bring the two forms closer and closer together, either by writing stories that are full of poetic qualities, or by writing poems that have much of the freedom, flexibility and realism of prose.

In the introduction to my *Selected Short Stories* of Tagore, first published in 1991, I organised my comments under three headings which I took from an early three-part selection of letters to his niece Indira Devi that Tagore himself made and published in a book called *Bichitra Prabandha* ('Miscellaneous Essays', 1907). These letters were later published much more extensively, and are crucial texts for an understanding of Tagore's life and work in the 1890s when he was managing the family estates in the Padma river region of what is now Bangladesh. An English selection of them was published in 1921 as *Glimpses of Bengal*. Tagore did not for these later collections use the headings that he used in the early selection of the letters, but the headings struck me as having great significance, which is why I use them in my introduction to the stories in my book, all of which were written during that same period, the 1890s. The headings are *sthale* (on land), *jal-pathe* (by water), and *ghāte* (at the mooring place). I argued in my introduction that the symbolism of earth and water and the meeting of earth and water at the *ghāt* was central to the meaning and effect of the stories. The flow of the river symbolises the spirit; the soil of the earth symbolises the world; and the *ghāt* symbolises the meeting of the two.

The spiritual dimension of the stories was their poetic dimension—for Tagore the poetic and the spiritual were always fundamentally the same. The deep feelings of love or longing or rapture that they contain carry the reader into a spiritual or transcendental realm, just as do many of Tagore's poems and songs. But the real world of day-to-day human experience is also strongly present in them, and that world—the world of the soil or the land and the lives of the mainly rural people depicted in the stories—is often a very bleak place indeed. It is full of loss and cruelty and suffering.

Take the story 'Exercise-book' (*Kāthā*), for example. A child bride Uma writes poems and stories in a beloved exercise-book. It is her most precious possession. When she is married off and suffers the cruelty of her husband and in-laws, it is her only solace, her only outlet. She is ridiculed for it: the very idea of a young housewife wanting to read and write is ridiculed. For a while she gives up writing, but one autumn morning she hears an adult woman singing an *āgamanī* song, a song associated with the *āgaman* or arrival of Shiva's wife Durga at her parental home at the beginning of Durga-*pūjā*. When she hears the song she writes it down in her exercise-book. The beauty of the song and its effect on Uma is a transcendental, spiritual moment in the story, but the spell is cruelly broken by Uma's sisters-in-law, who spy on her writing the song in her exercise-book and tells her husband about it. This is how the story ends:

> Pyarimohan came and sat down on the bed sternly. 'Give me that book', he thundered. When his command was not obeyed, he growled in an even deeper voice, 'Give it to me.'
>
> The girl held the exercise-book to her breast and looked at her husband, entreating him with her gaze. When she saw that Pyarimohan was about to force it from her, she hurled it down, covered her face with her hands, and fell to the floor.
>
> Pyarimohan picked up the exercise-book and loudly read out from her childish writings, as she listened, Uma tried to clutch the nethermost depths of the earth. The other girls collapsed into peals of laughter.
>
> Uma never got the exercise-book again. Pyarimohan also had an exercise-book full of various subtly barbed essays, but no one was philanthropic enough to snatch *his* book away and destroy it.[2]

In some of Tagore's short stories, there is some kind of resolution: the cruel or insensitive characters learn something from the kinder, more sensitive characters. But this story has no such resolution. This, to use the terms that were used in the poem *Nātak* that I took you through earlier, is pure *garjan*—roaring, howling, wailing. It is pure *besur* or disharmony. Uma's plight brings out all of Tagore's powers of empathy, which are so often displayed in his stories—and indeed in many poems too which have stories or characters—and often show a special identification with children or women.

[2] *Rabindranath Tagore: Selected Short Stories*, p. 145.

Empathy and sympathy have to be there, have to be mastered by him as a writer, in order to do justice to the reality of the world and the reality of human experience. As a poet and song-writer, Tagore had a kind of duty to himself: as he stressed in several letters in which he wrote about the highly personal poems that he chose for the English *Gitanjali*, in poetry he had to be true to himself, he had to express his deepest personal feelings. Prose, and especially prose fiction, took him out of himself. This must not only have afforded him relief, even escape, but also met his fundamental need and desire for wholeness, fullness, what he called *purnatā*.

The concept of *purnatā* seems to me more and more fundamental. The word occurs in many poems and songs and also in the religious sermons that Tagore delivered in Santiniketan and which were later collected into two volumes with that name. It is used for example the end of this very short poem in *Sphulinga*, the posthumous collection of very short poems that were published in 1945, and which I have translated in my book *The Jewel That is Best: Collected Brief Poems*:

Tumultuous days
    Rush towards night.
Seas are the goal
    Of streams of spate.
Impatient spring-flowers
    Long to be fruitful.
Restlessness strives
    To be calm and complete.[3]

Tagore has to be a master of empathy, he has to write about people other than himself, he has to write about the real world, because his fundamental goal of completeness or *purnatā* would not be achieved without it. *Purnatā* is not really the same as balance or harmony

[3] Rabindranath Tagore, *The Jewel That Is Best: Collected Brief Poems*, translated by William Radice, Penguin Books India, New Delhi 2011, p. 122.

which, in Bengali would be translated by the word *sāmanjasya*. I have noticed when hearing people speak at Tagore symposia about his ideas and ideals that the word 'harmony' often crops up. Tagore himself uses that word often enough in his English essays, but if *sāmanjasya* is harmony then the other meanings that the Bengali dictionary gives suggests that this is not as vast and comprehensive a term as *purnatā*. *Sāmanjasya* means 'proprietary, fitness; consistency, agreement; symmetry, harmony; mutual understanding, adjustment'.[4] It is harmony in those senses and not what is expressed by wholeness or fullness or *purnatā*. Actually, harmony in the western understanding may not really exist in India, because it is a metaphor derived from music, which in the West is based on harmony, unlike Indian music, which makes almost no use of it.

Purnatā includes *dis*harmony. This is the aesthetic and also philosophic and religious aspiration that lies behind the poem *Nātak*. Tagore would not have been the master of empathy that he was, if he had not aspired to embrace and express disharmony just as much as harmony.

Nātak and the other poems in *Punashcha* may have been a new departure, a turning point, and certainly stylistically they strike a new chord. But the basic aspiration that they express—that of bringing together world and spirit, prose and poetry, is something that is actually a constant throughout Tagore's long creative life. One may turn first to the short stories or novels or plays such as the famous *Dākghar* ('The Post-Office'), for Tagore's mastery of empathy. *Dākghar* especially teaches empathy, for the central character, Amal, the dying boy in whom Tagore embodied his love for his own younger son Samindranath and his terrible grief at his death in 1907, has powers or empathy beyond his years, and his adult characters in his play can be placed on a scale according to their own ability to feel or empathise. But in Tagore's poems and songs, even those that are not narrative and

[4] *Samsad Bengali-English Dictionary*. Revised & Enlarged Third Edition, Sahitya Samsad, Kolkata 2000, p. 1007.

do not have characters, even in the poems and songs as those he chose to include in the English *Gitanjali*, you will find plenty of empathy, plenty of focus on the lives and feelings of other people.

Let me end with two poems from *Gitanjali* which express Tagore's feelings for young children and for the mothers of young children. If I, as a poet, have learnt to empathise, then I would attribute a lot of that to the influence of Tagore's powers of empathy. The first poem is one of the sonnets that Tagore took from his book *Naibedya* (1901). Indra, king of the gods, was mentioned in *Nātak*. Here in this sonnet, he appears as the god of rain, and the sonnet is a plea for rain, for the life-giving waters of deep feeling, even if they come in a stormy destructive form. But notice how, although this is a deeply personal poem, in the imagery at the end Tagore's powers of empathy, his feelings for others, emerge with wonderful power and precision:

For so long, for so long such drought,
Indra, god of rain, in this heart of mine.
I scan the bleak horizon—nix, nought,
Nowhere even a fleck of a watery line—
Nothing anywhere bringing a cloud-cool,
Blue-green hint of impending rain.
If you so wish, lord, bring cruel,
Destructive, raucous, thunderous storms of pain,
Whip me with curved lightning to strip back
This still, sullen, carapace of heat, so vast,
So bitter, so lonely. Look at me, lord, like
A mother when she helplessly gazes with moist,
    Tender eyes at her child on horrible days
    On which its father's foulest rages blaze.[5]

Finally a gentler poem about children, about *Khokā*, the affectionate term that is used for the youngest boy in a family. This is one of the

[5] *Gitanjali* (2011), p. 91.

poems that Tagore also published in his book of poems about children, *The Crescent Moon*. It was not in the original manuscript sequence of his English *Gitanjali*, but was added later in England in 1912. I suppose being a grandfather myself now, with two grandsons in London aged three and one, and a granddaughter in Munich aged one, I identify very deeply with this poem:

The sleep that comes to Khoka's eye,
    Banishing all woes—
Can anyone tell me where it lives
    And how it comes and goes?
        I've heard that in some land of story,
        In forests firefly-bright yet murky
        Two parul-buds there make a cosy
            Nest for sleep to lie.
It floats from there to Khoka's eye,
    That's how it comes and goes.
The smiles that come to Khoka's face
    Waking him out of sleep,
Can anyone say from which far land
    Those sunny smiles leap?
        I've heard that in some cloud of autumn,
        Dewy infant sunbeams glisten—
        When Khoka's morning smiles open,
            They bear those sunbeams' trace.
That's how in his lips and face
    Those sunny smiles leap.

The gentle tenderness that brings
    Such grace to Khoka's skin,
Can anyone say where once it hid
    Before its birth within?
        The silent grace that in his mother's
        Body from her youth still lingers,

That wordlessly such sweetness utters,
That's from where it springs—
The gentle tenderness that brings
Such grace to Khoka's skin.

The blessings with whose kind caress
Khoka is wrapped around,
Can anyone tell me how they fell
Like fresh rain to the ground?
Springtime's new and soothing breezes,
Fragrance that the monsoon carries,
Paddy-fields that autumn hurries—
All of these express
The blessings with whose kind caress
Khoka is wrapped around.
Look at Khoka's fresh young form—
His face, his open eyes.
Tell me who will bear his weight
And where that cradle lies?
The One upon whose lap is rocking
The world with its resplendent cladding,
And sun and moon and stars is holding—
He will keep him warm.
Look at Khoka's fresh young form—
His face, his open eyes.[6]

Lecture in Leiden (Holland), 23 September 2011.

[6] *Gitanjali* (2011), pp. 120–22.

On the Seashore of a Great Poem

The title of this book, *On the Seashore of Humanity*, immediately evokes Tagore's famous poem in *Shishu* (1903), *Jagat-pārābārer tīre*. The poem is even more famous worldwide in Tagore's own translation, 'On the seashore of endless worlds children meet'. Here I focus on just this poem and its translation. Let me first reproduce the poem in Tagore's translation, and then in the translation that I have done for my new translation of *Gitanjali*.

Tagore's translation:

> On the seashore of endless worlds children meet. The infinite sky is motionless overhead and the restless water is boisterous. On the seashore of endless worlds the children meet with shouts and dances.
>
> They build their houses with sand and they play with empty shells. With withered leaves they weave their boats and smilingly float them on the vast deep. Children have their play on the seashore of worlds.
>
> They know not how to swim, they know not how to cast nets. Pearl fishers dive for pearls, merchants sail in their ships, while children gather pebbles and scatter them again. They seek not for hidden treasures, they know not how to cast nets.
>
> The sea surges up with laughter and pale gleams the smile of the sea beach. Death-dealing waves sing meaningless ballads to the children, even like a mother while rocking her baby's cradle. The sea plays with children, and pale gleams the smile of the sea beach.
>
> On the seashore of endless worlds children meet. Tempest roams in the pathless sky, ships are wrecked in the trackless water, death is

abroad and children play. On the seashore of endless worlds is the great meeting of children.

Gitanjali 60[1]

My translation:

On the shore of the world-sea,
  Children play.
Endless sky stretching
Above their heads unmoving;
Deep blue water foaming—
  Dances all day.
Merrily on the shore
They meet and play.

They build their sand-castles,
  They play with shells.
The leaves they gaily scatter
Upon the vast blue water
Are rafts, toy-boats that saunter
  While ocean swells.
On the shore of the world-sea,
  They join in play.

They don't know how to swim,
  Or how to fish;
The diver dives for pearls,
The busy merchant sails,
They make from clods and pebbles
  What they wish.
They crave not wealth or jewels;
  They do not fish.

[1] *Gitanjali* (2011), p. 196.

The ocean laughs and surges,
    The beach runs wild;
Awesome waves rolling
Are to the child's hearing
A rocking and a singing
    Of mother to child.
The ocean sports, plays games:
    The beach runs wild.

On the shore of the world-sea,
    Children play
Tempests rage with anger,
Boats sink in far water,
Death's messengers caper—
    The children stay.
On the shore of the world-sea
    They meet and play.[2]

Tagore's manuscript can be found at the end of the so called 'Rothenstein manuscript' of Tagore's translation of *Gitanjali*. This manuscript was given to William Rothenstein when he came to England in 1912, and has been preserved among the Rothenstein papers in the Houghton Library at Harvard. The manuscript is a 'notebook in blue roan' (according to the Houghton Libraries catalogue description), and most of it consists of 83 poems and songs in a carefully numbered sequence. I have argued in my new book that these 83 poems represent Tagore's original conception of the English *Gitanjali*. When *Gitanjali* was published by the India Society in London in November 1912, and then by Macmillan in February 1913, introduced and edited by W.B. Yeats, three poems were left out of the sequence. 23 poems were then added from miscellaneous sources, and no complete manuscripts of these have survived. Three of the 23 are

[2] *Gitanjali* (2011), pp. 131–33.

found on spare pages at the end of the Rothenstein manuscript: 'On the seashore of endless worlds' and two other poems from *Shishu*. Beautiful though these poems are, they do not really belong with the *Gitanjali* of the main sequence, which takes poems and songs from four Bengali books (*Gītāñjali, Gītimālya, Naibedya,* and *Kheyā*) and one play (*Āchalayatan*).

Shishu is a book of poems about children that Tagore wrote when he was looking after his youngest daughter and son after his wife Mrinalini Devi died in 1902. His son Samindranath was already ailing and was to die in 1907. *Shishu* was the source for Tagore's English book *The Crescent Moon* (1913), and the three translations from the end of the Rothenstein manuscript were reprinted there.

'On the seashore of endless worlds' is not among the poems where there are major differences between Tagore's manuscript version and the published text as edited by W. B. Yeats. The paragraphing and punctuation are the same, and the only differences are in the phrasing. The paragraph divisions correspond to the five verses of the Bengali poem. At the end of the third paragraph, 'Hidden Treasures' is 'Hidden Treasure' in the manuscript. The first sentence of the third paragraph reads, in the manuscript, 'the sea surges up with laughter and smiles the sea beach.' The last sentence of this paragraph reads in the manuscript, 'The sea plays with children and smiles the sea beach.' The expressive phrase 'and pale gleams the smile of the sea beach', which occurs twice in the published text, is therefore a departure from the manuscript. It is impossible to say whether this change was Tagore's own doing, or was suggested by Yeats. We have very little actual documentary evidence for Yeats changes, because the typed copy on which he is said to have made his alterations has been lost.

In the last paragraph of the translation, 'Are wrecked' is 'Get wrecked' in the manuscript. The manuscript version of this phrase survived in *Gitanjali* as published in 1912 and 1913 and in other subsequent, separate editions of the book. In *The Crescent Moon* and also in the *Collected Poems and Plays of Rabindranath Tagore* (Macmillan, London, 1936), 'get wrecked' was changed to 'are wrecked'.

Tagore's translation of *Jagat-pārābārer tīre* is very eloquent, has been loved by many readers across the world in numerous secondary translations, and has been much anthologised. The transition is mostly accurate, but some interesting differences emerge when one compares it closely with the original. The opening phrase, 'On the seashore of endless worlds' is more mystical than the Bengali phrase, *Jagat-pārābārer tīre*. The English suggest something transcendent—"worlds" beyond this world—but in the Bengali the ocean is a metaphor for the world that we actually live in. The children are playing in that world, but with a certain detachment from it, because of their innocence and limited experience.

The same metaphor of a world-ocean, with its waves of life and death, can be found in *Gitanjali* 69, which is a sonnet taken from *Naibedya*. This poem is about the stream of life (*prān*) which runs through the whole of nature and human existence. It contains lines that Tagore translated as: 'it is the same life that is rocked in the ocean-cradle of birth and of death, in ebb and in flow.' In the standard text, the next sentence reads: 'I feel my limbs are made glorious by the touch of this world of life.' The manuscript has 'this world-life' rather than 'this world of life', and this alteration—assuming it was Yeats' doing—seems to me insensitive. The world is for Tagore a living being, it is not a world that happens to contain life.

In line 6 of verse 1, *sārā belā* ('all day long') has been left out in Tagore's translation. This slightly weakens the meaning of the original: the fact that children continue to play all day long, whatever maybe going on around them, is an aspect of their innocent detachment. In verse 2, *nil* ('blue') has been left out of the description of the sea, and together with the addition of 'pale gleams the smile' in the next paragraph it makes the poem slightly less colourful—slightly pallid—compared to the original.

In verse 3, 'while children gather pebbles and scatter them again' is a rather puzzling departure from the Bengali, because children playing on a beach are much more likely to leave their careful arrangement of pebbles rather than scatter them again, and the Bengali *chelerā nuri kurāye peye sājāy basi dhelā* implies precisely that kind of careful arrangement. In verse 4, 'pale gleams the smile of the sea beach' is not in the original. What Tagore wrote in the manuscript of his translation, 'and smiles the sea beach' is not so expressive or poetic, but is actually closer to the Bengali original. It adds a slightly sinister note, which may distort Tagore's meaning here. In the Bengali original, the beach is for the children a place of joy, happiness and innocence. The sea with its ways of life and death may be more sinister, but the children are more oblivious to it. In the last verse, 'death is abroad' is a rather weak translation of *maran-dut uriyā chale*, but the full effect of the Bengali is very hard to translate here, so I certainly do not blame Tagore for his simplification.

Jagat-pārābārer tīre can be compared with William Blake's celebrated poems about childish innocence. But Tagore's conception of children was very different from Blake's. For Blake as a Christian, children in their innocence are born into a fallen world, a dangerous world of mortality and sin. In lyrics such as 'infant joy' and 'infant sorrow', the infant as a symbol of the Immortal Spirit is immediately threatened and corrupted when it leaps into the world, 'helpless, naked, piping loud'. In Tagore's poem, children bring their innocence and joy into the world as a counterforce to its dangers. Furthermore, their happy games help to put death in perspective. The simile of the 'death-dealing waves' (*bhīshan dheu*, 'terrifying waves' in the original) being like a mother 'rocking her baby's cradle' suggests not that death is a threat to life but is an almost reassuring simile. Tagore's world—the world on whose shore children innocently play—is not a fallen world. It may be flawed, imperfect, unjust, full of terrible and cruel things, but it contains the beauty of the seashore and the innocence of children playing on it as well as the turbulence of the sea and the dangers it presents to fishermen, pearl divers, or merchants.

Now for my own translation. The main difference between it and Tagore's is that mine is a verse translation: I have tried through the use of metre and rhyme to capture the rhythmic and formal qualities of the original. Tagore, not being an English poet, wisely chose to translate his poems and songs into poetic prose. Although Tagore is often apologetic about his translations when referring to them in correspondence, here he is, writing on 4 April 1915 to William Rothenstein in quite a confident mood. He had been arguing with the poet Robert Bridges about changes that Bridges wished to make to poems from *Gitanjali* for inclusion in the anthology *The Spirit of Man*. Tagore wrote:

> Of course, at that time I never could imagine that anything that I could write would find its place in your literature. But the situation is changed now. And if it be true that Yeats' touches have made it possible for Gitanjali to occupy the place it does then that must be confessed. At least by my subsequent unadulterated writings my true level should be found out and the faintest speck of lie should be wiped out from the fame I enjoy now. It does not matter what the people think of me but it does matter all the world to me to be true to myself. This is the reason why I cannot accept any help from Bridges excepting where the grammar is wrong or wrong words have been used. My translations are frankly prose,—my aim is to make them simple with just a suggestion of rhythm to give them a touch of the lyric, avoiding all archaisms and poetical conventions.[3]

I myself am an English poet, not a Bengali poet, so I make full use in my translations of technical skills that I have acquired over four decades. But the way in which I use these techniques is often mysterious even to me, just as the technique of a singer or instrumentalist can become mysterious and unconscious when it has been mastered through years of practice. Of course, it is not for me to judge the quality of my translations in comparison with Tagore's. But I feel, reading it again now, some months after I did the translations in Santiniketan in September 2010, that my version of the poem has a lighter, more innocent, more childish quality than Tagore's translation. That quality is present in the original, and emerges as much from the music and the form of the poem as it does from the language and imagery.

[3] *Imperfect Encounter: Letters of William Rothenstein and Rabindranath Tagore 1911–1941*. Edited by Mary M. Lago, Harvard University Press, Cambridge 1972, p. 195.

To achieve a translation of this sort, with the rhymes falling into place with the same kind of inevitability as they do in the original, one has to adopt an attitude of mind which is quite similar to that of the children playing on the seashore. It is a strange mixture of the conscious and the unconscious, the knowing and the innocent. The arrangement of words into rhythmic and rhyming patterns has to be playful, just as the children playing with pebbles on the beach are playful. One has to be oblivious of other things that may be going on as one does the translation. One has to forget about death and all the frightening and ugly things in the world, just as children are oblivious of such things as they play. One needs to be engrossed, but also detached. The emotions of the poem have to be absorbed and internalised in a deep and unconscious way. They have to do their work at one level, while at another level the mind, with precision and skill, finds the words that are needed to express the meaning and mood of the poem.

When speaking about creative translation I do often describe it as an 'interpretative art', quite similar to the performance by a musician of a work by a great composer. The difference between a translation and an original poem is that the poem has already been supplied, like a musical score supplied by a composer to the musicians who then perform and then interpret his music. With an original poem, one is creating the score as well as performing it. But many of the creative processes involved are the same.

Like all great poems, *Jagat-pārābārer tīre* is about far more than one might think at a first, superficial reading. When I did my translation, I certainly did not consciously think about its connections with the creative process. But thinking about it now, I begin to understand why this poem has been so widely admired and so much loved. It is about life and death, the strange and frightening world that we bring children into the mystery and innocence of creativity.

Reprinted with abbreviations and editorial changes from: 'On the Seashore of Humanity', in *The Sequi-Centenary Volume on Tagore*, edited by Suranjan Das, Biswanath Roy and Chinmoy Guha, University of Calcutta, Calcutta 2012, p. 117–26.

What I Have Learnt from Tagore

The title of this seminar, 'My Tagore: Why Tagore', invites us to reflect on Tagore in a personal way, and that is what I shall do in this talk. The 150th birth-anniversary is a milestone in Tagore's legacy to us, but also a milestone in my own life. I turned sixty last February, and at the end of August I retired from my academic position at SOAS, University of London. I am hopeful that 2011 will be the start of a whole new phase in my life and work—a phase in which I may focus on Rabindranath's achievements more deeply and more extensively than ever before.

What have I learnt from Tagore? The question is so big, that it is almost like asking, 'What have I learnt from living for sixty years?' But let me attempt to group what I have learnt under five main headings.

1. *Language*

There is a splendid poem on Rabindranath by Shamsur Rahman, the greatest poet of independent Bangladesh. Entitled *Suryābarta* ('Rotation round the sun': an allusion to the sun, *rabi*, in Rabindranath's name), it attributes much of the poet's own creativity to Rabindranath's influence. Rabindranath has taught Shamsur Rahman the joy of being alive; to look at the world afresh; to respond to nature's beauties. But at the climax and heart of the poem, he writes:

āmāke diyecho bhāshā, tar dhvani, pratiki hillol
astitver tate āne kato
aishvaryer tari pāl-tola, taranger smrti-snāta
dipta jalayan.

> You have given me language, its sound and symbolic ebb and flow on the shore of existence bring so many boats of rich merchandise, their sails raised, such shining ships bathed in the memories of waves.

Āmāke diyecho bhāshā, 'You have given me language'. As a native speaker of English, not Bengali, I have not received from Tagore a language in the way that he has given Shamsur Rahman and so many other Bengalis their language. But he has taken me into a vast and extraordinary linguistic world that has become a major part of my life. Tagore could not convey his astonishing linguistic and technical virtuosity in his own translations, and arguably it is impossible to convey it in any translation. But mastery of verse form, intricacy of metre and rhyme, breathtaking richness of vocabulary and imagery, yet haunting simplicity and lucidity of language too—these are qualities I have indeed tried to convey in my translations. When I was working on my new translation of *Gitanjali* at Santiniketan in 2010, I was constantly amazed by Rabindranath's craftsmanship and linguistic command, and somehow those qualities inspired me to do daring things with my own language, too.

Readers seem to like my translations of the sonnets in *Gitanjali* especially. These are mainly from *Naibedya* (1901), but among the poems that Tagore added to his original manuscript of the English *Gitanjali*, there is a sonnet from *Chaitāli* (1896), which came to me effortlessly in translation, and which has special, personal associations for me. I attempted to do a translation of this poem early on in my Bengali studies, in the 1970s. That draft translation must still be somewhere among my papers. I remember feeling very dissatisfied with it: the poem had a sublime simplicity that I could not capture in English without it seeming banal. But I also remember my mother, Betty Radice, who was a distinguished translator of Latin, looking over my shoulder as I wrestled with the poem, and saying that at last she could understand—even from my imperfect draft—what a truly great poet Tagore was. I hope I have come closer to the poem in this new translation. If it seems easy, then that is as it should be:

> One day this precious gift of sight will cease—
> My last blink will forever seal my eyes.
> The following day will dawn the same as this,
> The world will wake to see the same sunrise.
> The noisy play of the world will carry on—
> In homes, the time will gladly, sadly pass.
> Thinking of this, towards this world I turn
> And look at it with new-found eagerness.
> The simple things that didn't seem to count
> All now take on a value beyond price:
> Places or lives of which the least amount
> Of note was taken will now more than suffice.
> Away with all I've got or didn't get!
> Give me what's humble: things that I forget.[1]

2. *Feeling*

In two of his finest English essays, 'The Poet's Religion' and 'The Creative Ideal', published in *Creative Unity* (1922), Tagore discusses the 'mystery of unity' in art. In 'The Creative Ideal', he built his argument around three terms taken from 'an old Sanskrit book': *rupa-bhedāh* ('separatedness of forms'), *pramanani* ('proportions') and *bhava* ('the emotional idea'). The term *bhava* interests me particularly, and I very much like Tagore's translation of it as 'the emotional idea'. If you look up *bhava* (*bhāb*) in a Bengali dictionary, you will find that it has a host of meanings that incorporate many aspects of thought and feeling. The crucial thing about *bhāb* is that it *combines* thought with feeling, intellect with emotion. Tagore's conception

[1] *Gitanjali* (2011), p. 117. Originally in *Chaitāli* under the title *Durlabh Janma* ('Precious Life').

of a poem—or any work of art—deriving its unity from a union of thought and feeling is very profound, and for me has become an ideal not only in my translations but in my own poems too. Pure emotion is not enough to make a poem; but pure thought is too dry to make one either. One needs both. The problem that I had—and many readers have had—with Tagore's own translations is that they were full of emotion, but somehow they lacked intellectual coherence, a backbone of thought.

My research on the manuscript of Tagore's translations of *Gitanjali* has shown me that there might have been more intellectual coherence in his English translations had he been differently guided, or if he had been left to develop his English voice entirely unaided. But in most of the translations that we have there is something missing: an intellectual, rational dimension that is always present when one reads Tagore in Bengali. That dimension expresses itself as much in his control of form as in the content of the poems, and it was that formal dimension that was beyond his powers as a translator. Gradually, not only through my own translations, but through the work of many scholars and translators, Tagore the intellectual and thinker is, I believe, emerging more strongly. As his essays and discursive writings become more widely available, non-Bengali readers will be better able to find Tagore's intellect even in works of his that might seem quite un-intellectual—his songs, perhaps, or his paintings.

My heading above, however, was 'feeling', not 'intellect'. We seem in today's world to be bombarded with huge amounts of art and literature and music which lack deep feeling. What Tagore's works have shown me over the years is that, without *bhāb*, art is pointless. It has to stem from feeling, and it has to stir the feelings. But it will not do that convincingly or permanently unless it also engages the mind.

3. *Purnatā*

I have used the Bengali word *purnatā* rather than its English translation 'fullness', because 'fullness' does not seem full enough. In another English essay 'What is Art?', published in *Personality* (1917), Tagore commented on this problem—that abstract words can be richer in one language than their equivalents in another. He wrote:

> For instance, the English word 'consciousness' has not yet outgrown the cocoon stage of its scholastic inertia, therefore it is seldom used in poetry; whereas its Indian synonym '*chetanā*' is a vital word and is of constant poetical use. On the other hand the English word 'feeling' is fluid with life, but its Bengali synonym '*anubhuti*' is refused in poetry, because it merely has a meaning and no flavour.[2]

The more I have worked on Tagore, the more important his concept of *purnatā* has become for me. Tagore's extraordinary range of activities, and the simple fact that he was a master of prose as well as poetry, encourage me to think that a comprehensive vision, a cast of mind that we sometimes describe as 'renaissance', is still possible in today's ever more complex world. The splits between cultures, conflicts between religions and ideologies, squabbles between scientists and humanists, or atheists and religious people, that bedevil our world *can* be overcome. Tagore's tireless attempts to achieve a unified outlook that was rational, religious and moral, to keep abreast of developments of science just as much as changes in art or society, show that *purnatā*—wholeness of vision—is not impossible, and that we need it more and more.

People often talk about 'harmony' in relation to Tagore. At the unveiling of an imposing new bust of Tagore in Gordon Square in the Bloomsbury area of London on 7 July 2011 (installed and paid for by the Tagore Centre UK and its supporters), the Prince of Wales eloquently identified Tagore's outlook with 'harmony', and he himself has recently published a book with that word as its title. But I am not sure if 'harmony' (a word that derives from western musical tradition and which has no real Indian equivalent) adequately evokes Tagore's concept of *purnatā*. One of his short poems in the posthumously published collections *Sphulinga* (no. 38) reads in Bengali:

[2] *English Writings* (1996), vol. 2, p. 355.

kallolamukhar din
dhāy rātri-pāne.
uchchhal nirjhar chale
sindhur sandhāne.
basante ashānta phul
pete chāy phal.
stabdha purnatār pāne
chalichhe chanchal.[3]

In my translation of Tagore's collected *kabitika* or 'brief poems', this reads as follows:

Tumultuous days
Rush towards night.
Seas are the goal
Of streams of spate.
Impatient spring-flowers
Long to be fruit.
Restlessness strives
To be calm and complete.[4]

Notice how even in this short poem *purnatā* includes what is tumultuous, dynamic, incomplete and restless. I think Tagore did believe that the universe was ultimately balanced and harmonious, but the harmony of the universe is one that obviously includes a vast amount of disharmony and confusion—even chaos. His creative works are full of awareness of this. You find it in a great poem such as *Prithibi* ('Earth') in *Patraput* (1936), in which he writes of the earth:

You are mighty, and knowable only by the mighty;
You counterpoise charm and severity;

[3] *Rabīndra-rachanābalī*, vol. 14, p. 16.

[4] Rabindranath Tagore: *The Jewel That Is Best: Collected Brief Poems*. Translated by William Radice, Penguin Books, New Delhi 2011, p. 122.

Compounded of male and female;
You sway human life with unbearable conflict.[5]

It can also be found in the poem *Jāgāt-parabārer tīre* of *Shishu* (1903), which Tagore famously translated as 'On the seashore of endless worlds children meet'. In this poem the serene play of the children on the beach evokes innocence, beauty and harmony, but the dangerous waves of the sea represent the confusing and frightening world that we all have to grow up in. This poem was another that meant a great deal to me when I translated it in Santiniketan. Tagore's own translation is one of his best, but maybe the verse form that I was able to give it does convey the movement of the waves as expressed by the rhythm of his Bengali verse.[6]

The paradox of the 'Awesome waves rolling / Are to the child's hearing / A rocking and a singing / Of mother to child.'[7] makes me think of one of my favourite songs by Tagore:

ache duhkha, ache mrityu, birahadahan lāge.
tabuo shānti, tabu ānanda, tabu ananta jāge.
There is sorrow, there is death, there is the fire of separation;
yet there is peace, yet there is joy, yet there is eternity.[8]

This great song, which seems to encompass the whole universe in just eight lines of text, also contains the word *purnatā* in its last line: *sei purnatār pāye man sthān māge.*—'mind/heart seeks a place at the feet of that fullness'. *Man* in Bengali is as comprehensive as *bhāb* and includes both thought and emotion.

4. *Goodness*

At the symposium on Tagore at the Smithsonian Institution in Washington DC last May (2011), Uma Das Gupta in a moving

[5] *Selected Poems* (1985), p. 99.
[6] See *Gitanjali* (2011), pp. 131–32.
[7] *Gitanjali* (2011), p. 132.
[8] *Gītabitān*: Pūjā 248.

summing up quoted Tagore's comment: 'We become powerful with knowledge, but we attain fullness by sympathy.' I was touched to find recently that one of my PhD students, Mayurika Chakravorty, quoted that same comment in her acknowledgements at the beginning of her thesis on Bengali fantasy fiction, saying that I in my supervision of her work, had taught her that principle. If I did, then that must have something to do with my exposure to Rabindranath over so many years. Tagore's extraordinary powers of empathy, his ability to enter into the lives and feelings of people from so many different backgrounds, male and female and of all ages is closely related to his greatness as a prose and fiction writer as well as a poet. Tagore's mastery of both poetry and prose is something that is now taken for granted, but is not thought about sufficiently. It is actually very unusual—possibly unique. I know of no other writer for whom poetry and prose are of absolutely equal importance, two sides of the same coin. Prose and poetry for Tagore represented world and spirit, and it is part of his striving for *purnatā* that both should be brought into balance.

As a poet, Tagore found it difficult to shed the ego. In many of his poems and songs he is focussed on himself. But prose—especially short stories and novels—took him out of himself. It obliged him to focus on other people, to create believable characters and describe real life and society. This was essentially an altruistic endeavour, just as his practical work at Santiniketan and Sriniketan, and for Visva-Bharati, was altruistic. His short stories especially, therefore, are suffused with a quality of goodness, which is also quite unusual among writers.

For some readers, this can become oppressive. I remember a poet in Bangladesh—Abul Hossain—saying to me many years ago that he had a problem with the 'lack of grossness' in Tagore's poetry. Maybe we expect great writers to encompass grossness. There is plenty in Shakespeare, after all. But if we consider Tagore's novels as well as his short stories, we will find characters that are gross or sensual, even if Tagore avoided sexual explicitness. One thinks of Sandip in *Ghare Bāire* ('The Home and the World'; 1916), or Madhusudan in Tagore's late, unfinished novel *Yogāyog* (1929). But the shining quality of goodness that we find running through Tagore's entire creative output is something that is deeply precious to those who know and love his works. From it I have personally learnt that it is possible to be both great and good as an artist, that the tension between 'perfection of the life, or of the work' that Yeats spoke of in his poem 'The Choice' *can* be overcome.

I believe, in fact, that the destiny of all great artists, even if their journey takes them through the circles of hell, is ultimately to arrive at some conception of paradise. This was Dante's journey, but when we listen to Prospero's extraordinary epilogue at the end of *The Tempest*—lines in which Shakespeare for the first time in his plays seems to speak to us as himself. We feel that even Shakespeare arrives at that vision, in a way that is all the more humbling and moving because he cannot get there on his own:

> Now I want
> Spirits to enforce, art to enchant;
> And my ending is despair,
> Unless I be relieved by prayer,
> Which pierces so, that it assaults,
> Mercy itself, and frees all faults.
> As you from crimes would pardoned be,
> Let your indulgence set me free.

5. *Truth*

The vulnerability of Shakespeare's farewell to the world in those haunting lines is matched, I think, by Tagore in his very last poems—the poems in *Shes Lekhā* that he managed to pen on his deathbed. I did not include any of those in my *Selected Poems*; I still feel reluctant to attempt to translate them. Superficially, they might seem to be the most translatable of all of Tagore's poems, because of their freedom of form and simplicity of language. Indeed, many people have translated them, and I am not sure that I could do any better. For me, their very vulnerability and honesty and simplicity is precisely what makes them so hard to shift from one language to another. Translation in general is perhaps possible because, when we write, we put on clothes or costumes of one kind or another. An actor puts on a costume; another actor can come along from a different culture or background and put on a similar costume. But in these final poems, Tagore has achieved what he set out as an ideal in one of the most famous poems in *Gitanjali*, no. 7, which in my new translation reads as follows:

> This song of mine has thrown away
> all ornaments;
> It's kept for you no pride any more
> in garments.
> Trinkets that fall between
> Divide us like a screen;
> Their jingle-jangle pushes away
> what you say.
>
> My poet's vanity in front of you
> doesn't hold;
> Greatest of poets, I want to lay at your feet
> the world.
> If I can make from life a simple flute
> painstakingly,
> You'll fill all its holes with your own
> melody.[9]

The lack of ornament, a lack of any kind of costume, makes it impossible for these late poems of Tagore to be any other than his own voice, speaking his own language, Bengali.

Nevertheless, from the poems of *Shes Lekhā*, one can derive an unadorned commitment to the truth that I and all of us can learn from Tagore. As he put it in poem no. 11 of *Shes Lekhā*, he unforgettably

[9] *Gitanjali* (2011), p. 136.

tells us that *satya ye kathin* ('truth is hard'), yet he has 'loved the hard' (*kathinere bhālobāsilām*). Yes, truth is hard: it includes *duhkha* (sorrow) as well as *sukha* (happiness), disharmony as well as harmony, evil as well as good. Tagore has taught me that commitment to truth is the most important thing of all. Here in Ahmedabad, we are reminded of Gandhi, and his commitment to the truth, and the conception of his entire life as a series of 'experiments with truth'. Maybe those of us who work on Tagore, who attempt to communicate his genius through translation or through writing, or through seminars like this, are trying, in our humble and imperfect way, to do no less. Our experiments may fail; they may not last; others may come after us and perform them better. But we have to keep attempting them, and that is what I have above all learnt from Rabindranath Tagore.

Lecture at Ahmedabad, 15 October 2011.

The Possibilities and Problems of Tagore Translation

In 1986, on the 125th anniversary of the birth of Rabindranath Tagore, the Sahitya Akademi devoted the May-June issue of their journal *Indian Literature* to him. It included an article by me called 'Ten Rules for translating Tagore'. Reading it again now, I find I agree with most of it, but not all. I smiled when I saw that my first rule was 'The work must be done slowly'. I meant that the total work of translating Tagore's *Rachanābali* could not be done in a hurry—it would require an effort over many years, many generations. That of course is true. But my recent experience of translating *Gitanjali* was anything but slow. I started the translations in the summer of 2009, and at first I did progress fairly slowly, fitting them in round other work. But when I arrived at Santiniketan as a Visiting Professor at Rabindra-Bhavan at the end of August 2010, I only had two months to complete the book before Penguin India's end-of-October deadline. There were more than sixty poems still to translate, and the Introduction to write. Moreoever, the book grew into a far bigger enterprise than I had expected.

How I managed to complete this book—translating at the rate of more than one poem or song a day, and simultaneously researching in Rabindra-Bhavan for the Introduction and Appendices—will always be a mystery to me. The mystery was deepened by the fact that I had to write the book with one arm! I fell soon after my arrival in Santiniketan and badly dislocated and fractured my right wrist. The translations were therefore done on a laptop with my left hand, and the rest of the book was dictated. The digital recording machine that I almost did not bother to bring to India became my lifeline, with sound files of even the footnotes sent by email to my assistant Mrs Monwara Seetul in London, who typed them and sent them back.

My 'Ten Rules' in 1986 were largely a rationale for my *Selected Poems*. Today, I would hesitate to be so prescriptive. I now think of 'translation' in broader terms. Translation is not just the translation of a text into another language. Musical, dramatic or cinematic adaptations are also 'translations'. Satyajit Ray's great Tagore-based films are translations. Tanusree Shankar's electrifying dance version of Tagore's English poem 'The Child'—which I was privileged to see at the Indian Council for Cultural Relations' 'Tagore Beyond Frontiers' festival in Kolkata in December 2010—is a translation, too. So is the opera 'Snatched by the Gods' by Param Vir, with a libretto by me based on my translation of *Debatār Grās*. It has been performed in many European cities since its premiere in 1992 in Munich, in several different productions. In my view, it is one of the most powerful translations of Tagore that has ever been done, and it is unfortunate that it is not being performed again in the current 150th birth-anniversary year. *Rabīndra-bhakti* and the world of contemporary Western opera remain very separate worlds. The *Rabīndra-bhaktas* don't know about contemporary music, and the lovers of new music don't know about Tagore. I try, in my own writings and lectures, to join up the many different worlds where Tagore has a presence, but it is an uphill struggle.

In my articles and lectures during this anniversary year I am frequently focusing on translation in this broad sense. Musical settings of Tagore's poems in translation are another subject that I feel very close to, now that my own translations are being set by contemporary composers. Most Bengalis are unaware of the hundreds of settings of Tagore's own translations that have been done—in many different languages—by Western composers. The best known (in Germany, at least) is the massive *Lyrische Symphonie* of Alexander Zemlinsky (1871–1942), for Soprano, Baritone and enormous orchestra, written in a lush, romantic style quite similar to the symphonies of Gustav Mahler.

But there are many settings just for voice and piano. I recently took part in a seminar on Tagore in Germany at the Deutsche Literaturarchiv in Marbach, near Stuttgart (10–11 March 2011). The seminar was largely the initiative of my dear friend, Dr Martin Kämpchen. A fascinating concert was held as part of it, of settings of Tagore by composers from seven different countries: Jean Cras (France), Ottorino Respighi (Italy), Karol Szymanowski (Poland), Rued Langgaard (Denmark), Bernard Hughes (Britain), Hanns Eisler (Germany) and John Alden Carpenter (USA). All pieces were songs except the piano piece by Rued Langgaard. No one who was there will forget the brilliance of the performance (in four different languages!) by the young French soprano Marie-Pierre Roy and the South Korean pianist Hye-Yeon Kim, both music students in Stuttgart and giving—I was astonished to hear afterwards—their first public concert together. In the universe of Tagore translation, musical settings of this sort have just as much a place as linguistic translations of literary texts.

With my translation of *Gitanjali*, however, I was much concerned with textual matters, and my introduction took its lead from Sukanta Chaudhuri's recent book *The Metaphysics of Text* (Cambridge, 2010), which lays great stress on the 'afterlife' of texts. Anyone who is audacious enough to re-translate the poems that Tagore chose for his English *Gitanjali* cannot ignore Tagore's own version and its consequences: the stunning critical success of the book when published by the India Society in London in November 1912 and by Macmillan in March 1913, the Nobel Prize that directly followed that success, and the numerous secondary translations that were then made. I have argued in my book that the standard text of Tagore's translation as introduced and edited by Yeats has many shortcomings, but this standard text will not go away: it cannot be displaced by my new text or by anyone else's. It is part of literary history. Even the wrong question marks that were added to *Gitanjali* which made nonsense of what Tagore wanted to say are part of *Gitanjali*'s 'afterlife', and cannot be wished away, cannot be airbrushed from the past in the way that figures in official photos of the Soviet Communist era were sometimes removed after they fell out of favour and were sent to Siberia.

The story of the wrong question mark is among the many surprising discoveries that I made as I raced to complete my book, despite the pain and awkwardness of my broken wrist. It may seem a trivial, pedantic detail, but read the story as told by the Englishman John W. Rattray and you will see how deeply shocked and wounded Tagore was when the wrong question mark was revealed to him in 1938. Rattray's sensitive and moving account of his visit to Santiniketan and his meeting with the poet and with Amiya Chakravarty is appended to my translation of *Gitanjali*[1] Sadly, the mistake was not rectified in the Macmillan editions of *Gitanjali* till 1950, nine years after Tagore's death, and even more sadly it has cropped up again in a number of recent editions by other publishers.

For me, the story symbolizes the challenge of translating Tagore in a way that does justice not only to the Bengali originals but also to the reality of his global career, his unique place in the literary history not just of Bengal or India but many countries worldwide. I want in my book to recover 'the real Gitanjali', the original Bengali poems and songs, and the creative *ānanda* that Tagore felt when he first embarked on the experiment of translating his poems and songs into a foreign tongue. But I also want to understand why and how *Gitanjali* became what it did.

Rattray's account would make a wonderful film or opera. Such a work would be another kind of 'translation', an attempt to understand and convey to audiences in our century the 77-year old poet's distress on discovering that a song that was a profound expression of his feelings had circulated all over the world in a wrong and misleading form. But he would have been wise enough to accept that what had happened had happened, and in my 60th year I too am old enough to accept that new translations of Tagore do not displace or replace what has come before, they merely add to what has accumulated over

[1] 'I Shall Stand', by John W. Rattray, In: *Gitanjali* (2011), pp. 233–45.

time—an afterlife that is as much a part of his achievement as all he wrote and did when he was alive.

Who knows how that afterlife will develop in the future? I watch how my own translations are taking on new *avatārs* in the hands of composers, dancers and painters, and realize that the Golden Boat will eventually carry them away and leave me alone on the river-bank just as it carried away Tagore's original works. But while I am still here, and there is still a place in the boat for me, I'd be very happy to hear from any film maker or opera composer who agrees with me about the potential of the wrong question mark story....

First published in the bi-monthly *Desh* (Kolkata) 2 May 2011 (in Bengali).

Rabindranath, Maker of Paths

On 18 September 1927, during his tour of South East Asia, Rabindranath Tagore was about to leave Surakarta in Java by car, to drive to Jogjakarta along with Suniti Kumar Chatterjee, Surendranath Kar, Dhirendra Krishna Dev Burman, and Samuel Koperberg, the Dutch Secretary of the Java Instituut. Their departure was delayed a bit, as Tagore had been asked to open a bridge and a road named after him, Tagorestraat. Recalling this in letter no. 16 of his *Jāvā-yātrīr patra* ('Letters from Java', 1929), Tagore wrote (from Jogjakarta, on 19 September 1927):

> In Soerakarta they had just finished making a road with a bridge and I was asked to perform the opening ceremony. A length of tape was stretched across the entrance to the bridge, which I had to cut with a pair of scissors in order to declare the road open to traffic. The function gave me a peculiar satisfaction as being emblematic of my self-imposed task of path maker. The road was named after me.[1]

The phrase 'self imposed task of path maker', in Indiradevi Chaudhurani's translation here, is very telling, and the original Bengali even more so. Tagore writes: *kājtā āmār lāgla bhālo; māne hala, pather badha dur karāi āmār brata*, which means, 'I liked the task; removing obstructions to paths is my vocation'.

[1] *Letters from Java: Rabindranath Tagore's Tour of South-East Asia 1927*, Translated by Indira Chaudhurani & Supriya Roy, edited by Supriya Roy, Visva-Bharati, Kolkata 2010, p. 119.

It is not difficult to think of numerous ways in which this self-description was applicable to Tagore's works and activities. His journey to Singapore, Malaya, Bali, Java and Siam in 1927, and indeed all of his twelve tours abroad, were all about forging paths and building bridges. He embarked on them because of his universalist philosophy, because he believed in intercultural exchange, and he wanted wherever he went to foster the international ideals of his most precious creation of all, Visva-Bharati.

In his creative works, whether in poetry, prose, music, drama, dance or painting, Tagore was a relentless maker of new paths, a ceaseless innovator, constantly creating new forms and styles in his poetry, coming up with totally unprecedented narrative structures in novels such as *Ghare Bāire* or *Chaturanga*, moving Bengali literary language away from the *shādhu bhāshā* of the nineteenth century to the more colloquial *chalit bhāshā* of the twentieth century, developing his stage craft away from Shakespearean or proscenium theatre conventions to the radically stripped down dramaturgy of his later symbolic plays, transforming modern Indian painting from the mimetic and figurative to the abstract or expressionist, and so forth. The original Bengali sentence in the letter that I have just quoted also for me indicates his love for collaboration: he removed obstructions or opened new paths for others. Reading Utpal K. Banerjee's recent book, *Tagore's Mystique of Dance*[2] I was very struck by Tagore's generosity to other creative people. In his dramatic, musical and dance drama experiments, he was not a dictator, making everyone dance to his tune. Rather, he was a facilitator, inviting talented dancers such as Mrinalini Sarabhai to Santiniketan, giving maximum scope to Pratima Devi as a director of his dance dramas, or sending Santidev Ghosh to Java and Bali so that he could learn from dance traditions there.

Some roads and some bridges may lead to one place, but others lead to more roads and bridges spreading off in numerous different

[2] Niyogi Books, New Delhi 2011.

directions. If one was to single out acts of path-making or bridge-building that were particularly significant and fertile in Tagore's career, what would they be? For me there are two crucial moments without which we would certainly not be here today, discussing Tagore at Jorasanko in Tagore's 150th anniversary year; nor would numerous other anniversary events in many countries have taken place over the last few months.

The first was on 22 December 1901: the inauguration of the Santiniketan School. For those, like me, who work on Tagore's literature from afar, the institutions that Tagore founded and inspired and moulded at Santiniketan and Sriniketan, and which flowered into Visva-Bharati, inaugurated in 1921, might sometimes seem less important than his literary works, or his songs or his paintings. Institutions are fragile and always uncertain in their future; works of art, and especially literary texts, are as durable as anything is in this world. But I have come to understand that it would be very erroneous to discount or sideline Tagore's noble and courageous experiments in institution-building, if only because Santiniketan and Visva-Bharati were themselves the cradle for so many of his creative works. You cannot separate one from the other, and this is particularly true of his works of drama, music or dance. Moreover, reading Tagore's writings on education is a sure way to a true and deep understanding of his aims and identity as a poet.

This struck me recently when, reading the appendices to Supriya Roy's excellent recent edition of Tagore's letters from Java, I came across the superb address on education that Tagore gave on 25 July 1927 at the Victoria Theatre in Singapore. The large audience on that occasion included many school children and their teachers, and it is Tagore's ability to connect with people of all ages right down to the youngest that is so especially moving and striking. I would happily spend the rest of this lecture simply reading out Tagore's own address, because it says so much and he says it so beautifully. But let me content myself with a few quotations:

They have asked me to talk to you because they know that I have a great love for children, and, it is true, I have more friends among our children, who are some of them of your age, than among those of my own age.

In my own school my children come around me. I sit with them on the same level, very often in the open air.

I had three classes under me, very young boys they were, and girls too. All of a sudden they would sometimes feel restless, and I would allow them, that very moment, to climb up the trees, or do something very irregular according to the regulations that we have in schools and colleges.

Young children are restless all round; their bodies are restless, and their minds are in sympathy with the body. When the body is having its movement, the mind also has its own movement, and a moving mind has more power to assimilate facts, to gather knowledge from the outside world.

We try to create an atmosphere of activities, and we make the whole surroundings full of surprises for these young boys. And through constant curiosity their mind becomes more and more active.

The best method of education for boys would be to let them travel, and along with that have their lessons. Let them come to fresh facts in their lives. Let their schooling be like a perpetual picnic party, and let them have what they are daily accustomed to. Thus every day they would come upon new facts quite naturally, not through books, and along with that stream of experience.

You can all picture in your minds the surroundings of these boys, the beautiful natural surroundings. But one thing which I cannot make plain to you is the atmosphere— that is the best part, the principal feature of my institution. It is an atmosphere not merely of teaching and studying, but of other sides of culture as well. We have artists, some of the best artists in Bengal,—and the girls and boys have the opportunity to watch them doing their work, producing their masterpieces day by day. I am a poet and I have to do my literary work every day and very often I read to my students and to my teachers my new play or my new story, or my poems, or I sing to them my latest song. That is not a regular class, but it is better than a class.

I also tried to explain to an audience the other day, not merely about the atmosphere of learning and the natural beauty, but of the atmosphere of love, what we call *maitri* in Buddhistic language, universal sympathy, both intellectual and emotional.

I have tried my best to give not only the natural environment of culture to our students but also to create that atmosphere, of mutual sympathy, international sympathy, which is absolutely necessary for the students of the present day.

The child brings its own God-given gift of life and growth in this world, but very often as we grow up we squander away that great gift, we lose the child which has brought to us the introduction to this great world and which should accompany us to the end of our days, we become cynical. Fortunately for me as a poet I have this child fresh within myself, this child which always has its living curiosity for all things, its sense of wonder for this great universe.[...] Therefore I am certain I have the right to be in the company of children.

Most adult people do not have the right because they cannot keep a real and natural sympathy for the children. They impose upon the children their own ideas of the grown-up mind without realizing the needs of the child mind. If I could live among them they will discover in me a companion of their own age, but I had not the opportunity, and I am unfortunate that they should carry away with them the impression that I am an old, possibly a wise man, talking words that are not comprehensible. This is a wrong introduction. I am not a wise man, but I am a poet.[3]

The thoughts and ideas in this speech go far beyond the institutional structure or curriculum of Patha-Bhavan in Santiniketan itself. They can be an inspiration to teachers and people working with children in a great range of institutions and systems. In this way, Tagore's aims and aspirations as an educationist open doors, make paths, and build bridges, for anyone, anywhere in the world, concerned with the welfare and the future of our children. No wonder Tagore did lay such emphasis on his school when he gave his Nobel Prize acceptance speech

[3] *Letters from Java* (2010), pp. 156–62.

to the Swedish Academy in Stockholm on 24 May 1921. There is a kind of magic ball here which people, whatever their background or culture, can pick up and run with. It is a bridge to the life and feelings and imagination of the child that all of us need to cross.

The second crucial moment for me and indeed for all of us who care about Tagore was his decision, in March 1912, while recuperating at Shelidah from the illness that had postponed his planned voyage to England, to start translating selected poems and songs into English. Again, for those of us working on Tagore's Bengali writings, and trying in recent decades to widen the understanding of his achievements as a writer in his mother-tongue through new translations, there has been a tendency—one that I have certainly had myself—to discount or ignore Tagore's own English translations. But through my own recent new translation of *Gitanjali,* I have come to understand much more deeply Tagore's sincere attempts to make paths and build bridges through his English translations. It turned Tagore into an international celebrity—and the subsequent expansion of his career across at least three continents is unimaginable without it. But were the directions in which people ran, with *Gitanjali* in their hands, actually, over time, the right directions? My conclusion as I completed the book was that they weren't really, and the aspect of Tagore that was above all concealed by the restructuring of the text of his translations and the packaging of it by Yeats was the personal aspect. Near the end of my introduction to *Gitanjali* I quote a paragraph from an essay of Tagore written in 1917 that Tagore included in his book *Ātmaparichay* (1943):

> A person's reputation is based on the way he is known to the outside world. If this external identity does not agree in any way with his inner truth then a split enters his existence. Because a person is not only what he is inside himself, he exists largely in the way he is known to all. 'Know thyself' is not the final truth; 'let thyself be known' is also of great importance. The attempt to let oneself be known is everywhere in the world. So it is that my inner religion fails to lock itself up within itself—it must necessarily go on making

itself known to the outside in various ways that are both apparent and still not apparent to me.[4]

When I read the manuscript of Tagore's *Gitanjali*—I feel strongly that he was trying—and to a large degree succeeded—in making himself known. My book is an attempt to help others to get to know Tagore's inner self and feelings as expressed not only in the original Bengali poems and songs but in his English translations.

If there has been an underlying, though perhaps not fully conscious, purpose behind all the 150th birth-anniversary celebrations and publications that have gone on over the last year, then I would say that they have all been dedicated to the goal to getting to know Tagore better: to getting to know the real Rabindranath, in all his activities and manifestations. My *Gitanjali* book is my own contribution to this, but there are many other people who have made significant contributions too. The image of picking up a ball and running with it, seems to be the one that I want to adopt here. I am hoping of course that people will pick up my *Gitanjali* book and run with it. With Penguin India's decision to include it among twenty-five books they have brought out (in Penguin's original orange covers) to celebrate their twenty-fifth anniversary, perhaps this is already happening.

At many events and performances that I have attended, I have seen young creative artists and performers pick up aspects of Tagore's music, drama and dance in new and exciting ways. I have also noticed, particularly at the Tagore festival that Satish Kumar organised in Dartington last May, how inspiring many of Tagore's ideas can be today to campaigners for peace or progressive education or the preservation of the natural environment.

Let me end with mentioning an achievement by the Tagore Centre UK. Their crowning achievement of their quarter century of existence was the unveiling of a bust of Tagore in Gordon Square in London by

[4] RabindranathTagore, *Of Myself (Ātmaparichay)*, translated from the Bengali by Devadatta Joardar and Joe Winter, Visva-Bharati, Kolkata 2006, by arrangement with Anvil Press Poetry, London, p. 21.

the Prince of Wales on 7 July 2011. The importance of this bust in the heart of the city that many people regard as the ultimate world city, cannot be underestimated. In neighbouring Tavistock Square there is a statue of Gandhi. Of course statues of Gandhi can be found all over the world, but the statue in Tavistock Square has had as big an impact as any statue of Gandhi anywhere. The same will, I believe, be true of the bust of Tagore. Just before coming to Bangladesh and India on this trip, I went and had a look at it again. I said to Dr Kalyan Kundu of the Tagore Centre UK at the time, and I re-iterate it now, that the choice that he and his colleagues made of the first poem in *Gitanjali* (the first poem in the standard text, but no. 3 in the manuscript) as the text for the plinth of the bust was an inspired choice. Even more inspired was it to have this text in Tagore's own manuscript hand, in both Bengali and English, beautifully reproduced from the Rothenstein manuscript:

> Thou hast made me endless, such is thy pleasure. This frail vessel thou emptiest again and again, and fillest it ever with fresh life.
>
> This little flute of a reed thou hast carried over hills and dales, and hast breathed through it melodies eternally new.
>
> At the immortal touch of thy hands my little heart loses its limits in a great joy and gives birth to utterance ineffable.
>
> Thy infinite gifts come to me only on these very small hands of mine. Ages pass and still thou pourest, and still there is room to fill.[5]

Of course when Tagore wrote this celebrated song and its equally celebrated English translation, he was addressing his God, his maker, his *jīban-debatā*. But the songs and poems of *Gitanjali* are so open-ended that it is perfectly possible to apply the words of this song to Tagore himself. If we do, then we not only realise what an infinite resource Tagore himself is, and how it can fill us over and over again with new life, but it also makes us aware of our humility, of the *littleness* of the heart that can lose its limits in a great joy.

[5] *Gitanjali* (2011), pp. 171–72.

Many are the paths that Tagore continues to open for us, and many are the bridges that we can cross, thanks to him. But we should always remember that each one of us is but one of many. The sentence that I quoted at the beginning of this address reminds us of Tagore's own humble sense that his vocation or vow or *brata* or chief object in life was to remove obstacles from the paths not just of himself but of others.

Lecture at Rabindra-Bharati University, Kolkata 10 February 2012.

The Balance of Complexity and Simplicity

When I started my work on Tagore in the early 1980s, he was, in the West, an almost forgotten figure. I had a strong feeling that the old impression of Tagore, based largely on his own translations and their numerous secondary translations into other languages, was false and incomplete. I wanted to establish his reputation on a new basis: to show not only through new translations but through an introduction and notes that he was a poet of enormous range and sophistication. I wanted to open a new door, and maybe I was successful in that aim, for my *Selected Poems* of Tagore which first came out in 1985, has been constantly in print since then, and nowadays many people who cannot read Bengali get their first impression of Tagore from this book rather than from *Gitanjali* and the other translations that Tagore did himself.

The impact of *Selected Poems* and of other books that have been done by me and by others means that we remember Tagore today not just as he was a century ago when *Gitanjali* was published, but through new translations and adaptations. He has become, far more than when I began my work, a living presence: his impact is continuously unfolding, just as the impact of Shakespeare and other great writers continues to unfold through new performances, films and books.

For me, remembering Tagore is deeply bound up with the presence that my own books now have in my mind. Not just the books: every talk I have given, every poem or story by Tagore that I have read with my students at SOAS, every musical or dramatic performance that I have been involved in—all of these contribute to what I remember when I think about Tagore today.

Tagore writes about the crucial role of the audience in his beautiful poem 'Broken Song' (*Gān-bhanga*), which you can find in my *Selected Poems*. The King Pratap Ray asks his beloved old court singer Baraj Lal to sing, even though the courtiers are now only interested in the flashy younger singer Kashinath. When Baraj tries to sing, he disastrously forgets the words of the song. This is deeply humiliating for him, but the King comforts him and takes him out of the court. The poem ends with lines that move me every time I read them:

'Come, let us go from here,' he says with kindness and love.
They leave that festive hall with its hundreds of blinding lights.
The two old friends go outside, holding each other's hands.

Baraj says with hands clasped, 'Master, our days are gone.
New men have come now, new styles and customs in the world.
The court we kept is deserted—only the two of us are left.
Don't ask anyone to listen to me now, I beg you at your feet, my lord.
The singer alone does not make a song, there has to be someone who hears:
One man opens his throat to sing, the other sings in his mind.
Only when waves fall on the shore do they make a harmonious sound;
Only when breezes shake the woods do we hear a rustling in the leaves.
Only from a marriage of two forces does music arise in the world.
Where there is no love, where listeners are dumb, there never can be song.'[1]

If people in the Western world now remember Tagore not just as a figure in the past but as a living presence in their literary and cultural

[1] *Selected Poems* (1985), p. 55.

life, this is because his writings are finding a responsive audience. They are no longer being ignored in the way that poor Baraj Lal is ignored by the courtiers when he tries to sing because his King has asked him to do so. What is the audience for Tagore today, why is it growing, and why will it, in my opinion, continue to grow?

Tagore does not yet feature very often in the pages of our serious newspapers or in journals such as the *Times Literary Supplement*. Programmes on Tagore on BBC radio have been few and far between, and I do not recall a single television programme. We may see a few articles appearing in connection with the 150th birth-anniversary, and maybe he will be mentioned on the radio. But I do not expect to see a sudden explosion of attention, in the way that happens when anniversaries are reached for major writers, painters, or composers in the Western tradition. For the British literary and cultural establishment, Tagore remains a marginal figure, and I do not expect this situation to change.

However, it is striking to me that Tagore is increasingly reaching an audience in a way that bypasses conventional channels. This is partly because of the power of the internet; it has also to do with the way our society has changed because of immigration from overseas, and the way in which school education is evolving too as a result of this change in society.

It is astonishing to see how popular some of Tagore's poems have become on the internet. Perhaps the most popular of all is 'Unending Love' (*Ananta Prem*).[2] If you Google this poem, you will find that it appears on thousands and thousands of websites. It always appears in my translation, and more often than not, my name as the translator is not given. I do not mind this, in fact I am pleased, because it shows that the poem has a power and appeal that go beyond any translation, just as the great plays of Shakespeare appeal to audiences all over the world regardless of what language and what translation they are being performed in.

'Unending Love' has become particularly popular at weddings. My wife read the poem out at our own younger daughter's wedding, and my daughter tells me that friends of theirs have chosen it for their weddings too. People also find it a moving poem to read out at funerals. This seems to me almost a definition of universal appeal: a quality in a poem that makes it appropriate for both weddings and funerals! Musical settings of the poem have been done by at least five composers including my friend, the Indian-born composer Param Vir, and by the distinguished British composer Jonathan Harvey.

What is it about 'Unending Love' that appeals so widely and deeply? And who is it appealing to? Turn to 'Broken Song' again, and you will find the answer. The courtiers in Pratap Ray's court like the singer Kashinath because he is clever and fashionable. But this is not Baraj Lal's style, and not what appeals to his old friend the King. I quoted the end of the poem; here is how it opens:

> Kashinath the new young singer fills the hall with sound:
> The seven notes dance in his throat like seven tame birds.
> His voice is a sharp sword slicing and thrusting everywhere.
> It darts like lightning—no knowing where it will go when.
> He sets deadly traps for himself, then cuts them away:
> The courtiers listen in amazement, give frequent gasps of praise.
> Only the old King Pratap Ray sits like wood, unmoved.
> Baraj Lal is the only singer he likes, all others leave him cold.
> From childhood he has spent so long listening to him sing—
> Rag Kafi during *holi*, cloud songs during the rains,
> Songs for Durga at dawn in autumn, songs to bid her farewell—
> His heart swelled when he heard them and his eyes swam with tears.
> And on days when friends gathered and filled the hall
> There were cowherds' songs of Krishna, in rags Bhupali and Multan.[2]

What Tagore is emphasising here is the emotional appeal of Baraj Lal's style of singing. It appeals to the heart because it is sincere and simple; the songs that he has sung through the years have also resonated

[2] *Selected Poems* (1985), pp. 53–54.

with crucial moments in Pratap Ray's life. 'Unending Love' and other poems by Tagore that have become so popular in recent decades make a similar appeal to the heart, and many people find them relevant to the most crucial and memorable days in their lives: weddings and funerals.

The people who are enjoying Tagore's poems and other writings are, so far as I can tell, 'ordinary people'. They are not people who perhaps read literature very much at all, or rush to keep abreast of the latest literary trends and fashions. They may not be readers of the *Times Literary Supplement*, or of the book reviews in the Sunday newspapers. They undoubtedly include many people of Bengali or Asian origin, but the readership that Tagore is finding today is certainly not limited to such groups. I suspect that Tagore's poems and stories are being read in many British schools, usually in my translation, because Tagore's writings at their best meet the essential criteria for success with both teachers and pupils. 'Teachability' is a good test of quality in a literary work. Teachers are always on the look-out for poems and stories that they can put across well to their pupils. There has to be something in them that appeals at different levels to different age groups; there has to be complexity, so that there is something to analyse and discuss; but there also has to be a quality of clarity and simplicity.

I recently completed a new translation of Tagore's most famous book, his English *Gitanjali*. As I worked on this book, I was constantly struck by the balance that all great poetry achieves between complexity and simplicity. In my view, works of literature—or of art or music—will not appeal to a wide general audience unless they achieve this balance. Technical complexity alone may be of interest to professional writers or literary critics, but will not strike a chord with the ordinary reader. Simplicity alone can have a temporary or sentimental appeal, but will not endure, because there will not be enough for teachers or pupils or future generations of readers to ponder over or discuss.

In everything Tagore wrote, there is a breath-taking technical virtuosity. Often those who want to translate his works underestimate this technical element. I get sent a lot of translations of Tagore's poetry by native speakers who certainly know and love the poems deeply, but simply do not have the English verse technique that is required in order to do justice to the poems in translation. I sometimes—gently, I hope—point out to them that translation is an interpretative art. It is rather like the performance of a piece of composed music. You cannot play Bach on the violin unless you can already play the violin. Baraj Lal in 'Broken Song' may be past his prime, and the words of the songs that he used to sing so well may no longer be fixed in his memory. But he is an *Ustād*, a master, with a much greater technique than the flashy young singer Kashinath, because his art would have been 'the art that conceals art'.

One of the paradoxes of the work of translators is that the better they get at translating, the more it is taken for granted by readers. 'Unending Love' is a prime example: the readers who have passed it around to each other on the internet (unfortunately often with the last verse missing because they have copied it from each other) seem completely oblivious of the fact that it is a translation they are reading and not the original Bengali. That is as it should be. John Keats said of poetry. 'If poetry comes not as naturally as the leaves to a tree, it had better not come at all.' Some of you may have heard this in Jane Campion's recent and beautiful film about Keats and Fanny Brawne, *Bright Star*. The same is true of translation. There is actually in my translation of 'Unending Love' a great deal of complexity and sophistication in the use of metre and rhyme; but those who read and listen to the poem at weddings and funerals are unaware of it.

My translation of Tagore's short poems is available with the title *The Jewel That Is Best: Collected Brief Poems*. There are nearly 500 poems in the book, each one of which presented a technical challenge. I was amazed when I worked on them how Tagore hardly ever repeats himself in formal or technical terms. Almost every one of the little poems in *Lekhan* (Jottings) and *Sphulinga* (Sparks) is in a different verse form.

Somehow, in my translation, I had to match up to that technical range and virtuosity, while at the same time catching the effortless simplicity of the poems. Here are four poems from 'Sparks':

117
Great work bears
  Its own burden.
Great grief supplies
  Its own consolation.
Small tasks, small hurts, small troubles
  Crush the life-spirit
    To near suffocation.

118
How easy it is
To mock the sun:
The light by which it's caught
  Is its own.

119
Rain on a monsoon night
  Knocks petals off the jasmine-creeper.
Their scent makes the watery breeze
  Kind and tender.

120
Sit yearly under a *shiuli*-tree,
  And offer its flowers in prayer.
Weave a garland of fallen blooms,
  And of this be sure:
Its petals will quickly fade
But its beauty will not depart:
  If you look you will find it
  Somewhere in your heart.

It will stay as if locked in a chest:
Opened, the scent is released
Of times past. [3]

In each of these brief poems there is much to discuss. In no. 118 for example, Tagore seems to be commenting wistfully on himself: his name Rabi means the sun, and despite his immense fame and success, Tagore always suffered mockery—and still does—precisely because of the sincerity and simplicity with which he wrote. The fourth poem seems to say something about what a translation or a re-reading of a poem from the past can do. The poem is locked in the past as in a chest, but it can be opened up again, and when it does an extraordinary and beautiful fragrance can emerge.

One of the questions that I am most frequently asked about Tagore is what makes him relevant today. I suspect that when people ask that question they expect me to talk about the relevance of his ideals—of his work as an educationist, ecologist, and internationalist. These aspects of Tagore are certainly important, and as a thinker and activist he undoubtedly has much to teach us. But what makes him above all relevant today—and will make him increasingly relevant as time goes on and his works become better known—is the power and beauty of his art. Many Bengalis, with access to his works in the original, despair of their beauties ever really being communicable to those who can only read him in translation. I don't think they should be so worried. In fact, the greater the poet, the *more* translatable he is, not the less. There are many beautiful details in Shakespeare's Elizabethan English that must be impossible to translate into other languages. But Shakespeare is so great that the power of his plays survives almost any translation. In a way, translation is like a sieve: there is much that will run through the sieve and be lost through the process of translation, but the gold

[3] Rabindranath Tagore: *The Jewel That Is Best, Collected Brief Poems*. Translated by William Radice, Penguin Books India, New Delhi 2011, pp. 144–45.

in the work will be retained. My experience as a translator of Tagore has taught me that the difficulties are immense, but the solutions to those difficulties are often quite simple.

When I did the *Selected Poems* of Tagore I believed that the songs could not be translated, because they needed the melody. As Tagore said himself, a song without a melody is 'like a butterfly whose wings have been plucked'. I preserve the repetition of the lines that occur when the song is sung. If one does this, it is immediately apparent to the reader that this is a song not a poem. The language of Tagore's songs is quite simple—much simpler than his prose or much of his poetry. I find that the words of the songs can be translated very straightforwardly; their repetitions will be enough to give the translation a satisfying shape and a 'music' which is not the same as the melody but which nevertheless takes on a beauty of its own.

In conveying the genius of Tagore, success is achievable if the same balance of simplicity and complexity as we find in the original can also be transmitted in translation. Translation does not just mean the translation of texts; with his songs or plays or dance dramas, translation means performance and adaptation as well. Exciting experiments in that direction have already taken place, and there will be many more in the future. Each new translation, each new production or performance, is an act of remembrance. It is in this way that we should remember him today. Correct, scholarly understanding of his life and international career is certainly important; but is not enough. Once again, Tagore has himself, in one of his most famous poems, indicated the correct approach. In 'The Golden Boat' (*Sonār tarī*), the speaker of the poem is left behind as the mysterious golden boat carries away his harvest. Remembering Tagore as he was in the past and in his lifetime is like focussing on the speaker in that poem, left behind 'on the bare river-bank'. It is the harvest that matters: where it travels to, and what is done with it. Remembering Tagore today means bringing in that harvest.

Lecture at Glasgow, Tagore Centre, in 2011.

Tagore before and after 1912

In 2011, the 150th anniversary of Tagore's birth. In 2012, the centenary of the publication of Tagore's English *Gitanjali*. In 2013, the centenary of his Nobel Prize for Literature. All these anniversaries bring to mind a famous and beautiful poem that Tagore wrote in the spring of 1896. It was included in his book *Chitrā*, and given the title *1400 Sāl*, that is the beginning of the 15th century in the Bengali calendar, 100 years after Tagore wrote the poem. In English translation the poem has been given the title '1996', but it is also known as 'A Hundred Years from Today'. The poem is full of the imagery and emotions of spring, and I find it an appropriate poem to read now that spring has come to England, taking us by surprise, as always, with its greenness and beauty. In the poem, Tagore forms a connection in his mind with a poet a hundred years in the future, who might be responding to the beauties of spring in the same way as Tagore himself has in 1896.

Reading the poem now, after all that has happened in the world since then, and with all that we know about what happened to Tagore's career after 1912 and to his standing in the world in the decades after his death in 1941, one wonders how the poem would have been if he had written it twenty or thirty years later. In the poem that we have, the context that he imagines for his fellow poet 100 years hence is entirely Indian or Bengali. The flowers, birds, bees, and southern spring breeze that Tagore hopes the future poet will respond to are exactly the same as what Tagore experiences in the Bengal that he knew and loved so well. The poem is both universal—in its focus on experiences available to all poets of whatever time or place—and also intensely local. It is not a poem by a poet who could ever have imagined in 1896 that he would become a world figure, that his own English translations of his poems and songs would spread to every corner of the earth through numerous secondary translations, and that he would in 1913, become the first non-Westerner to be awarded the Noble Prize.

1912 was undoubtedly the watershed in Tagore's life, but it is only recently that I have come to appreciate the true significance of that year. When I started translating his poems in the 1970s, I really wanted to forget about *Gitanjali*, the Nobel Prize and everything that followed. I took my lead from a letter that Tagore wrote on 26 November 1932 to William Rothenstein—a letter that continues to make a deep impression on me every time I read it. Tagore in this letter casts his mind back to *Gitanjali*, with mixed feelings that surface in many other letters as well in which he refers to his own English translations and to his western career generally:

> It was not at all necessary for my reputation that I should find my place in the history of your literature. It was an accident for which you were also responsible and possibly most of all was Yeats. But yet sometimes I feel almost ashamed that I whose undoubted claim has been recognised by my countrymen to a souvereignty in our own world of letters should not have waited till it was discovered by the outside world in its own true majesty and environment, that I should ever go out of my way to court the attention of others having their own language for their enjoyment and use.[1]

As a translator and reader of Tagore, I have been trying to discover Tagore's poetry 'in its own true majesty and environment'—to fulfil what, when he was in this kind of wistful mood, he wished could have happened had history been different. Some progress has been made by me and other translators since then. The Tagore that is available to

[1] *Imperfect Encounter*. Letters of William Rothenstein and Rabindranath Tagore 1911–1941. Edited by Mary M. Lago. Harvard University Press, Cambridge 1972, p. 346.

non-Bengali readers across the world is a richer, fuller and more varied figure than he was when I began my work. But the current spate of conferences, festivals and publications will empathetically show that the Tagore of *Gitanjali* and the Nobel Prize is very much still part of the international picture, and will always be so.

In my new translation of *Gitanjali* I have tried to recover what was actually in Tagore's mind and heart when he began the translations that were to change his life and the world of literature. I have tried to bring out the variety of the poems and songs that he chose to include in the English *Gitanjali* (which was a very different book from the Bengali *Gītāñjali* of 1910). In my long introduction, I have constantly stressed the personal character of the poems and songs that he chose: how they were, as he said in another letter to William Rothenstein, 'revelations of my true self to me'.[2] My new translations alternate with a radically new text of Tagore's own translation, based on the manuscript that has been preserved among the 'Rothenstein papers' at the Houghton Library in Harvard, following wherever possible Tagore's original selection, order, paragraphing, punctuation and phrasing. I have examined the extensive differences between the manuscript and the published text as edited by W. B. Yeats, and have tried to understand how *Gitanjali* as published could have moved so far from Tagore's original conception of the book. I argue that Tagore's frequent expressions of ambivalence and even regret that he had done the translations at all arose not so much from doubts that he had about his command of English (though he frequently expressed such doubts), but from a deep seated feeling that his work had been taken out of his hands, that the success of *Gitanjali* and the award of the Nobel Prize a year later unleashed an unstoppable chain of events over which he had little control.

I have done all this in the hope that perceptions of *Gitanjali* worldwide can gradually be altered, and Tagore as a man and as a poet can gradually be better understood. But I also have no illusions about

[2] Ibid., p. 82 (30 December 1912).

how entrenched the Tagore of 1912 and 1913 still is. Like it or not, Yeats' introduction and editing, the numerous secondary translations, and the Nobel Prize and its aftermath will not go away. They are part of the story, and will certainly form a major part of the celebrations this birth-anniversary year and in the two years to come.

As always, Tagore himself has the last word on this. On 20 August 1915, he wrote to Rothenstein about a dispute he had had with the poet Robert Bridges over alterations that Bridge's wanted to make to translations by Tagore that he was including in his anthology *The Spirit of Man*. Quoting from his letter to Bridges, Tagore wrote to Rothenstein:

> Please do not think I have the least conceit about my English. Being not born to it I have no standard of judgement in my mind about this language—at least, I cannot consciously use it. Therefore I am all the more helpless in deciding whether certain alterations add to the value of a poem with which my readers' minds have already become familiar. I know, habit gives a poem its true living character, making it seem inevitable like a flower or fruit. Flaws are there but life makes up for all its flaws.[3]

Habit has indeed made the *Gitanjali* of 1912 seem 'inevitable like a flower or fruit', and no translation that I or anyone else can do, and no new text based on Tagore's manuscript, can do anything to change that simple fact.

To return to Tagore's poem of 1896, what answer should we give to my question about how the poem might have been different if Tagore had written it after 1912? Tagore's universalism, inseparable from his international identity in the post-Nobel Prize phase of his career, was always rooted in the local, and he continued to write numerous poems and songs in which the natural beauties of Santiniketan were to the fore and the rest of the world might not have existed.

But *1400 Sāl* is about Tagore's core identity as a poet, which for him is also the centre of the universe. The poem's central phrase is

[3] Ibid., p. 212.

nikhiler marma, 'the heart of the universe', a place where both Tagore and his fellow poet a hundred years hence can find common ground. A poem post-1912 reaching out to that common ground would have to take in more than the birds and bees and scented flowers of Bengal. It would embrace the numerous other subjects that came to preoccupy Tagore: Indian freedom and social development, world peace, education, science, religion—just about everything, in fact. The *nutan kabi* ('new poet') who Tagore imagines would be singing his own songs and responding to Tagore's songs as well, might well be a poet in another country or language. After 1912, Tagore's literary horizons embraced translations and readers in many lands. The poet of a hundred years hence might even be a poet-translator such as myself, attempting to discover Tagore's poetry 'in its own true majesty and environment', just as distinguished translators into other languages such as Martin Kämpchen into German are doing. Or it might include older translators such as Gide into French or Jimenez into Spanish, who were reliant on Tagore's own English versions. Exactly what kind of poem Tagore would have written post-1912 is impossible to say, but I think it would have been more complex, more burdened with moral preoccupations, and quite possible more tormented than the joyous poem of the spring that he wrote in 1896.

The other question that arises from this poem is what Tagore would have made of the world and of his place in it if he had himself lived to 1996 or indeed to 2011? This question brings us slap up against the festivities that will soon be in full swing. Looking through the programmes of the many events that have been planned, I am struck by a tension or dichotomy that has, in a way, been present ever since Tagore leapt on to the international scene in 1912. On the one hand, we have the people who see in Tagore what they want to find. Their arch-priest was and still is W. B. Yeats, who wrote in his famous introduction to *Gitanjali* that 'A whole people, a whole civilization, immeasurable strange to us, seems to have been taken up into this imagination; and yet we are not moved because of its strangeness, but because we have met our own image, as though we had walked in

Rossetti's willow wood, or heard, perhaps for the first time in literature, our voice as in a dream'.

On the other hand, we have those who are trying to see and understand Tagore as he actually was. Of the events about to come up in Britain, the Tagore Festival in Dartington (1 to 7 May) looks like being very much a celebration of the Tagore that people wish to see. An anthology called *A Taste of Tagore* that is being published has a foreword by Deepak Chopra that is in the same vein as Yeats' Introduction. Chopra writes, 'Although Rabindranath Tagore grew up in Edwardian times, he is more relevant today than ever before. His contribution to our understanding of spirituality as a domain of human awareness that is universal is deeply needed to repair our wounded soul and heal our planet.'

The London conference that is being organised by the Tagore Centre UK (7 and 8 May 2011), by contrast, will attempt to contribute to our historical and critical understanding of who Tagore was and what he achieved—a goal that has inspired all the Tagore Centre's activities and publications since its inception in 1985.

I belong more to the second tribe, and I have argued that it can be misleading to read Tagore's complex literary works through the filter of his moral ideals, or of our own moral ideals. Like all great works of literature, they are too many-sided for that, too full of light and dark, the ominous rivers of the underworld being as ever present in them as the ambrosial rivers of heaven. But I do not wish to pour scorn on the idealists. Their enthusiasm for Tagore was a major reason for his success in 1912, and is a major reason why his 150th birth-anniversary is being celebrated with such fervour today.

If Tagore were alive today, if he were himself a poet of a hundred years hence, he would be sympathetic to both groups. As he said so eloquently in one of his last poems, he knew that truth was hard, *satya ye kathin*. He loved it for its complexity, and never imagined that the world could be reduced to a simple set of moral ideals. But he undoubtedly also did have those ideals, and constantly strove for the qualities of peace and harmony and unity with the natural world that his present generation of idealistic admirers find in him.

I believe that the two tribes—the idealists and the realists—can find common ground and meet each other at the upcoming Tagore events in friendship and sympathy, so long as they always remember that Tagore was fundamentally a poet. As a great poet he was fated to be both an idealist and a realist, agonizing though it often was to reconcile the two.

In poems by Tagore whose themes seem particularly relevant to our contemporary worries and problems, such as *Pakshī-Mānab* ('Flying man'), *Briksha-Bandanā* ('In Praise of Trees'), *Ghar-Chārā* ('Leaving home'), or *Prithibī* ('Earth'), we find strong echoes of our concerns about technology, the environment, migration, and evolution, whether we are idealists or realists. We are also including his extraordinary poem *Nagar-Sangīt* ('Song of the City'). This poem is extraordinarily prophetic of the vast and relentlessly expanding cities of the 21st century—the horror of them, but also the intoxicating excitement of them. The threats to the natural world, the ever growing gulf between urban and traditional ways of living, would be shocking and alarming to Tagore were he alive today, just as they are to many of us. Maybe he would have had doubts now about the confidence he expressed in 1896 that a poet of a hundred years hence could relate to an eternal and unchanging natural world in the same way as he himself had done. But his poem as written—in innocence, as it were, in 1896—takes on a new poignancy and urgency in our present world-context. We know that the natural world cannot be as it was for him, that we cannot rely on it anymore but instead must take responsibility for it. But each time the spring comes round, so surprisingly, and with its exuberant promise of hope and renewal, we cling to the hope that the natural world may yet be there for us.

In Japan, while engineers desperately struggle to bring the damaged Fukushima nuclear reactor under control, the citizens of Tokyo and other big cities are still travelling out to see the Cherry Blossom, just as they have done for generations, and with the same hope and belief in the ultimate beneficence of nature. Tagore is a poet that we can turn to with the same spirit of hope. The 'joyous greeting of the spring' (*basanter ānanda-abhibādan*) will be present, as if sent to us by Tagore in 1896.

First published in *Tagore 150 Years: A Tribute,* Supplement of *The Statesman,* Kolkata, 4 June 2011, pp. 9–16.

Tagore's Sense of Rhythm

My pictures are my versification, in lines. If by chance they are entitled to claim recognition, it must primarily be for some rhythmic significance of form which is ultimate and not for any interpretation of an idea or a representation of a fact.[1]

In an article in Bengali on *Rabīndrasangīt*, published in 1967, the great film director Satyajit Ray distinguished between Tagore the poet, Tagore the composer of songs, and Tagore the painter, according to his technical proficiency. As a poet—and indeed as a writer of fiction and drama—Tagore was an absolute virtuoso. He could do anything with language, could write in any number of verse-forms and metres, and invented many new forms of his own. As a singer and composer, Tagore was extremely accomplished too. His knowledge of India's musical traditions, both classical and folk, was profound, and recordings that have survived show him to be a singer of great flexibility and subtlety. He was however somewhat impatient with rigid musical orthodoxy, adopting an innovative and creative approach in his use of *rāga* and *tāla*. As a painter, Tagore was largely self-taught. He lacked academic training in draughtsmanship (though some early sketches that have been discovered show him to be more skilled in that area than was previously thought), and by his unique, expressionist style he made a virtue of his technical limitations.[2]

[1] 'My Pictures' (1), 28 May 1930, in Prithwish Neogy (ed.): *Tagore on Art and Aesthetics*, Subarnarekha, Kolkata 2005, p. 88.

[2] See Satyajit Ray: 'Some Reflections on *Rabindrasangeet*', in Krishna Dutta

I agree with Satyajit Ray's threefold analysis, but it should be possible to find some unifying factor, some special characteristic or instinct that went beyond technique. Many scholars of Tagore have sought a unity in his universalist philosophy, in his humanism and international ideals. Others have pointed to his overall pursuit of harmony, his quest for *purnatā* or 'fullness', a completeness of vision that would reconcile art and morality, science and religion. I have never felt quite comfortable with this approach, partly because his literary works, like any great works of literature, are full of complexity and contradiction. For every positive current, there is a darker undercurrent; joy is always mixed with sorrow, life with death. There is also a problem with his paintings.

Many people have been puzzled by an apparent gulf between the paintings and his literary works. I myself, in my *Selected Poems* of Tagore, saw in the paintings an escape from the moral preoccupations that often burdened Tagore the writer and thinker. Much the same idea crops up in Flavia Arzeni's recent book, *An Education in Happiness: The Lessons of Hesse and Tagore*, which presents Tagore and Hermann Hesse very much as thinkers whose idealistic philosophy can help our troubled world. She writes of the paintings:

> What is most surprising, apart from the sheer mass of the work, is that it went in a completely different, indeed radically opposed direction to that which he pursued in his literary work. In his poetry, as in his prose, Tagore always kept to the model of beauty and harmony which he himself advocated and which he expressed faithfully in both content and style. His painting seems to come from a different world, as if it were the product of someone else's mind. His visual universe is dark, often anguished, his self-portraits cruel and grotesque, his figures disturbing, his landscapes crepuscular. Parallels could be drawn, with some justification, with certain styles of the European avant-garde, especially German expressionism.[3]

---

and Andrew Robinson (eds.): *Purabi: A Miscellany in Memory of Rabindranath Tagore 1941–1991*, The Tagore Centre UK, London 1991, pp. 177–89.

[3] Flavia Arzeni: *An Education in Happiness: The Lessons of Hesse and Tagore*, tr. Howard Curtis, Pushkin Press London 2009, pp. 178–79.

I no longer see this disjunction. I find, rather, that more and more points of contact with the paintings emerge, the more deeply one goes into his literary works. At the same time, I recognize the need for some unifying principle that goes beyond Tagore's moral outlook. We need a principle that goes to the heart of his creativity, for whether in poetry, prose, songs or paintings, Tagore was always creative, and his works, however diverse, were the product of a unified creative impulse. He himself gave this impulse a name; he called it his *jīban-debatā*, his 'life-god'. But the *jīban-debatā* is itself elusive of explanation. Is there some simpler principle, which may be mysterious but which we can all feel and recognize, even if we are reliant on translation? I have for a long time felt that a unique sense of rhythm is what gives fundamental unity to all Tagore's creative endeavours. In the Introduction to *Selected Poems*, I said that I hoped my translations, as well as being varied in form and metre, would have an overall quality of rhythm that would run through the entire book. I have said the same in the Introduction to my new translation of *Gitanjali*, Tagore's most famous book. As a poet myself, I have tried to capture that rhythm by using my own creative instincts. I have not till now tried to analyse it, though I was certainly aware when I started translating Tagore's poetry that I was introducing into English poetry many forms and metres that were new and which owed a lot to the rhythmic influence of the original. I now feel ready to attempt some analysis of Tagore's rhythmic distinctiveness, though what I will say in this article is provisional and tentative.

In order to do so, I started to read Tagore's essays on rhythm and metre. There are a considerable number of them, gathered together in *Chhanda* ('Metre'), first published by Visva-Bharati in 1936. Many of these essays are highly technical, as one would expect from a poetic virtuoso. But they also contain many general insights into metre and rhythm, which have implications for our understanding of Tagore's work in all fields—literary, musical and artistic. In an essay called *Chhander Artha* ('The Meaning of Metre'), first published in the journal *Sabuj-Patra* in 1916, Tagore discusses how words alone express meaning, but metre and rhythm express feelings that go beyond the meaning of the words. He recalls the famous story of how the metre of the *Rāmāyana* was discovered by the poet Valmiki after he heard a bird in the forest piteously grieving for its mate that had just been killed by hunters. In order to express the pain and grief that the bird was suffering, a metre that became the metre of the whole *Rāmāyana* miraculously came to Valmiki's mind. Tagore says that although metre ties down words, in another way it sets them free. It is like the tight strings on a *sitār* on which beautiful music can be played. Words on their own are like a bow, but when given new life and music by metre they are like arrows that can go straight to the heart. The metaphor of the arrow is like a lovely little poem in Tagore's book *Kanikā* ('Particles', 1899), which in my translation of Tagore's collected 'brief poems' is as follows:

Poetry and Prose
'You're heavy, Club, ' says the nimble dart.
That's why you're always so stiff and straight.
Do what I do: cut through debate!
Instead of head-clobbering, pierce the heart.[4]

In this essay and in all the essays in the book *Chhanda*, Tagore uses *chhanda* as the equivalent of the English word 'metre'. As a frequent word in his poetry, however, *chhanda* can mean a more general quality of rhythm. His essay on the meaning of metre uses a number of other words too: *beg* for 'force' or the energy that metre can convey; *abeg* for the passion and excitement that metre can raise in the mind of the reader; *spandan* for 'pulse', a regularity of beat similar to a heart-beat. He also makes a fascinating distinction between *chal* and *chalan*. These two words are used in his famous play *Tāser Desh* ('Card Country', 1933, rev. 1939). In the play, there is a contrast between the inhabitants of the Card Country, who are

[4] Rabindranath Tagore: *The Jewel That Is Best: Collected Brief Poems*, translated by William Radice, Penguin India, New Delhi 2011, p. 53.

playing-cards and the human beings who arrive on the island where the cards live and quickly start to subvert their society and way of life. To the cards, the human characters are capable of *chalan* but not *chal.* In my translation of the play, published by Visva-Bharati in 2008, I translated *chalan* as 'movements' and *chal* as 'moves'. In the essay, I would translate them the other way round, but maybe the distinction between the two is somewhat arbitrary.

In his analysis in this essay of how Bengali metre works, Tagore uses *chalan* for the metre of the separate 'feet' in a verse line, and *chal* for the rhythmic effect and impetus of the whole line. An appendix to the book *Chhanda* includes some interesting letters in English between Tagore and J. D. Anderson, a British scholar of Bengali based in Cambridge. The letters were exchanged in 1918, and they go into considerable technicalities. Anderson had evidently just read Tagore's essay on the meaning of metre, and Tagore gives him a summary of his arguments. He writes:

> In my paper I have discussed about the short divisions and long divisions of a metre. The long divisions are the divisions generally represented by lines in the printed form. But the shorter divisions within those lines are more important for the rhythm. They are what the bars are in music, and can be measured by beats—the beats which, according to the rhythm of the particular metre, contain a particular quantity of sound-units.[5]

In his essay, Tagore distinguishes between three types of *padakshep*, the Bengali word he uses for 'foot' or 'short division' and which he says represents the *chalan* or 'moves' in the line. The first type he calls *samachalaner chhanda* ('evenly moving metre'), and has two *mātrās* or beats. The second type is called *asamachalaner chhanda* ('unevenly moving metre'), and has three *mātrās*. The third type is called *bishamachalaner chhanda* ('mixed-measure metre'), and alternates between two and three *mātrās*.

[5] Rabindranath Tagore: *Chhanda*, Visva-Bharati, Kolkata 1936, pp. 483–84.

The technicalities of all this are of course hard to explain without knowledge of Bengali poetry and the Bengali language. There are, however, two points of fundamental interest that I want to extract from this essay, which I hope I can illustrate with examples from my own translations. The first concerns the role of the *yuktākshar* or 'conjunct consonants' in the Bengali script. The Bengali poetry of the pre-modern period (i.e. up to the early 19th century) was nearly all written in a metre called *payār*, a regular pattern of two beats, forming a seven-foot line with a caesura after the fourth and seventh foot. (Tagore regards *payār* as having eight feet, counting the break after the seventh as an 'empty' foot.) The rhythm is trochaic: *tum-tee tum-tee tum-tee* etc. In this metre, combined or conjunct consonants are treated in exactly the same way as single consonants; they do not cause any hold-up or delay in the steady progress of the metre. When modern Bengali poetry began to develop in the mid-19th century, poets became much more aware of how conjunct consonants cause a slight hold-up, and therefore disrupt the progress of the line in a way that can be highly expressive. The great pioneering poet and dramatist Michael Madhusudan Dutt (1824–1873) invented a form of Bengali blank verse in which the conjunct consonants play a vital role. The very first word of his masterpiece, *Meghnādbadh kābya* ('The Poem of the Killing of Meghnad'; 1861) has a double 'mm'-sound that immediately causes a captivating hold-up in the line, and which establishes that in every line thereafter conjunct consonants will have a crucial effect. The first three words of the line are *sammukh samare pari* ('having fallen in open combat'), and it is essential to hold the double 'mm' as one would a double consonant in Italian.

Tagore did not like Madhusudan's poetry in all its aspects, but he did acknowledge his contribution to Bengali metrics, and his essays in *Chhanda* contain several appreciative references to Madhusudan as a metrist, with quotations from his works. There are plenty of poems by Tagore, particularly from the earlier part of his creative life, where he uses *payār* metre with its characteristic ignoring of the conjunct consonants. But when he started to create metres of his own, many of them influenced by folk-poetry, the conjunct consonants started to be given their full weight, and in his essay on the meaning of metre he is careful to say that a conjunct consonant counts as two *mātrās* (beats) and not as one.

The second point that I want to extract is that of the three types of metre that Tagore defines, the 'mixed-measure metre' seems to be the one that appealed to him most profoundly. His poems are full of 'short divisions' which alternate between two or three beats, just as the *tāla*s (rhythmic cycles) of Indian music are full of similarly mixed measures.

Looking back through the translations of Tagore's poetry that I have done over the last three decades, I find that using my own poetic ear and somehow picking up distinctive features of Tagore's Bengali verse, I have frequently created mixed measures in my English lines. I have also—and this is something that I have not realized consciously until very recently—often counted the combined consonants that occur very frequently in English as more 'held' or 'stopped' than they would be in normal pronunciation and in most kinds of English metre. For example, my translation of Tagore's poem 'New Rain' from his book *Kshanikā* ('The Flitting'; 1900) begins with the lines:

> It dances today, my heart, like a peacock it dances, it dances.
>   It sports a mosaic of passions
>   Like a peacock's tail,
> It soars to the sky with delight, it quests, O wildly
> It dances today, my heart, like a peacock it dances.'[6]

Not only do these lines contain a varying pattern of three-beat (*titty-tum*) and two-beat (*tee-tum*) sound units, there is also a kind of holding or checking on the combined consonants that we get in words like 'dances', 'quests' and 'wildly'. This now seems to me to be very Tagorean. Let me strengthen the point with an exceedingly short poem

[6] *Selected Poems* (1985), p. 66.

from his posthumous collection of brief poems, *Sphulinga* ('Sparks'; 1945). This is poem no. 105 in the first edition of *Sphulinga*:

Buds
  Bring solace
    To the woods.[7]

I could in theory have translated this into what Tagore called an 'evenly moving', two-beat metre, in which case it would have come out something like this:

The buds
  Bring gifts
    To woods.

Or I could have done it using an 'unevenly moving', three-beat metre, in which case it would have been like this:

Flower-buds
  Give delight
    To the woods.

Both these alternative versions can be rejected on grounds of accuracy, but they also lack a quality of rhythm that I now see (and hear) as typically Tagorean. In my published translation of this brief poem, I have within those three very short lines, a mixture of measures. It thus becomes a translation of the form and sound of the original poem, as well as its literal meaning. In his essay on the meaning of metre, Tagore says that the peculiar charm and excitement of 'mixed-measure metres' is that they stop and start. The constant checks and hold-ups in the movement of the line, many of them created by conjunct consonants, are what give his Bengali poetry its vital, dancing

[7] *The Jewel That Is Best* (2011), p. 140.

and energetic quality. Here is another poem from *Sphulinga* which has in my translation a 'mixed-measure', stop-start character, but is also about stopping and starting as a crucial characteristic of music and, therefore by implication, of the musical aspects of poetry:

> Music is made
> From blocks in the road,
> Frustration, confusion,
>   Stop, start.
> The rhythm of sadness
> Creates transcendent delightfulness
>   Through musical art.[8]

I have completed my new translations of *Gitanjali* so recently that I have not yet been able to analyse them objectively. But I am sure that when I do, I will find that they are full of mixed-measure metres, and particularly interesting to me as a poet is how, when I use a traditional English form such as the sonnet—which is an obvious equivalent of the 14-line poems from *Naibedya* ('Offerings'; 1901) that were included in the English *Gitanjali*—my lines contain subtle variations that depart from the Shakespearean norm, but which give the poems a life and a movement—a *chal*, to use Tagore's own word—which owes a lot to the movement of Tagore's Bengali verse.

When I prepared my new translation of *Gitanjali*, I found that when I followed Tagore's original manuscript as closely as possible, there was a rhythmic energy in his English that was not so different from his Bengali sources. This energy comes about through a much more sparing use of commas than in the published text, and also through far fewer paragraph divisions.

There are also many places where the phrasing was changed by Yeats to produce a result that I find rhythmically inert, when compared to Tagore's original version.

[8] Ibid., p. 127.

Have a look at a poem from the English *Gitanjali*, no. 70 in the standard published text, no. 15 in my new text. The standard text comes first:

> Is it beyond thee to be glad with the gladness of this rhythm? to be tossed and lost and broken in the whirl of this fearful joy?
>
> All things rush on, they stop not, they look not behind, no power can hold them back, they rush on.
>
> Keeping steps with that restless, rapid music, seasons come dancing and pass away—colours, tunes, and perfumes pour in endless cascades in the abounding joy that scatters and gives up and dies every moment.[9]

> Is it beyond thee to be glad with the gladness of this wild rhythm? To be tossed and lost and broken in the whirl of this fearful joy? Listen, canst thou hear from every direction of the sky, from all the sun, moon and stars, the harp player of death smiting forth a fiery round of music pulsing in burning joy!
>
> The hurricane of maddening tunes is carrying onward all that ever is. Everything moves, they stop not, they look not behind, they can never be kept bound in bonds—they are snatched and swirled and borne on by the liberating joy.
>
> Keeping steps with that restless rapid music seasons come dancing and pass away–colours, tunes and perfumes pour in endless cascades in the abounding joy that scatters and gives up and dies every moment.[10]

In this particular poem, the paragraphing in the published text is the same as in the manuscript, but Tagore's draft has been drastically cut and commas have been added, with considerable loss of rhythmic energy. Even though his English translations of *Gitanjali* are in prose, not verse, as he rightly knew that he would not be able to handle English verse rhyme and metre, his marvellous ear for rhythm, which is always evident in Bengali whether he is writing in verse or prose (in *Chhanda* there is an essay on the rhythm of prose), is present in

[9] *Gitanjali* (2011). Appendix C.

[10] Ibid. (main poems section).

his English translation, and far more present in his own unaided draft than in the published version as edited by Yeats.

Let me now add my own translation of the poem, which is actually a song, and therefore as with all my translation of the songs in *Gitanjali*, I preserve the repetitions of the lines that occur when the song is sung, and I also indicate the four main parts of the song by line breaks. The italics indicate that the second and fourth parts of a Tagore song always have the same melody:

Can you not join in this rhythm?
Can you not join in this rhythm?
The jettisoning, drifting away and dissolving joy of it?
Can you not join in this rhythm?
Can you not join in this rhythm?

Can you not open your ears
Can you not open your ears
To the music the vīna *of death plays*
all over the sky
in the sun, the stars, the moon?
Can you not feel the fire that cascades
with the joy of its burning?
Can you not join in this rhythm?
Can you not join in this rhythm?

With mind-blowing flurries of song
It hurtles who knows where
It never looks back
The racing, rolling joy of its forward movement
can never be checked
With mind-blowing flurries of song
It hurtles who knows where
It never looks back
The racing, rolling joy of its forward movement
can never be checked

With the stamping of the feet of that joy
With the stamping of the feet of that joy
The six seasons wildly dance, a flood is unleashed
in the world,
a symphony of scent and colour
Because of the joy of letting go,
of casting aside, of dying
Can you not join in this rhythm?
Can you not join in this rhythm?[11]

Both the content and the rhythmic energy of this poem convey more effectively than any analysis how wide and deep Tagore's sense of rhythm ran. In his essay on the meaning of metre, he writes that some people find metre artificial and restrictive. But he finds it liberating, and compares it to natural cycles such as the 24 hours of the day and the 365 days of the year. He says that metre is no more artificial than those great natural rhythms, and it is through metre that the force (*beg*) of feeling expresses its own *gati*—another word that he uses for movement or progression.

It therefore seems to me that if we are looking for some kind of overarching principle uniting all Tagore's creative works, then a focus on rhythm could be very fruitful. In the article on Tagore's songs that I mentioned at the beginning, Satyajit Ray examines the complex relationship between the metre of the words and the rhythm of the music in Rabindrasangit. But rhythm is equally relevant to the analysis of his paintings, and Tagore's own comments on his art indicate that he wanted critics to look at them in that way. I have used one such comment above as an epigraph, and in another he writes: But one thing which is common to all arts is the principle of rhythm which transforms inert materials into living creations. My instinct for it and my training in its use led me to know that lines

[11] Ibid.

and colours in art are no carriers of information; they seek their rhythmic incarnation in pictures.[12]

In the analysis of Tagore's paintings, colour will not play as big a part as in the discussion of Bonnard or Renoir, and portraiture, social content, or topography will not feature at all. But the rhythm of his lines belongs as much to the description of his paintings as to the discussion of his poetry. Particularly in the case of Tagore, it is not an accident that in many languages the same word is used for the lines of a poem and the lines of a drawing or painting. (Bengali has adopted the English word 'line'.) As is well known, his art emerged from erasures and doodles in the manuscripts of his poems, and there is an intimate relationship between the visual shape of his poems on the page and the drawings and paintings that he later came to make. His free verse poems with lines of varying lengths spread out across the page— always with a general movement from left to right—have a shape as distinctive as his drawings and paintings. In a lecture that I gave some years ago I referred to such poems as 'sari-poems', because the shape of them on the page reminded me of the asymmetrical way in which a sari is wrapped round the body.[13]

In Tagore's overall vision, rhythm, creativity, nature and the *jīban-debatā* are one and the same. It is impossible to imagine the *līlā* (sport) or *khelā* (play) of the universe without the rhythmic energy which found its expression in countless poems, songs and paintings by Tagore. It is something that goes beyond technique, beyond morality, and beyond the meaning of words. In a way, all my work as a translator and interpreter of Tagore over the years has aimed to bring out that central and distinctive rhythmic quality with ever greater power and clarity. Exhibitions of his paintings such as the present one are a further

[12] 'My Pictures' in *Tagore on Art and Asthetics*, p. 90 (see note 1)

[13] 'Poetic Engineering—Lessons Learnt from Tagore', in William Radice: *Poetry and Community: Lectures and Essays: 1991–2001*, DC Publishers, New Delhi 2003, p. 29.

contribution to the communication of that power. So much of what he writes about metre can be related equally well to the paintings: the stop–start nature of 'mixed-measure metre'; the way in which lines in poetry have different speeds according to which metre is employed; and the way in which the fixed stillness of words as dictionary items acquires movement and life through their rhythmic combination, whether in verse or in prose. In another beautiful metaphor, Tagore says in his essay on the meaning of metre that the meaning of words is like the trunk of a tree, and the rhythm of words is like the fluttering of leaves of the tree. A painting may seem a static object compared to a poem or song, but if we do not sense in Tagore's lines and forms a movement as dynamic as his poetry, then we have missed what his paintings are about.

First printed in *The Last Harvest*, Paintings of Rabindranath Tagore [Catalogue], Edited by Raman Siva Kumar, Mapin Publishing, Ahmedabad 2011.

Tagore and Christianity

I am the proud custodian of a manuscript letter from Rabindranath Tagore, written in 1914. It was given to me by Tony and Jean Brown, who now live in Ludlow, Shropshire. From 1961 to 1967 they worked for the Baptist Missionary Society in East Pakistan (now Bangladesh). Tony became the administrator of the Arthington Mission Hospital in Chandraghona, Chittagong Hill Tracts. They both learnt Bengali well. Later, after returning to the UK, Tony became Senior Tutor and then Principal of Woodbrooke College in Selly Oak, Birmingham, the international Quaker College. A previous Senior Tutor of the College, Rendel Harris, had acquired a copy of Rabindranath Tagore's *Gitanjali* (the reprint of January 1914) and had pasted into the book a letter from Tagore that was clearly a reply to a letter from him. Tagore wrote:

> Shanti Niketan
> Bolpur. Bengal
> Feb. 16. 1914
>
> Dear Sir,
>
> Thank you for your kind letter of appreciation. The poem about the woman by the well, referred to in your letter, had been written when I was not acquainted with the story of the Samaritan woman. The expression "lash of lightning" has its obvious meaning.
>
> Yours truly
> Rabindranath Tagore

Mr Harris must have been alluding to *Gitanjali* no. 54, which begins, 'I asked nothing from thee; I uttered not my name to thine ear.' The reference to 'lash of lightning' is harder to place: the only comparable phrase in *Gitanjali* is in poem, no. 40: 'Send thy angry storm, dark with death, if it is thy wish, and with lashes of lightning startle the sky from end to end.' I do not know what, if any, biblical reference Mr Harris was making here, as in the Bible the normal phrase is 'flash of lightning'.

Tagore's polite dismissal of any connection between his poem and the encounter between Jesus and the Samaritan woman by the well, described in St John's Gospel, ch. 4, is perfectly reasonable. Other than the fact that a thirsty traveller meets a woman at a well, there is really no connection between the Gospel story and Tagore's poem. The Samaritan woman does not give Jesus any water, but gets immediately interested when he starts to talk about the water of everlasting life. The English style that Tagore adopted for his translation of *Gitanjali* and subsequent books and poems often seemed biblical to its readers, and it was natural for Rendel Harris and others to look for allusions to the Bible. But in the original Bengali this poem is written in ballad-like stanzas, and in my own new translation of *Gitanjali*, I have tried to capture the form and tone of the original:

I didn't ask for anything,
    I didn't speak my name.
When you took your leave of me,
    Bashful I became.

I sat alone beside the well,
    Deep in the neem's shade;
Others had with water-pots
    Returned to where they stayed.
They had on leaving called to me,
    'Come, it's noon, it's late.'

Somehow I could not shake off
  My silent, pensive state.
I didn't hear your footsteps when
  You hobbled close and said,
With weary voice and plaintive eyes,
  'I'm thirsty, nearly dead—'
At once I rose and rushed to fetch
  Fresh water from the well
To pour into your outstretched hands,
  Your thirstiness to quell.
Koels somewhere chirped amidst
  The rustling of the trees;
Acacia-blooms along the paths
  Scented the midday breeze.
When you asked me for my name,
  I suddenly felt shy.
What had I done that you should want
  A name to know me by?
I had simply given you
  Some water from the well:
To ask my name rewarded me
  More than I can tell.
It's late and by the well-side still
  Koels keep up their tune;
The neem still rustles; I just sit
  And linger long past noon.[1]

From this translation, it will, I think, be clear that the poem does not allude to any text or tradition. It is a pure product of Tagore's imagination, and is all the more poignant and beautiful for being so. Tagore's letter reflects the kind of misunderstanding that frequently

[1] *Gitanjali* (2011), pp. 128–30.

arose from his own translations, from their secondary translation into other languages, and from the extraordinary international fame he enjoyed after winning the Nobel Prize for Literature in November 1913. Tagore was not a Christian. Readers who thought his poems seemed Christian were wrong, and they would instantly have seen that they were wrong if they had been able to read the poems in the original Bengali.

This, among readers and critics who know Bengali, would be the standard view. In my reading, over the last four decades, of what has been written about Tagore, in Bengali or in English, I have very rarely encountered much reference to Christianity. Even the careful and scholarly researches of Jose Chunkapura S.D.B., whose book *The God of Rabindranath Tagore*, based on his doctoral thesis at the Pontifical Gregorian University in Rome, relegates connections between Tagore and Christianity to a nineteen-page section at the end, and concludes: 'In our opinion, the influence of Christ and Christianity on Rabindranath's understanding of God consisted primarily in deepening, strengthening and confirming the ideas that he already had.'[2]

Yet if one goes really deeply into the poems and songs of *Gitanjali*, as I have inevitably done through doing my new translation, and if one reads many other works by Tagore, including the six heartfelt and penetrating essays on Christianity that he delivered as Christmas Day sermons at Santiniketan, one is inclined to think hard about whether it is correct or fair to leave Christianity so firmly on the periphery of Tagore's life and work. My purpose in this article is to make an initial and tentative survey of this 'yet', and to argue that among the many influences on Tagore's sensibility and creative achievement Christianity deserves to be given serious and respectful attention.

It is a difficult topic, one that I myself have shirked for a long time. The reasons for shirking it are obvious. They go back to the many

[2] Jose Chunkapura: *The God of Rabindranath Tagore*. Visva-Bharati, Kolkata 2002, p. 304.

sensitivities that were aroused in India by Christian missionaries. In the early years of East India Company rule, the British authorities were well aware of the trouble that missionaries could cause, and did their best to keep them out. In Bengal, the famous Baptist missionary, William Carey (1761–1834) was obliged to base his activities as a scholar and printer of Bengali and other Indian languages at Serampore, a Danish trading station up the Hooghly from Calcutta and outside British control. Pressure from Charles Grant and the evangelical Clapham Sect on the Court of Directors of the East India Company eventually led to the insertion of a 'pious clause' in its renewed charter of 1813, allowing missionaries and churches to operate freely. From then on, Christian churches became significant threads in the complex tapestry of nineteenth century Calcutta, and their contribution to education remains influential to this day. But relations between Christianity and the predominantly Hindu culture of modern Bengal were never easy, and became even more strained with the growth of nationalism and Hindu revivalism at the end of the nineteenth century. Tagore's stance on nationalism and revivalism was critical, and at times scathing, but as his oeuvre and standing grew, he came to be seen, and is still seen, as the powerful embodiment not only of modern Bengali culture but of the whole civilization of modern India. The Christian churches are now an established part of modern Indian life, and their rights and freedom are respected under India's secular constitution. But it is fully understandable that in the Bengali and Indian context—a context to which I myself must be constantly sensitive—Tagore's relationship to Christianity is not a topic on which his countrymen are inclined to put much stress. I doubt if it has featured at a single one of the numerous celebrations and symposia that have been organised in many parts of the world in 2011, the 150th anniversary of Tagore's birth.

That Tagore himself was aware of the sensitivities is readily apparent from the first of his sermons on Christianity, dated 25 December 1910. Tagore gave regular sermons in the *Kāñcher Mandir* or 'Glass Temple' which continues to play a central role in the life of the Santiniketan community today. His Christmas Day sermons began as a result of a decision in 1910 to honour the birth or death anniversaries of great religious teachers with special festivals. His sermon of 1910 entitled *Yisucharit* ('The character of Jesus') was the longest and most wide-ranging of the essays that were later gathered into a book called *Khrishta* (1959). It was also published as an introduction to a book with the same title by Ajit Kumar Chakravarty, a young teacher at Santiniketan, who went to Britain in September 1910 to study at Harris Manchester College, Oxford. The sermon's first appearance in print was in the *Tattvabodhinī Patrikā*, the journal that became the main mouthpiece of the Brahmo Samaj when Tagore's father Debendranath took over and reconstituted that movement in 1843. The Brahmo Samaj (founded as the Brahmo Sabha by Ram Mohun Roy in 1828), Unitarianism, Harris Manchester College: there are important connections and cross-currents here that a complete account of Tagore and Christianity would certainly have to include. It was at Manchester College that Tagore gave his lectures on the *Religion of Man* in 1930, and by and large he remained loyal to the 'Unitarian' aspects of his Brahmo heritage, even if he personally moved away from what he himself called the 'Brahmo church'. But the Unitarian dimension, interesting though it is historically, does not, I think, take us to the poetic heart of Tagore, which is what I want to focus on here.

1910 was the year in which Tagore published his Bengali book *Gītāñjali*, a collection of 157 lyric poems, many of which were songs. Fifty-three of those poems were used by Tagore as sources for his translations in the English *Gitanjali*, which he began early in 1912. (The rest of the 103 poems in the English *Gitanjali* were taken from a total of ten other books.) If Tagore's whole 'Gitanjali phase' began in a year in which he also wrote his first disquisition on the character of Jesus, then it is not unreasonable to look for connections between the two—connections far more profound than were noticed by western readers and critics reminded of Christianity by the English *Gitanjali's* 'biblical' prose style.

In Tagore's eighteen-page sermon, Bengal's modern history, Christian missionaries, Indian nationalism, Judaism, the Roman

Empire, and Tagore's interpretation of the life and teachings of Jesus are woven together with wonderful grace and skill. Beginning with the problem of casteism and sectarianism, he writes of how such attitudes have been extended to Christians and Christian missionaries. In the early days of British rule, criticism by Christian missionaries of evils and abuses in Hindu society had demoralised the Bengali elite, and had alienated them from their own society. With the growth of nationalist feeling in the later nineteenth century, Bengalis had swung from one extreme to the other, and were now inclined to leap to the defence of all aspects of their society and dismiss criticism by Christians as an imperialist imposition. This attitude of strident self-justification had blinded them to the true nature of Christ and his teaching. Tagore argues that their situation was not dissimilar to that of the Jews under Roman rule. They too, as a subject people, leapt to the defence of their traditions and scriptures, and rejected the challenging teaching of Jesus Christ as a threat to their society. Tagore in this essay, as in all his writings on Christianity, is not interested in the Christian churches: his focus is on Jesus Christ as a revolutionary preacher of what he later came to call *Mānusher dharma* or the 'Religion of man'.

The poems that Tagore chose to include in the English *Gitanjali* were intensely personal poems. They stemmed from a period in which Tagore suffered an appalling series of bereavements: the deaths of his wife in 1902, his daughter Renuka in 1903, his father in 1905, and his son Samindranath in 1907. In his comments on the *Gitanjali* poems, Tagore always stressed their personal aspects, describing them in a letter to his friend William Rothenstein on 30 December 1912 as 'revelations of my true self to me'. This deeply personal aspect was perhaps not very well understood by W. B. Yeats, who in his famous and influential introduction to *Gitanjali* saw the poems very much as a product of an alternative, pre-modern culture, 'as much the growth of the common soil as the grass and the rushes'. But reading the poems alongside *Yisucharit*, one soon senses that their personal nature is closely allied to Tagore's equally personal response to the character and teachings of Jesus.

Let me now pick out some points at which the poems in *Gitanjali* and Tagore's great sermon of Christmas Day 1910 connect and touch. They show that western readers who found Christian echoes in the poems were not unjustified, even if Tagore himself, as in his reply to Rendel Harris, might have dismissed a direct connection.

Poem no. 10 in *Gitanjali* has impressed many Christian readers. In the standard text of *Gitanjali* as edited by Yeats it begins: 'Here is thy footstool and there rest thy feet where live the poorest, and lowliest, and lost.' Tagore's translation is among many in *Gitanjali* where I prefer what he wrote in his manuscript to the version that was later published. The manuscript begins: 'There is thy footstool and there rest thy feet where live the poorest and lowliest and lost.' Changing 'there' to 'here' seems to me confusing, and the insertion of commas upsets the natural flow of Tagore's prose. In the original Bengali, this poem is a song, and as with all my translations of Tagore's songs I have, in my new translation, tried to preserve the musical structure of the song by reproducing the repetitions of lines and indicating the song's four-part structure with line breaks:

Humbler than all and lower than the low
That is the place where your feet reign
    behind all, beneath all
Among those who have lost all
Humbler than all and lower than the low

I bow down before you
    but my bending gets stuck somewhere
I bow down before you
    but my bending gets stuck somewhere
It doesn't reach down to the place below shame
    where your feet reach

Behind all, beneath all
Among those who have lost all
Humbler than all and lower than the low

Arrogance finds no perch in the realm where you wander
Shorn of ornaments, dressed in the rags of the poor
Arrogance finds no perch in the realm where you wander
Shorn of ornaments, dressed in the rags of the poor

We count on companionship with you
in places of wealth and grandeur
We count on companionship with you
in places of wealth and grandeur
But you make friends with those who have no companions
in a region my heart doesn't reach

Behind all, beneath all
Among those who have lost all
Humbler than all and lower than the low[3]

Shorn of biblical phraseology, this translation does, I hope, connect with a passage in *Yisucharit* in a clear and moving way. Tagore has been describing Satan's temptation of Jesus in the desert:

> But the extraordinary thing is that he cut through this all-encompassing web of illusion and clearly perceived God's Kingdom of Truth. He did not see it in pride and wealth; he didn't see it in the arrogant glory of empire; he saw it in poverty and its lack of outward possessions, and he fearlessly flung before all rich people the strange idea that those who are lowly shall inherit the earth.[4]

This poem is followed in the published *Gitanjali* (though not in Tagore's manuscript, where they are nos. 24 and 28 respectively) by

[3] *Gitanjali* (2011), pp. 35–36. My italics indicate a melodic connection between the second section (*antarā*) and fourth section (*ābhog*) of nearly all Tagore's songs. The melody rises higher than in the first section (*sthāyi* or refrain), and when it returns later with different words it brings the song to its climax.

[4] Rabindranath Tagore: *Khrishta,* edited by Pulinbihari Sen, Visva-Bharati, Kolkata 1959, p. 21. This and other quotations from *Khrishta* are my own translations.

a poem that is a poem not a song and which seems to have a more Hindu context. In Tagore's translation it begins 'Leave this chanting and singing and telling of beads!' The Hindu references are even clearer in the original Bengali, and in my own new translation:

Prayer and worship and rite—
    cast them aside.
In a nook of the closed temple,
    why hide?
Groping in your mind's dark,
What pooja-object do you seek?
Open your eyes and look:
    God doesn't stay inside.

He's gone to where farmers labour
    to hack the soil,
To where stone-breaking for a road
    takes a year of toil.
He's there in the flood and the heat;
His hands are plastered with dirt;
Be like him, strip off your shirt
    to be level with all.

Release? Where will you gain it?
    Where is it found?
Taking on shackles of creation,
    God himself is bound.
Forget about trances or poojas
Throw away trays of flowers;
Rip clothes, get grimy, get sweaty;
    get down to his ground.[5]

[5] *Gitanjali* (2011), pp. 40–41.

Despite the Hindu references, this poem connects strongly with the following passage in Tagore's sermon. This passage builds on a distinction that Tagore has been making between what in human nature is *baro* (big) and what is *choto* (small):

> When man is small in this way, then his aims and activities all become small too; his capacities are diminished, and he merely meanders in futility. Therefore the Son of Man did not see custom or scripture as greater than man himself, and said that the worship of God is not achieved through rituals and offerings, but the heart's devotion. He then touched those who were untouchable and ate with those who were impure—and he did not abandon sinners but called them to the way of salvation.[6]

These aspects of the life and teachings of Jesus also, of course, made a great impression on Mahatma Gandhi. Gandhi's relationship to Christianity lies beyond the scope of this article, but in my view what Gandhi valued in Jesus and what Tagore valued were fundamentally the same.

It is noticeable that when one looks further for connections of this kind, often a statement which in the sermon is presented in general terms is articulated in the poems in a highly personal way. In the paragraph before the passage from the sermon that I have just quoted, Tagore writes:

> When man sees himself properly then he sees God in himself; and when he looks at himself and only sees wealth or status, then he demeans himself and his whole way of life becomes a denial of God.[7]

This reminds me of *Gitanjali* no. 29, which in Tagore's translation begins: 'He whom I enclose with my name is weeping in this dungeon.' It is a poem, not a song, and in my new translation it reads:

[6] *Khrishta* (1959), p. 24.
[7] Ibid.

He who by my name is kept in hiding
Within the prison of that name is dying.
Everything else by day and night forgetting,
Towards the sky that name forever piling,
    I lose within its dark
        My own true spark.

Dust on dust, layer on layer impacting,
Higher and higher that name of mine I'm rearing.
Lest anywhere a crack or hole is forming,
My heart is ever fearful and unresting.
    As I this lie refine,
        I lose what's mine.[8]

Other similar shifts from the general to the personal suggest that in certain moods Tagore was able to identify himself with Christ—which is not to say that he thought of himself, even for a minute, as some kind of messiah or prophet, though many of his western admirers thought of him in that way. The identification is with Jesus as a Man of Sorrows, with the religion of love that he imparted through his own suffering. Tagore endured great inner loneliness and suffering in his life, and as I have already said the poems and songs of the 'Gitanjali phase' grew out of a period of devastating loss and bereavement. Furthermore, his travels all over the world, and his meetings with people from many sorts of background, made him able to identify with Christ's ability to connect with people from different communities. In the beautiful concluding paragraph of the sermon, the phrase *ye par tāhāke āpan kariteche* ('He who is foreign he makes his own') reminds me of *Gitanjali* no. 63, which in the original is a very well-known and well-loved song (*Kata ajānāre jānāile tumi, / kata ghare dile thāi*). In my own translation the song reads:

[8] *Gitanjali* (2011), pp. 44–45.

So much of the unknown
    you've made known to me
You've given me a place in so many homes
You've made the distant near, my friend,
    and made the stranger a brother
So much of the unknown
    you've made known to me
You've given me a place in so many homes

When I leave my familiar surroundings
I worry about how it will be
When I leave my familiar surroundings
I worry about how it will be
I forget that amidst the new
    you are always there
You've made the distant near, my friend,
    and made the stranger a brother
So much of the unknown
    you've made known to me
You've given me a place in so many homes

Wherever and whenever you take me
    in life, in death and throughout the world
You who are familiar with everything
    will make me know all
Wherever and whenever you take me
    in life, in death and throughout the world
You who are familiar with everything
    will make me know all

When you are known, no one is alien
There are no obstructions, no fears
When you are known, no one is alien
There are no obstructions, no fears

You are wide awake in everything—
I feel that I always see you
You've made the distant near, my friend,
and made the stranger a brother
So much of the unknown
you've made known to me
You've given me a place in so many homes[9]

For me, the sermon and the song touch at the phrases 'He who is foreign he makes his own' and 'You've…made the stranger a brother'. But the whole last paragraph of the sermon, so eloquent and poetic in its phrasing and especially in its metaphor of a spreading tree, shows clearly that the spiritual worlds of *Gitanjali* and of Tagore's sermon on the character of Jesus are united at a deep level:

> God is expressed through man—this message of Jesus is not imprisoned in a theory or a verse of scripture. Because he embodied its overwhelming truth in his life, it remains alive today like a tree that forever extends new branches. Every day he is engaged in cutting through the barrier of hundreds and thousands of superstitions in the mind of man. Every day the drunkenness of force insults him, the arrogance of knowledge dismisses him, the worshippers of power despise him for his weakness, the cruel rich reject him as a coward: yet he humbly and silently spreads through man's profoundest thoughts, makes sorrow his aid and service his companion—makes those who are foreign his own, lifts up those who have fallen, endlessly dedicates himself to those from whom there is nothing to receive. In this way, the Son of Man has made the world and all people great—has given them power over hatred and extended their rights; and with the news that they live in their father's house he has removed from human society the fear of being despised. This is his gift of freedom.[10]

Reading through the rest of Tagore's Christmas sermons, given in the years 1914, 1923, 1926, 1932 and 1936, one can find many other

[9] *Gitanjali* (2011), pp. 11–12.
[10] *Khrishta* (1959), pp. 26–27.

connections, not just with *Gitanjali* but with other works by Tagore from all periods of his long creative life. Space does not permit me to describe these comprehensively, but let me pick out a few that I have found particularly striking.

There is a powerful poem in an early book by Tagore, *Mānasī* ('The Lady of the Mind', 1890) called *Dharmaprachār* ('The preaching of religion'). A note at the beginning of the poem says it was inspired by a newspaper report. It is a poem with dialogue—almost a mini-play—in which a gang of fanatical young Hindu thugs mock and attack a Salvation Army preacher who has adopted Indian dress. Written at a time (1888) when nationalism and Hindu revivalism were growing apace, the poem is a passionate indictment of bigoted and sectarian attitudes to Christianity. In his sermon entitled *Khrishtadharma* ('The Christian religion') of 1914, Tagore speaks out against the arrogance of some Christian missionaries and sects and writes:

> Therefore one must specially aspire to rescue man [*mānush*] from the hands of Christian sects, Vishnu from the Vaishnavites, Brahman from the Bhrahmos.[11]

But when he writes, as he does in his sermon of 1926, in praise of the Christian spirit of service and self-sacrifice, he praises missionaries for their courage in going out and preaching the gospel even to cannibals. This is in marked contrast, he says, with an Indian tendency to be concerned only with one's immediate community:

> They [the missionaries] go even among those who eat human flesh and ask, 'You are human—what are doing? What are you thinking of?' And us? We take no interest even in those who live next door. We have no curiosity about them, no respect for them.[12]

The Salvation Army preacher in *Dharmaprachār* embodies the courage that Tagore admired in the best Christian missionaries. When

[11] Ibid., pp. 28–29.
[12] Ibid., pp. 45–46.

the preacher prays to God as the thugs assail him, there is a reference to making the stranger one's own that is very similar to what we noticed in *Gitanjali* no. 63:

Pleasure, comfort, the love of women,
    The chatter of friends—
I've forgone them all and taken on my head
    My great vow to you.
I still can't forget them,
    Often I think of them—
The bonds of pleasure and home
    Still tug all one's life.
But then, when I look at your blood-stained face,
    Turn towards your love,
Familiar and strange become nothing,
    No own or foreign any more.
You spread that love
    Through my heart—
Let those who come to throw poison at it
    Go back with nectar.
Let those who have come with sin in their lives
    Come to your breast—
Let the sweet light of your love
    Fall on their furious faces![13]

Another recurrent theme in Tagore's Christmas Day sermons—a theme that is related to the brutal assault on the Salvation Army preacher—is the perpetual nature of Christ's crucifixion. Tagore argues repeatedly that it is wrong to link Christ's teaching and passion to particular historical circumstances. (Nineteenth-century Christian missionaries often argued that Christianity was superior to Hinduism

[13] *Rabīndra-rachanābali*, West Bengal Government edition, vol. 1, Kolkata 1980, p. 398.

because it was based on actual historical events. Brahmos from Ram Mohun Roy on argued against that kind of narrow historicism. In rejecting it too, Tagore is being loyal to a distinctively Brahmo tradition.) In his sermon of 1932, entitled *Barodin* ('Christmas Day'), he writes:

> Shall we say that today is his birthday by consulting a calendar? If we do not feel that day in our hearts, can we feel it through a temporal calculation? The day on which we renounce in the name of truth, on which we are able to call people our brothers in a simple spirit of love—that's the day on which God's son is born in our lives, that is Christmas Day, on whichever date it falls. His birthday comes at specially happy moments in our lives, but his death by nailing on the cross comes day after day. I know that on today's special day praises are ringing out in many churches in many lands for him who has brought to the children of men the message of his supreme father—and outside those churches the world is awash with the blood of brother slaughtering brother.[14]

The perpetual nature of Christ's crucifixion, and the hypocrisy of conventional worshippers who ignore it, connects with passages of bitter irony in Tagore's poetry, such as lines from his famous poem 'Africa' (1936), which contrasts the brutality of Africa's colonial violators with church services going on back home (note that church bells are described as 'temple bells', implying that hypocritical Christians are more 'heathen' than the peoples they have set out to convert):

> Meanwhile across the sea in their native parishes
> Temple-bells summoned your conquerors to prayer,
> Morning and evening in the name of a loving god.
> Mothers dandled babies in their laps;
> Poets raised hymns to beauty...[15]

[14] *Khrishta* (1959), p. 48.
[15] *Selected Poems* (1985), p. 102.

Tagore returned to the theme of the perpetual crucifixion of Christ, arising from human cruelty and violence, in a song that is also simply called *Barodin*, composed near the end of his life on Christmas Day 1939. Its tone is very similar to his agonised 'Crisis in Civilization' speech (1941) that was read on his last birthday before he died, and was published internationally as the world collapsed into the disaster of the Second World War. Tagore himself supplied a translation of this song:

> Those who stuck Him once
> in the name of their rulers,
> are born again in this present age.
> They gather in their prayer-halls in a pious garb,
> they call their soldiers,
> 'Kill, Kill' they shout;
> in their roaring mingles the music of their hymns,
> while the Son of Man in his agony prays, 'O God,
> fling far away this cup filled with the bitterest of poisons.'[16]

The theme of the song and its use of the repeated *maro maro* ('Kill, Kill') is almost identical to a powerful poem called *Manab-Putra* ('The Son of Man') which Tagore wrote in 1932.[17]

But Tagore finds themes of joy and love in his reflections of Christianity just as much as *duhkha* (sorrow) or hypocrisy or crucifixion. An aspect of Christianity that he valued particularly highly was the centrality it gives to the father-son, God-man relationship. For him, Jesus Christ is not the unique son of God, but an embodiment of the way in which we can all become sons of God. In this passage from his sermon of 1923, entitled *Khrishtotsab* ('Christ's Festival') he identifies divine love (*prem*) and our relationship with God to the Indian concept of *ānanda* ('joy') running through all things:

[16] *English Writings* (1994), vol. 1. p. 387.
[17] Included in *Khrishta* (1959), pp. 73–74.

> This supreme bond at the root of the universe that gives fullness to emptiness and enables a stream of joy to flow over the grief of death—that bond of sweetness must today be felt in our hearts.[18]

Ānandadhārā ('stream of joy') will immediately evoke for Bengalis one of Tagore's most beautiful and best-loved songs: *Ānandadhārā bahiche bhubane* ('A stream of joy flows through the world').

The exercise of finding links and connections between Tagore's reflections on Christianity and his poems, songs and other literary works could be extended almost indefinitely. His English poem 'The Child', written in 1931 after he had experienced the passion play at Oberammergau near Munich, which he saw in July 1930, would certainly need to be brought in, though Christian references in that poem, if any, are not precisely linked to either the nativity or the passion of Christ. The symbol of the King, too, in plays such as *Dākghar* ('The Post-Office', 1916) or *Rājā* (1910, translated as *The King of the Dark Chamber*, 1914) probably owes more to Christian conceptions of Christ the King or God as the King of Heaven than it does to Hindu traditions. If one extends the discussion to Tagore's social and educational work, to the ideals of Visva-Bharati with its emphasis on service to the community and mankind; and if one takes into account close associates of Tagore, especially the Reverend C. F. Andrews (whose initials, as Tagore himself pointed out, stood for 'Christ's faithful apostle') then 'Tagore and Christianity' becomes a very extensive topic indeed—far bigger than can be handled in a short article like this.[19]

[18] *Khrishta* (1959), p. 36.

[19] Tagore's friendship with Andrews deserves a separate article, but it needs to wait until a complete and revised edition of the Tagore-Andrews correspondence is published. An edited selection was published long ago as *Letters to a Friend* (Allen & Unwin, London 1928). Tagore's leading biographer of recent times, Prasanta Kumar Paul, was working on a new edition before his untimely death in 2007. Meanwhile, Hugh Tinker's biography of Andrews: *The Ordeal of Love: C. F. Andrews and India* (Oxford University Press, New Delhi 1979) is recommended.

Of course the exercise of finding connections between Tagore's thoughts on Christianity and his creative and practical work can be equally well done with his numerous reflections on other religious traditions. In the collected sermons that he delivered in the *Kāñcher Mandir* at Santiniketan, published by Visva-Bharati in two volumes in 1949 with the title *Sāntiniketan*, the religious texts that are referred to most frequently are the Upanishads, and it is probably possible to find many more poems and songs by Tagore with Upanishadic echoes than there are poems and songs with Christian ones. Buddhism, too, was another religion that Tagore valued very highly indeed, and when writing or reflecting on *ahimsā* ('non-violence'), or caste or bigotry, it was often to Buddhist *jātāka* tales that he turned, especially in plays such as *Chandālikā* ('The Untouchable Girl', 1933) or *Natīrpūjā* ('Worship by the Dancing Girl', 1926). Tagore was eclectic in his religion, just as Visva-Bharati was eclectic in its creation of a universal centre of learning and culture in a rural Bengali setting. For him, the great religions of the world (including, let it be remembered, Islam, on which he wrote a number of essays) were all among the 'diversities of gifts' through which the Spirit expressed itself in the world.

To use a somewhat Tagorean metaphor, different religions, including Christianity, were like tributary streams that together formed a single great river. Nevertheless, I would want to argue that the stream of Christianity was one that Tagore liked to sit beside and contemplate when he was in particular moods: of *duhkha* (sorrow), or horror at the way human beings can crucify each other, or *ānanda* (joy) when he felt a personal, filial relationship with God, or *sebā* (service) when he felt a strong desire to serve humanity. It does not surprise me that Nirad C. Chaudhuri, in his provocative yet insightful chapter on Tagore in his massive autobiography *Thy Hand, Great Anarch!*, writes of Tagore's conception of God:

> Dominantly, it was of a deity who was both transcendental and personal. There can be no doubt that he was a fervent Deist of the

> Christian type, who was always ready to say: *In la sua volontate à nostra pace*, and who was always seeking guidance from God. But on the other hand, he was also thoroughly pantheistic, if not animistic. His capacity to see God in everything animate or inanimate on earth was unlimited, and it was accompanied by a habit of seeing divine movements in the motions of water or wind.[20]

I began with a brief encounter between Tagore and an Englishman in the form of a letter that he wrote that was dismissive of a direct connection between a poem in *Gitanjali* and the story of Christ's meeting with the Samaritan woman by the well. Let me end with another encounter, one that deserves to be better known. I did not know about it at all until I started researching for the introduction and notes to my new translation of *Gitanjali.* In 1938 an Englishman called John W. Rattray visited Tagore in Santiniketan. (I do not know who Rattray was, or why he was in India, and would welcome information on him if any readers of this article have any.) Rattray had been a fan of *Gitanjali* for many years, and wanted to meet the great man not only so that his copy could be signed but because he also had a query about poem no. 76. In the standard text of *Gitanjali,* which by 1938 had been reprinted innumerable times and had been translated into all the major languages of the world, this poem began as follows:

> Day after day, O lord of my life, shall I stand before thee face to face? With folded hands, O lord of all worlds, shall I stand before thee face to face?

Rattray had for a long time been puzzled by the question marks in this poem, and he asked Tagore why they were there. Tagore and the poet Amiya Chakravarty, who acted as Tagore's secretary at that time, were shocked when they looked at the poem and saw these question marks. They immediately broke out spontaneously into the song that

[20] Nirad C. Chaudhuri: *Thy Hand, Great Anarch! India: 1921–1952.* Chatto & Windus, London 1987; The Hogarth Press: 1990, pp. 618–19.

was the translation's source—a song which expresses faith, or rather a determination to have faith, and is not a poem of questioning or doubt at all. In my new translation it reads:

Every day I shall,
    O master of my life,
Stand before you
Every day I shall,
    O master of my life,
Stand before you
Pressing my hands together
    O lord of the world
Pressing my hands together
    O lord of the world
I shall stand before you
Every day I shall
Beneath your uncrossable sky,
    alone and secluded
Beneath your uncrossable sky,
    alone and secluded
With humble heart and tears in my eyes
I shall stand before you
Every day I shall
In this multi-dimensioned world of yours
On the shore of this ocean of action
In this multi-dimensioned world of yours
On the shore of this ocean of action
In the midst of world-scurrying crowds
I shall stand before you
When my work in this world
    is finished
When my work in this world
    is finished

O king of kings, silent and alone
I shall stand before you
Every day I shall[21]

It seems that in preparing *Gitanjali* for publication, Yeats—or maybe someone else in Tagore's English circle—was misled by the inversions in Tagore's own translation ('Day after day, O lord of my life, shall I stand…') into thinking that all the statements in the poem were questions. We know from Rattray's vivid and moving account of this meeting with Tagore that Tagore was deeply shocked to discover that this error had circulated in print all over the world for so long.

Rattray wrote:

> I saw him scan the lines of his own creation with an interest and eagerness that seemed to be suffused with pain, and in the ticking seconds I had time to fear that I had distressed him. How long a few seconds can be! A silence enwrapped us. Both poets seemed as those to whom something has been revealed. I was astonished, and even a little frightened by the effect of my query and the confirmation that I had sensed the true attitude of the poem.[22]

Of course there is nothing specifically Christian about this song. The God that Tagore stands before face to face every day of his life is a universal God, not a Christian or Hindu God. But frankly, it is impossible to imagine that this song and the translation of it that was done by Tagore himself into English (with no question marks at all in the manuscript) could have been written without the entry of Christianity into India's infinitely varied and complex religious world. A complete understanding of Tagore's spirituality, and of the profound links between his religious life and his poetic life, has to embrace and include Christianity, though always with the proviso that

[21] *Gitanjali* (2011), pp. 81–82.
[22] *Gitanjali* (2011), Appendix E: 'I Shall Stand', John W. Rattray, p. 243.

Christianity as understood and expounded by Tagore in his Christmas Day sermons was not the Christianity of any particular Christian church. Might one dare to suggest that the freedom of Christianity, in Tagore's conception of it, from any suggestion of 'Churchianity' is precisely what gives it meaning and relevance to Christians today, struggling to make sense of their religion in our ever more complex and interconnected world?

Reprinted from *One in Christ*, vol. 45 (2011), no. 2. Turvey and Rostrevor Monsteries, UK.

The Wakening of Shiva
Rabindranath Tagore's Spanish Incarnation

There is a wonderful poem by Tagore called *Tapobhanga*. It was published in a book called *Pūrabī* (1925), a book that has connections with the Hispanic world, because many of the poems in the book were written during Tagore's stay with Victoria Ocampo in Buenos Ares in 1924, or on the voyage back to Europe. The title means the breaking of *tāpas*. *Tāpas* means penance or austerity, and is an important concept in Indian tradition. There are many Hindu myths in which Brahmins or *rishis* achieve power over the gods themselves through their extreme acts of penance or austerity. Because Tagore's poem is based on the *Kumārasambhava* of Kalidasa, a famous work by Sanskrit literature's greatest poet, and because Kalidasa's poem is based on a myth about the god Shiva's own periods of *tāpas*, my translation of Tagore's poem is called 'The Wakening of Shiva'. The poem is of a kind that Tagore did not attempt to translate himself, because in its classical complexity of language, form and imagery it was beyond his power as a translator. Many would say that you need to know Bengali—and maybe Sanskrit too—to fully appreciate this poem, and some would regard it as untranslatable. But I myself revelled in translating it for my *Selected Poems* of Rabindranath Tagore.

The poem is about Shiva's fluctuations between phases of intense creative energy and periods of *tāpas* or quiescent austerity. In it, Tagore associates his own phases of creative energy with those of Shiva. Writing the poem when he was 61 years, he harks back to his energy as a youthful poet:

Wildly you roamed through the woods with your pulsing dances,
To whose rhythm and tempo I constantly matched my tunes—
Dancing beside you.
In my eyes there were dreams of paradise, moonlit by your brow;
The ever-renewing force of your *līlā* filled my heart…[1]

But brilliantly, he also identifies himself in this poem with the god of love, Kama, who was sent by Indra to break Shiva out of his trance so that the great god's power could be employed to rescue the universe from a demon who was threatening it with total destruction. Through this identification with Kama, Tagore speaks of the poet's power constantly to recover youth, energy and creativity. The climactic tenth stanza in this fifteen-stanza poem has always been an inspiration to me as a poet and a translator:

For I am Indra's messenger: I come to break your penance,
O Shiva, fearsome ascetic; I am heaven's conspiracy against you.
Age after age I come,
A poet, to your hermitage. I fill my basket with garlands of victory;
Irrepressible conquests shout through the plangent rhythms of my verse.
By the force that drives my feelings, roses open;
By the impulse of ecstatic discovery that opens new leaves,
I hurl forth my songs. [2]

I have thought about 'The Wakening of Shiva' during this year of the 150th birth-anniversary of Tagore because there have been active and quiescent phases in Tagore's reputation worldwide ever since he won the Nobel Prize for Literature in 1913, and because it is the hope of the people who have organised anniversary celebrations—including of course the celebrations here in Spain—that 2011 might be the start

[1] *Selected Poems* (1985), p. 88.
[2] Ibid., p. 89.

of a new, active period in Tagore's reputation and influence. Will we see a new wakening of Shiva? How will it come about? Will it take the same form as it did when Tagore's reputation was at its height during the teens and twenties of the last century?

In this lecture I want to look first at how Tagore became internationally famous; then at the particular nature of his fame in the Spanish and Portuguese speaking world; and finally think about ways in which his reputation could revive in Spain and elsewhere.

When Tagore was awarded the Nobel Prize for Literature in 1913—the first time to a non-Westerner—he fully deserved it for his extraordinary achievements as a Bengali poet and writer. However, he was not given the Prize for his Bengali writing. He was awarded it for his English translations of some of his poems and songs: translations which he began experimentally early in 1912 and which were published in London in November of that year as *Gitanjali: Song Offerings.* With its introduction by W. B. Yeats, *Gitanjali* was what won him the Prize, though the Nobel citation also made a mention of his follow-up volume, *The Gardener.* Tagore brought a completed notebook of these translations with him when he arrived in London in the summer of 1912, and also a second notebook of translations that he had been filling on the voyage. He showed these translations to his friend, the English painter William Rothenstein, who in turn showed them to W. B. Yeats. At a famous soirée hosted by Rothenstein in his house in Hampstead in North London on 7 July 1912, the great Irish poet read out Tagore's translations, and so strong was their impact on the gathering of writers and intellectuals who were there, that within days the recently established India Society in London agreed to publish the translations. Without Yeats' support and *imprimatur*, the publication of *Gitanjali*, its sell-out success, its re-publication in March 1913 by the major publishing house Macmillan, and the award of the Nobel Prize in November of that year, would probably not have happened.

Yeats did not just support and introduce the book: his influence on its selection, arrangement, paragraphing, punctuation and language was, in my view, extensive. When Tagore won the Nobel Prize, and translations of *Gitanjali* and subsequent books were rapidly made into all the major languages of the world, including Spanish, it was the 'Yeats version' of Tagore that prevailed. Even though Yeats' direct role in shaping Tagore's English translations after *Gitanjali* rapidly declined, nevertheless, by setting the ball rolling, he had a lasting impact on the way Tagore was perceived internationally, and on the English style in which Tagore chose to do his translations.

Tagore's international success relied on major writers in other languages too, such as André Gide in French and Frederik van Eeden in Dutch. But it was in Spanish that Tagore's success was linked, as it was in the English-speaking world, to a great poet. Readers in the English-speaking world got the 'Yeats Tagore'; in the Hispanic world they got the 'Jiménez Tagore'. Juan Ramón Jiménez was without question one of the greatest Spanish poets of the 20th century, just as Yeats was one of the greatest poets in English. Yeats and Jiménez in due course joined Tagore as recipients of the Nobel Prize for Literature. So there is a real parallel here, though there are also some interesting and striking differences.

Let me consider some of these differences briefly. Firstly, Yeats, unlike Jiménez and his English-speaking wife Zenobia Cambrubí Aymar, was an editor, not a translator of Tagore. Yeats' precise editorial role is complex and difficult to assess, because although the main manuscript of Tagore's English *Gitanjali* (the so called 'Rothenstein Manuscript'), has been preserved among Rothenstein's papers at Harvard in the USA, the typed copy of which Yeats is said to have made his emendations is lost. In my new translation of *Gitanjali*, which includes a new text of Tagore's own translation based on his manuscript as well as my own translation of all *Gitanjali*'s songs and poems, I have in a lengthy introduction and several appendices reached my own conclusions about Yeats' role. But for the purposes of this lecture, more important than the minutiae of Yeats' editorial interventions was a major difference in attitude to Tagore between Yeats and the Camprubí—Juan Ramón (wife and husband) team. This was the second big difference, and it stemmed from the basic fact that Yeats was an editor whereas Zenobia and Juan Ramón were translators.

Yeats met Tagore not only at Rothenstein's soirée, but at subsequent meetings to discuss and prepare the text of *Gitanjali* for publication, and he also exchanged a dozen letters with him. They never became friends, but Yeats was acquainted with Tagore in a way that was not possible for Zenobia and Juan Ramón. Yeats also undoubtedly loved *Gitanjali*, and his love and respect for it remained with him throughout his life, even though he rapidly became disillusioned with Tagore's subsequent English books. But in his eloquent Introduction to *Gitanjali*, there is hardly any emphasis on Tagore as a person. Yeats did not read the poems as the personal expression of a poet, but instead saw them as representative of a culture and a civilization whose qualities he saw as a model for the Irish literary renaissance that he wished to lead. He wrote in his Introduction:

> These lyrics—which are in the original, my Indians tell me, full of subtlety of rhythm, of untranslatable delicacies of colour, of metrical invention, display in their thought a world I have dreamed of all my life long. The work of a supreme culture, they yet appear as much the growth of the common soil as the grass and the rushes.[3]

In other words, Yeats saw Tagore as a representative of a pre-modern poetic culture, and was ignorant of the complex, modern, hybrid culture of nineteenth-century Kolkata to which the Tagore family belonged. Moreover, Yeats' Introduction presented Tagore as much as a saint as a poet. He quotes a Bengali doctor whom he met as saying of Tagore, 'He is the first among our saints who has not refused to live, but has spoken out of Life itself, and that is why we give him our love.'[4] This perception of Tagore as a sage and a saint had a huge influence on the way people flocked to hear him on his world tours—more interested, it seemed, in his religious and moral message than they were in his poetry.

[3] *English Writings* (1994), vol. 1, p. 39.
[4] Ibid., p. 38.

By contrast with this, the prose poem by Jiménez that replaced Yeats' Introduction in the Spanish translation of *Gitanjali* was highly personal, and presented Tagore totally as a poet, not as a sage or saint. True, Jiménez sees Tagore in this poem—as in all the prefatory poems that he wrote to his wife's translations—as a poet of an exceptionally spiritual and exalted kind. But the emphasis is on Tagore's use of words to express his heart's deepest feelings, and Jiménez' concern is that the translations should go some way towards matching those words and feelings:

> *Hemos intendado dar un cuerpo nuevo a tu gran corazón, a este libro donde tú quisiste recojer tu corazón completo y verdadero. ¿Lo moverá tu corazón con su sangre y con su ritmo? ¿Latirá tu corazón, libre, en nuestro cuerpo? Di, ¿cómo se encuentra en este cuerpo nuestro tu corazón?*
>
> *¿Echa nuestra palabra, un poquito, su sombra en tu alegría inmensa, en ese arenal de gozo, hermano sólo del mar del paraíso? ¿Es estrella grande y baja de tu noche de ventura? ¿Puedes alzar con ella al cenit tu fuego; puedes callar con ella, como con un agua subterránea, tu amor pensativo?*
>
> *¡Vas a ser oído en las palabras nuestras - ¡dicha de otros más! – por tu Dios! ¿Serán ellas suficientes para que tu Dios se venga a oír tu corazón al cielo de nosotros? ¿Puedes tú habarle a gusto, con nuestra voz española, a ese Dios tuyo, cercano, visible, humano, que oye las palabras bellas?*

> *It is our desire to give a new body to your great heart, a new form to your work wherein you had placed your heart in all its fullness and truth. Will our book move your heart with its new blood and rhythm? Will your heart beat within this body of ours? Tell us, how does your heart feel to reside in this body of ours!*
>
> *Does our word cast a shadow over your immense joy, in that garden of pleasure, which is second only to the sea of paradise? Is it a great star that descends from your night of ethereal happiness? With our words can you raise your fire to the zenith; can our words, like the deep waters of the earth, temper your thoughts of love?*
>
> *You will now be heard through our words, in our tongue—which makes us luckier than others! And that is how we seek your God! Will our words be good enough for your God to come and listen to your heart which will now dwell in our heaven? Would you be at ease while conversing with*

Him in our Spanish voice, your God who is so close, visible and human, who forever responds to beautiful words?

(Translation by Malabika Bhattacharya)

I am struck by the intimacy of this poem: its use of the familiar pronoun 'tú', and the way Jiménez writes to Tagore as one poet to another. The poem immediately suggests that he and Zenobia were on the wavelength of the *Gitanjali* poems, and understood how deeply personal and introspective they were, far more than did W. B. Yeats.

The third big difference between the relationship between Tagore and Yeats and the relationship between Tagore and the Jiménezes was that their commitment to him was sustained through some twenty volumes of translations. As well as his prefatory poems in these volumes, Jiménez wrote five other poems to Tagore[5] Not only did Yeats become disillusioned with Tagore, his own poetry moved in directions that were very different. There is no indication that Tagore knew or liked Yeats' own poetry. Of course, as he did not know Spanish, he had no access to Jiménez' poetry, but I am confident from my limited reading of Jiménez that there is a great deal in his extensive oeuvre that Tagore would have appreciated. Some critics (including Ganguly and Das) have pointed to the direct influence of Tagore on Jiménez, and certainly the British scholar R. Johnson's well-known article published in 1965, 'Juan Ramón Jiménez, Rabindranath Tagore and "La Poesía Desnuda"', in which he argued that Jiménez' poem 'Vino, primero, pura' in his book *Eternidades* (1917) was influenced (as was Yeats' poem 'The Coat') by poem no. 7 of *Gitanjali* ('My song has put off her adornments'), was a useful contribution.

However, I would be inclined to side with those critics who have been sceptical about any direct influence, and instead put the emphasis

[5] They are discussed and translated by Shyama Prasad Ganguly and Sisir Kumar Das in their excellent book in Bengali on Tagore and Spain: *Saswata Mouchak* ('Eternal Honeycomb'), Papyrus, Kolkata 1987, republished by Dey's Publishing, 2011.

on affinity or sympathy. In Jiménez' celebrated and delightful *Platero y yo*, most of which was written well before his work on Tagore began, we can find a love of nature and children and of rural life that is quite Tagorean, and when I read the short poems in *Eternidades*, I feel I am close to the many short poems by Tagore that I translated comprehensively in my book *The Jewel That Is Best.*[6] Many of these short poems gave rise to Tagore's English aphorisms, collected in his books *Fireflies* and *Stray Birds*. Jiménez admired these aphorisms. *Stray Birds* ('Pájaros Perdidos') was one of the books that he and Zenobia translated. Jiménez himself wrote aphorisms, and some people have suggested a connection between the aphorisms of Tagore and Jiménez. Jiménez' aphorisms seem very different from Tagore's, yet Jiménez' very short poems—such as the poems in *Eternidades*—are often strikingly similar to Tagore's *kabitikā* or 'brief poems', even though Jiménez did not have access to them.

It is also very interesting to compare closely the Jiménezes' translation of *Gitanjali* (and subsequent books) with Tagore's English original. Theirs is a very subtle and careful translation indeed. It is never slavishly literal. As Ganguly and Das have noticed, many alterations are made in sentence structure and phrasing. Although it is probably impossible to establish how much was Zenobia's work and how much came from her husband, it is nevertheless clear that Juan Ramón's mastery of rhythm and language always played an active role. To take just one example, I was very interested to see what they did with the most famous poem in *Gitanjali*, no. 35, 'Where the mind is without fear'. In the manuscript of Tagore's English translation of this poem, it is written as a piece of continuous prose without any paragraph divisions. In the revised version, as edited by Yeats, the poem was chopped up into short verses, which as elsewhere in *Gitanjali* makes for a somewhat 'biblical' effect. By and large, the

[6] Rabindranath Tagore: *The Jewel That Is Best: Collected Brief Poems,* translated with an Introduction by William Radice Penguin India, New Delhi 2011. This is a new edition of a book that was first published in Delhi and London in 2000/2001 with the title *Particles, Jottings, Sparks.*

Jiménezes stick to the paragraph divisions of the standard published text of *Gitanjali*, but in this particular poem the lines are connected into a long paragraph, and this—though they would not have known it—makes their translation closer in its effect to Tagore's manuscript version and to the Bengali original, which is actually a sonnet.

The second part of this lecture will consider the effect of the Jiménez Tagore on Tagore's reputation in the Hispanic world and how it affects his reputation today.

The Hispanic and Lusophone world is large and diverse, embracing more than twenty countries, and I am well aware that the connection between Tagore and the Jiménezes is by no means the end of the story. A comprehensive survey would have to touch on important figures such as Victoria Ocampo in Argentina, Pablo Neruda in Chile, and Octavio Paz in Mexico. Even in mainland Spain, the story is complex, with different Tagore legacies in the different regions. The Jiménez Tagore is an Andalusian Tagore as Jiménez himself liked to put it. But there is also a Catalan Tagore, and excellent articles by José Paz Rodríguez, who in his home in Ourense has a large private collection of Tagore books, have made me aware of the Galician Tagore, and in particular the important role played by Vicente Risco.[7] But in none of these countries and regions would anyone deny the central role that Juan Ramón and Zenobia played, and any discussion of Tagore's Hispanic legacy has to start with them.

For a great poet to be linked, outside his homeland, to another great poet, has advantages and disadvantages. When I started my own work on Tagore in the 1970s, I quickly realized that it was essential,

[7] See José Paz Rodríguez: 'Tagore and his Relationship with the Latin World (the Iberian Peninsula and Latin America)' in Amalendu Biswas and Charles Gordon-Graham ed.: *Rabindranath Tagore: A Creative Unity*, The Tagore Centre UK, London 2006, pp. 132–49; and 'Education Values of the Pedagogy of Rabindranath for Today's World' in Amalendu Biswas, Christine Marsh and Kalyan Kundu (eds.): *Rabindranath Tagore: A Timeless Mind*, The Tagore Centre UK, London in collaboration with the Indian Council for Cultural Relations, 2011, pp. 289–98.

if Tagore's reputation was to be re-established in the English-speaking world, that he should be 'de-linked' from Yeats. For many years I wanted myself to have nothing to do with *Gitanjali* and the whole image of Tagore, as presented by Yeats, that was based on it and on Tagore's other English translations. Indeed, I have come to respect Tagore's own translations much more, now that I have studied his manuscript and understand better what he was trying to achieve as a self-translator. But all those who have worked on Tagore in recent decades in the English-speaking world are aware of Tagore's enormous diversity and inventiveness as a poet, prose writer, song-writer, playwright and painter, and have been trying to convey something of that richness and variety in essays and translations.

In the Hispanic world, by contrast, Tagore has not, I suspect, been de-linked from Jiménez in the way that he has, to some extent, been de-linked in English from Yeats. I imagine therefore that attitudes to Tagore today in Spain, are very closely related to attitudes to Jiménez himself. José Paz Rodríguez, in his articles, indicates that among those concerned with progressive education or with peace movements there may be people with a new and special interest in Tagore. But such movements are probably somewhat outside the mainstream.[8]

What is Jiménez' standing as a poet today? From my reading of him, I can see what a great and dedicated poet he was, but I can also see there are aspects of his entire poetic enterprise that may seem alien to contemporary readers. His relentless focus on the transcendental and the spiritual; his undogmatic yet deep religiosity; his love of nature and rural life; his apparent indifference to political affairs, even though he lived through such a turbulent period and was forced, like my great friend the Majorcan translator and thinker Juan Mascaró, to flee Spain when the civil war broke out, all these things may not be to everyone's taste. If Tagore in Spain is permanently linked to Jimenez' poetic taste and ideals, then this may be a problem for his ultimate reputation here.

[8] Ibid., especially his second article.

Let me return to the great poem that I mentioned at the beginning, *Tapobhanga* or 'The Wakening of Shiva'. In the next stanza after the climactic tenth stanza that I quoted, Tagore alludes to the burning of Kama by Shiva with fire from the third eye in the centre of his forehead. This he did in anger when Kama tried to wake him from his trance by arousing his desire for his wife Parvati, also known as Durga, Uma or Kali. Tagore says in his stanza that although Shiva burns up Kama, he actually *wants* to be defeated by love and beauty, and always himself revives Kama again. Comparing himself to Kama, Tagore then says that poets are sent into the world to ensure that that revival and renewal take place. The stanza reads:

O bark-clad anchorite, I know all your deceptions.
Your bark is illusory armour: you joyfully anticipate defeat
  At the hands of beauty.
You may burn up Kama again and again with your fire,
But you always restore him to doubly blazing life;
And because I fill and refill his quiver
With passion, I am come with my snares of music, a poet,
  Into the lap of earth.[9]

Jiménez knew that there was a rhythm and music in Tagore's Bengali poetry that he could not hear. (Yeats also knew this.) He tried without success to find a Bengali who could read the original poems to him. It was a bitter disappointment to him and Zenobia that Tagore's planned visit to Madrid, Toledo and Andalucía (including Jiménez' home town of Moguer), planned for April 1921, was suddenly cancelled by the poet. Had Tagore come, the Jiménezes and others in Spain might have heard Tagore recite or sing.

There has been much discussion about the various aspects of Tagore that might attract new interest today. Some people want to put the emphasis on his ideals, on his ideas about education, rural

[9] *Selected Poems* (2011), p. 90.

development, or international relations. At conferences in India outside Bengal, emphasis is often put on Tagore's novels and stories, because good translations of these are available not only in English but in other Indian languages, and many teachers and students of literature rightly see in those novels and stories themes and ideas that are relevant to present-day society. A third aspect of Tagore where there is certainly scope for an expansion of international interest is his work as a painter.[10] In 2011 there had been a touring exhibition starting in Berlin, and a complete edition of all the drawings and paintings by him that are held by Rabindra-Bhavan, Santiniketan, has been published in four large volumes.

But Tagore himself constantly stressed the centrality of his poetry and particularly his songs to his whole creative identity, and as I myself am a poet—and have a keen interest in music as well—it is with his poetry that I want to remain as I bring this lecture to a conclusion.

In 'The Wakening of Shiva', the revival of energy and youth and creativity is seen as part of the natural fluctuations or *līlā* (sport or play) of nature. Shiva as the *mahādeva* or greatest of gods is ultimately in control of those fluctuations, but the poet—identified in the poem with Kama, the god of love—is active in this process. What I am trying to get at here is that a revival of interest in Tagore, here in Spain or anywhere else in the world, needs to come from the discovery of Tagore's inner energy. It cannot come from a revival of interest in what others have made of him. Here in Spain, it cannot come from a return to the 'Jiménez Tagore', any more than Tagore's revival in the English-speaking world can come from the 'Yeats Tagore'. Juan Ramón, with his mastery of the Spanish language, and Zenobia, with her fluency in English, succeeded in putting Tagore into a beautiful, gleaming showcase: one that those who know Spanish can continue to admire. But Tagore in 'The Wakening of Shiva' talks about 'how he can smash fossilised discipline', and I would like to suggest that if

[10] *Rabindra Chitravali* ('Paintings of Rabindranath Tagore'), edited by R. Siva Kumar. Pratikshan, Kolkata 2011.

we are to be true to Tagore and to his creativity then we will have to, here in Spain, smash the glass of the exquisite showcase that Jiménez and his wife put round him.

Am I going too far? Even if we do not smash the glass, we should, at least, respectfully open the showcase, to release the energy that could not express itself while Tagore was confined within it. One can range through many manifestations of that energy, which include his mastery of prose as well as poetry, his feeling for narrative and character, his empathy, his love of children, his interest in science, his paintings, his *desh-prem* (patriotism), his sensitivity to the rights and feelings of women, and more. But running through all of these was a fundamental quality of rhythm, *chhanda*. Here in Spain, where you have musical traditions that are so rich in pulsating rhythmic energy, you have tremendous opportunities for the discovery of this aspect of Tagore and for its integration into the literary and musical culture not only of Spain but of the entire Hispanic world. Yes, you need more translations direct from Bengali, not just secondary translations from English. But translation, in its broadest sense, is not just the translation of texts from one language into another. Translation can embrace adaptation, musical setting, film, opera, and ballet.

I recently saw in London an extraordinary dance production presented by Akademi, a long-established centre for the study of South Asian dance. The founder and director of Akademi, Mira Kaushik, is a woman of vision and open-mindedness. For Akademi's contribution to the 150th birth-anniversary celebrations, she wanted to put on something new, and to that purpose she recruited a young choreographer of exceptional talent, Ash Mukherjee, who is trained both in Bharatanatyam and western ballet. The idea was to devise a dance performance that would relate to contemporary urban life, and would use a sequence of songs by Tagore, arranged and interpreted by one of our leading young jazz musicians, Arun Ghosh, who is himself of Bengali origin. I was brought in to do English translations of the songs that Ash and Arun wanted to use, and I translated the songs in a way that has now become my normal practice, though I only arrived at this method about five years ago. When I translate Tagore's songs, I preserve the repetitions of the lines that you get when the songs are sung, and I am also careful to indicate with line breaks the four part structure that most songs by Tagore have. Here, in my translation, is one of the songs that was used:

He gambhīr
Nīla anjanaghana punjachāyāy sambrita ambar, he gambhīr

Deep collyrium-blue sky heaped up with shade
O solemn, O solemn
The woodland goddess atremble, her heart aquiver
The woodland goddess atremble, her heart aquiver
Her anklets of crickets humming
Her anklets of crickets humming
O solemn, O solemn
Deep collyrium-blue sky heaped up with shade
O solemn, O solemn

The song of the rains rumbling with thunder's rhythm,
with thunder's rhythm
Kadamba-trees thick with the joy of fragrance
Your festive temples ecstatic
Your festive temples ecstatic
O solemn, O solemn
Deep collyrium-blue sky heaped up with shade
O solemn, O solemn

The parched earth was raging with thirst on a bed of fire
You sent her news of the waters of Indra's heaven
The parched earth was raging with thirst on a bed of fire
You sent her news of the waters of Indra's heaven

The soil's harsh walls have cracked, dissolved all around,
dissolved all around,
The world is awash with new shoots unfolding their victory banner

Smashed are the prisoner's chains
Smashed are the prisoner's chains
O solemn, O solemn
Deep collyrium-blue sky heaped up with shade
O solemn, O solemn[11]

It seems to me that by this simple use of repetitions the songs take on a whole new life. The many songs from *Gitanjali* and other books, that were translated by Zenobia and Juan Ramón Jiménez, could take on new life in Spanish too, if the repetitions and the musical structure were similarly honoured. Combined with access to the melodies of the songs, which are increasingly available in this age of digitization and the internet, poets, musicians, and dancers in Spain will immediately see and hear the potential, just as these young artists in London have been able to see and hear it

For Bengalis used to Tagore's dance dramas performed in a style that has, over time, become traditional and conventional, Akademi's production in London was a surprising, even shocking experience. But for me it was an example of the wakening of Shiva—a wakening that we urgently need in Britain, in Spain, in India and all over the world.

This is the revised English text of a lecture delivered in Spanish (translated by Pilar Ordin) in Salamanca and Barcelona as part of the 'Tagore en España'—Festival, 27 September–4 October 2011). First published in: *The Kindred Voice: Reflections on Tagore in Spain and Latin America*, edited by Shyama Prasad Ganguly, Centre of Spanish, Portuguese, Italian and Latin American Studies, Jawaharlal Nehru University, New Delhi 2011, pp. 107–21.

[11] *Gītabitān: Prakriti* (Barshā) 55.

The Teacher of Poetry and Life

Most of you will know about Rabindranath's recollection of the impact that particular lines and phrases from nursery rhymes made on him when he was a very young child. He mentions this in his *Jībansmriti* ('My Reminiscences'), but a fuller discussion of it can be found in chapters 1 and 2 of *Lok-Sahitya* ('Folk Literature', 1907), in which he collects and analyses Bengali nursery rhymes. But to get into the subject let me recite the extraordinary poem no. 20 from *Janmadine* ('On my Birthday', 1941):

> Today I imagine the words of countless
> Languages to be suddenly fetterless—
> After long incarceration
> In the fortress of grammar, suddenly up in rebellion,
> Maddened by the stamp-stamping
> Of unmitigated regimental drilling.
> They have jumped the constraints of sentence
> To seek free expression in a world rid of intelligence...[1]

In *Lok-Sahitya* Tagore writes of the nursery jingle *brishti pare tāpur-tupur, nadi ela bān* ('the rain falls pitter-patter, the river has overflowed') that 'this nursery rhyme was like a magic spell to me in childhood, and I still cannot forget its enchantment.' He goes on to argue that nursery rhymes 'are born spontaneously' and reflect our

[1] *Selected Poems* (1985) p. 124.

minds 'in their natural state' before the conscious mind, through logic and grammar, imposes order on our thoughts. Thus:

> If the reflected stream of all the dream-like shadows and sounds that wander about like endlessly-forming clouds in the sky of our mind in its simple state, sometimes combining, sometimes separating, going through various shapes and colours, moving at the chance dictate of invisible winds, could be projected on to some non-conscious screen [*achetan pat*], then we would see a considerable resemblance between that projection and these rhymes that we are discussing. These rhymes are nothing but shadows of our ever-changing inner sky; they are like shadows projected on to the clear waters of a lake by clouds playing in the heavens. That is why I said they are born spontaneously.[2]

Tagore's fascination with the spontaneity of nursery rhymes can be connected with many aspects of his life and work: with his love of children and desire to create a system of education that would develop the mind and imagination of the child in a natural, compassionate and spontaneous way; with his books on nonsense writing in his very late years—*Se* and *Khāpchhārā*; with the whimsy of the doodles in his manuscripts; and with his whole approach to painting, which involved a kind of suspension of the conscious will. But I believe his response to nursery rhymes can be linked to his conception and practice of *poetry* in general at a very deep level. It helps us to understand what poetry actually *is*, and what, therefore, we can learn from it.

When I came up with my title and abstract for this paper, I had it in mind to range widely through Tagore's literary works and consider the various things that they can teach us. In other papers during this birth-anniversary year I have focused on a number of qualities that we find in his output—qualities that make him the great poet and writer that he was. They include qualities such as empathy—his profound ability to enter into the lives and feelings of all kinds of people, male or female, young or old, rich and poor; or far-sightedness—a

[2] Ibid., Appendix B, p. 185.

prophetic ability to engage with themes that resonate strongly with our contemporary fears and concerns.

These and other qualities have much to teach us, but they are not limited to his poetry—they can be found in all the genres that he mastered. What I want to focus on here are qualities that can be recognised as uniquely poetic, which can therefore be found *only* in Tagore's poems, not in his prose or dramatic writings—even though it may often seem that there is a great deal of overlap between all his works. He was essentially a poet in everything he wrote and did. I would further like to ask if there is a way of distinguishing his poetry from his songs, something that might seem, after my recent experience of translating *Gitanjali*—extremely difficult to do, since so many of the poems in *Gitanjali* are songs, and arguably (this is Shanka Ghosh's view) during the 'Gitanjali phase' of Tagore's creative output 1910–14 the distinction between poetry and song all but disappeared.

Among Tagore's best known and best loved poems—for Bengalis, that is: they remain entirely beyond the ken of those who do not know the Bengali language—are the verses of *Sahaj Pāth* ('Easy reader', 1932), his wonderful primer for children in four volumes. Generations of Bengalis have grown up with these books, have learnt to read and spell from them. They include many passages of delightful prose, but I would guess that when Bengalis think of *Sahaj Pāth* they think of its verses. They alone are an extraordinary gift to Bengali culture and society. How many children in other countries learn to read from *poetry*? For poetry is what you get from the first page of Book One of *Sahaj Pāth*, in the magical verses that introduce the Bengali vowels and consonants. Let me remind you of what they sound like:

choto khokā bale 'a' 'ā'
shekheni se kathā kāoyā

[The baby boy says *'a' 'ā'*
he has not yet learnt to talk.]

hrasva 'i' dirgha 'ī'
base khāy kshīr khai

[Short *'i'* and long *'ī'*
sit and eat *kshīr* and *khai*.]

hrasva 'u' dirgha 'ū'
dāk chāre gheu gheu

[Short *'u'* and long *'ū'*
bark and howl *gheu gheu*.]

shāl muri diye 'ha' 'ksha'
kone base kāshe 'kha' 'ksha'

[With shawl wrapped round, *'ha'* and *'ksha'*
huddle in a corner and cough *'kha'* and *'ksha'*.]

I am sure that Tagore was trying, in these verses, to replicate some of the 'spontaneity' of nursery rhymes—to find a way of teaching the letters of the Bengal alphabet to children that would be as enchanting as nursery rhymes and reflect the human mind in its 'natural state'. Let us consider what the qualities of these verses are, for if we can define them they may tell us a lot about what poetry in general is, from a nursery rhyme to an epic.

Firstly, poetry is *rhythmic*. Of course the rhythms of poetry encompass far more than the simple, regular metres of these verses in *Sahaj Pāth*. In the twentieth century, poets in all languages became so carried away with the possibilities of 'free verse' that this today has become the norm, rhymed or metrical verse being the exception. Tagore himself, with his development of *gadya-kābya* ('prose poetry') in the poetry of his last decade, announcing in his preface to *Punashcha* (The Post-Script, 1932) a desire to bring poetry and prose together, contributed massively to this development in Bengali poetry.[3] But poetry without any rhythm at all, without the poet choosing his or her words with an ear to their sound and their rhythm as well as their meaning—seems to me a contradiction in terms. The fact that poetic rhymes are hard-wired into our brains at an extremely young age—through the nursery rhymes we hear from our mothers or (in the case of Bengalis) from the verses of *Sahaj Pāth*—links them intimately with the mother-tongue, and makes the *translation* of poetry into a second or acquired language extremely challenging.

Secondly, poetry is *serendipitous*. By this I mean that there is a 'lucky', 'unplanned', 'haphazard' aspect to it. This quality is expressed *par excellence* through *rhyme*. The fact that words rhyme with some words in a language and not with others may sometimes appear to have

[3] The preface to *Punashcha* is a key statement by Tagore on his poetic development. Note that for Tagore, *gadya-kābya* is a term that incorporates both 'the prose poem' without line-endings (as in *Lipikā* or the English *Gitanjali*) and free verse or *vers libre* with line-endings (as in *Punashcha* and subsequent books). Tagore's preface to *Punashcha* gives us more details:

'I translated the songs of *Gitanjali* into English prose. This translation was regarded as poetic. Since then the question has been in my mind: might it be possible to to give to Bengali prose—free of rhyme and metre's explicit sound effects—a similarly poetic flavour [*rasa*]? I remember I asked Satyendranath to attempt this, but he never did. Then I myself had a go, in a few compositions in *Lipikā*. When they were printed they were not, however, broken up into lines—probably through timidity on my part.

Later, at my request, Abanindranath undertook the same experiment. In my view, these writings fell within the definition of poetry, but were let down by their linguistic excess. I decided to try again myself.

Let me make one thing clear. In prose poetry [*gadya-kābya*], it is not enough simply to dispense with fixed metre, its movement into the free world of prose becomes natural only if one discards the ornate and over-modest coverings that pertain to the language and expression of poetry. I believe it is possible greatly to extend the claims of poetry to the frankness of prose, and I have written the poems published in this book with this aim in view. There are some unrhymed poems among them that still have metre, but I have tried to get away from special poetic diction. Thus *tare* [for *janya*], *sane* [for sange], *mor* [for amar] and other words that are not used in prose have been avoided in all these poems.'

something to do with meaning—either similar meanings (e.g. 'quake, shake' in English) or opposite meanings ('light, night'; 'spark, dark') etc.—but essentially rhyme seems to be a matter of chance. For poets who delight in rhyme, the unexpected images and ideas that rhymes throw up are endlessly fascinating—fascinating for readers too, and a perpetual source of wit and humour in poetry. Indeed, the more that poetry depends on rhyme for its effects, the wittier it becomes, which is why it is impossible to write a tragic limerick.

In the opening verses of *Sahaj Pāth*, one of the most brilliant and appealing things is the way in which the letters, through the ideas thrown up by rhymes, morph into living beings. Without rhyme how could even Rabindranath come up with the notion that *hrasva 'u'* and *dirgha 'ū'* are like dogs barking, or *'kha' and 'ksha'* are like people with a hacking cough, huddling in a corner with a shawl round their shoulders? The price one pays for writing poetry without rhyme is that it is harder to achieve such serendipitous effects, though the greatest masters of blank verse such as Milton in English or Michael Madhusudan Dutt in Bengali do manage to achieve them—and be witty too. Indeed, it is even possible to achieve them in free verse or *gadya-kābya*—and I will return to this point presently.

Thirdly, poetry is *inevitable*, or should seem so, if it is good. For me, one of the tests of great poetry is: Does it seem so inevitable that one cannot imagine a single word being changed, added or removed? With mediocre poetry, one often feels that lines could be added or taken out, without much loss. With Rabindranath, I *never* feel this. Even in his 'freest' verse, every word and every line seems as inevitably in place as every note and every bar with the music of Johann Sebastian Bach. There is an inexhaustible, effortless virtuosity about it.

This third quality of inevitability applies to the *sequence* of poems as well as to the individual poems. You can read the 21 'alphabet' poems in *Sahaj Pāth*, or get learners to chant them as I have done with my students at SOAS, and feel that the individual verses build up into a larger structure that itself is a poem.

All three of the qualities that I have just defined can be found in innumerable poems by Rabindranath, including many challenging and complex poems that are not meant for children at all. I have found them in many of the poems of *Gītāñjali*, having recently translated them all. It is to *Gitanjali* that I would like to turn now as I address the questions: i) What do these three qualities of a poem teach us? ii) Is there a quality that can even distinguish poetry from song?

One thing that impelled me to make the book not just a new translation of all the poems that are in the English *Gitanjali* but also the new texts of Tagore's own translation, based on his manuscript, is that in his manuscript I actually found these three qualities—of rhythm, of serendipity, and inevitability—to be present: qualities that have always seemed to me absent from the standard text of his own translation as edited by W. B. Yeats. Their absence was, I suspect, the reason why for years I wanted to keep away from *Gitanjali*., This is also, I believe, the reason why Tagore's own translations have not stood the test of time for many readers across the world, have not convinced them that he was a great poet.

The obvious reason for this failure to convince might seem to be that they were *translations*, that he was not an English poet, and could not do in English what he could do in Bengali. As he himself said, in a letter to William Rothenstein of 4 April 1915 in which Tagore bridled at changes that Robert Bridges wanted to make to some poems from *Gitanjali* that he wanted to include in his anthology *The Spirit of Man*:

> My translations are frankly prose—my aim is to make them simple with just a suggestion of rhythm to give them a touch of the lyric, avoiding all archaisms and poetical conventions.[4]

But to my amazement, when I started to study Tagore's translation of *Gitanjali* in detail, in the manuscript he completed in 1912

[4] *Imperfect Encounter: Letters of William Rothenstein and Rabindranath Tagore 1911–1941*, edited by Mary M. Lago, Harvard University Press, Cambridge, Massachusetts 1972, p. 195.

before he arrived in England and before Yeats and others started to interfere with it, I found ample evidence—in its *gadha-kābya*—of the qualities that I have just defined as poetic. I found rhythmic energy and power, I found lively and serendipitous choice of words; and I found inevitability not only in individual poems and songs but in the *sequence*—the carefully arranged sequence of 83 poems and songs that we find in the 'Rothenstein Manuscript'—a sequence utterly different from the random, arbitrary sequence that we have in the standard text.

Let me give you just one example of the occurrence of these three qualities, rhythm, serendipity and inevitability, in a poem, the most famous one in *Gitanjali*, endlessly quoted in India and by visitors to India such as President Obama wanting to make the right impression.: But does it, in the standard text, convince people elsewhere that Tagore was a great poet? The standard text, as you all know, reads as follows:

Where the mind is without fear and the head is held high;
Where knowledge is free;
Where the world has not been broken up into fragments by narrow
    domestic walls;
Where words come out from the depth of truth;
Where tireless striving stretches its arms towards perfection;
Where the clear stream of reason has not lost its way into the dreary
    desert sand of dead habit;
Where the mind is led forward by thee into ever-widening thought
    and action—
Into that heaven of freedom, my Father, let my country awake.

In the manuscript, it is like this:

Where the mind is without fear and the head is held high; where knowledge is free; where the world has not been frittered into fragments by narrow domestic walls; where words come out from the depth of truth; where sleepless striving stretches its strenuous arms towards perfection; where the clear stream of reason has not lost its way in the dreary desert sand of dead habit, and where the mind is led

> forward by thee into ever-widening thought and action—there wake up my country into that heaven of freedom, my father![5]

Notice the differences! The translation in the manuscript is a piece of continuous prose, unbroken into the short paragraphs that slow it down and make it pompous and incantatory. Read naturally and passionately, it flows with a powerful *rhythmic* energy—a quintessentially Tagorean rhythm that I never felt in his English translations till I discovered the manuscript of *Gitanjali*. There is *serendipity* in Tagore's felicitous use of alliteration (influenced no doubt by the alliteration in his source, sonnet no. 72 in *Naibedya*) in 'frittered into fragments' (weakened into 'broken up into fragements' in the edited version) and 'sleepless striving stretches its strenuous arms' (reduced to 'tireless striving stretches its arms'). The conclusion is much more climactic, much more *inevitable* than the edited version, the direct imperative of 'wake up' being much closer to the Bengali. All in all, I see no need to change anything in the manuscript other than the three small corrections I have made in the text above—'<u>in</u> the dreary desert sand' rather than '<u>into</u>', 'wake up' rather than 'waken up', and 'ever-widening' rather than 'everwidening'.

What about the question I raised by my title? What does poetry, the essence of poetry, teach us? And what about the other question I raised earlier, whether the defining qualities of poetry can be distinguished from those of song? Let me tackle this second question first. In his book of English lectures *Sādhanā* (1913), Tagore wrote eloquently about 'the eternal law of harmony that is everywhere'.[6] It seems to me that in *poetry*—genuine poetry—this fundamental law is constantly undermined by the serendipitous element, and maybe, paradoxically, by the rhythmic element too—whereas in music—and certainly in the songs of Tagore—the law of harmony becomes dominant. One part of Tagore certainly believed that the universe was ultimately harmonious, as did Albert Einstein, who famously discussed the nature of truth

[5] *Gitanjali* (2011), p. 95.

[6] *English Writings* (1996), vol. 2. p. 335.

and beauty with Tagore. Tagore also believed that in his songs he came closest to that harmony. The texts of his songs may have all the qualities of poems, but as soon as they are sung a different aesthetic takes over—metre and rhyme cease to be so evident or apparent, and the harmony, law and balance inherent in the four-part *sthāyi*, *antarā*, *sanchari*, and *abhog* structure, and in the regularity of the *tāla*, take over.

In poetry it is different, and the reason why for Tagore nursery rhymes (and the rhymes of *Sahaj Pāth*) represent poetry in its purest form is precisely because of that element in them that *defies* law or harmony or regularity. Moreover, Tagore's sense that the rhythms of poetry included irregularity—and were thus different from the regular or repeated patterns of rhythm that you get in music—helps to explain why he constantly strove to expand the rhythmic possibilities of poetry so that they incorporated even prose. In his essay on metre, *Chander Artha* ('The Meaning of Metre', 1916) he writes of the charm that *bishama chalaner chhanda* ('mixed-measure metre') had for him, and in his poem *Nātak* in *Punashcha* he explicitly picks up the programme announced in his preface by imagining a style in which the *besur* ('tunelessness') or *garjan* ('roar') or prose will be combined with the *sur* ('tune') and *gān* ('song) of poetry.[7]

[7] For more on Tagore and metre, see my essay 'Tagore's Sense of Rhythm' (see pp.145–158 in this volume)

Since writing the present paper, I have come to feel that fundamental to Tagore's wish to bring poetry and prose together was deep-seated longing for *convergence*. In his songs, as conventionally sung with *tablā* accompaniment, the rhythms may seem to be stricter than in his poetry. But when you hear recordings by Tagore himself—such as his celebrated recording of *Tabu Mone Rekho*—his rhythmic flexibility is striking. It is as if he wants his music, even where there is an underlying *tāla*, to have the natural flexibility of speech. Professor Lars-Christian Koch, who has completed a major study of *Rabīndrasangīt* in German (*My Heart Sings: Die Lieder Rabindranath Tagores zwischen Tradition und Moderne*, LIT Verlag, Berlin etc. 2011), stressed in a lecture which he gave at 'The Many Worlds of Tagore: An International Conference' at the University of Chicago, 27–28 October 2011, that the notation of the songs—their rhythmic definition in *akar-matrik* notation in the *Swaralipi*—has led to

But what does poetry, defined by the qualities I have described, teach us and why does Rabindranath want it to be used in the teaching of very young children? *The fundamental thing that we can learn from poetry is the actual nature, stuff or fabric of reality.* This, so far as very young children are concerned, is certainly worth learning. Without it, the world will remain utterly confusing and baffling, as it does for children with disorders such as autism who remain disconnected from reality. The *rhythms* of reality remain exciting, engaging, they arouse our delight and curiosity. The *serendipity* of reality gives us the hope and optimism and faith that things will somehow be okay, fall into place, work out for the best. Without that faith, life would be too terrifying to endure. The *inevitability* of reality makes us accepting of even the most dreadful things that can happen, so that we can pick ourselves up and live to fight another day. It seems to me that a firm grounding in the kind of reality that poetry teaches us gives us a basis for a healthy attitude to life: helps us to see through illusions or dogma or fanaticism. Don't we often feel when we talk to a religious or political fanatic that he or she lacks any kind of poetic sensibility? Fanatics lack humour too, and the fact that we were all laughing at *Sahaj Pāth* shows us that poetry and wit are closely connected. Above all, fanatics in their narrow-mindedness lack an ability to see the *multi-faceted* nature of reality, and poetry is nothing if not multi-faceted. It was this poetic focus on reality that made Tagore—always at heart a poet—so interested in science, especially physics and evolution.[8]

---

a rhythmic rigidity that Tagore himself did not want. Thus, though I continue to believe that the songs of Tagore display a tendency towards harmony, order and transcendence, whereas his poetry shows a constant expansion of limits so that disharmony, disorder and immanence can be incorporated, both tendencies can be found in both, and it may be best to think of his poetry and music as a continuum, rather than contrasting with each other.

[8] See my essay 'Particles and Sparks: Tagore, Einstein and the Poetry of Science', in *India International Centre Quarterly*, vol. 25 nos. 2&3, Summer-Monsoon 1998, pp. 131–50.

Of course, poetry can teach us many other moral, aesthetic or historical lessons. But as I said earlier, these things can be learnt too from other kinds of literature or art or study. Only poetry, it seems to me—and I believe that this was Tagore's view too, expressed explicitly in his essay on nursery rhymes—can take us as deep into the stuff of reality as quantum or particle physics. Maybe it probes even more deeply than physics—but with that provocative and unprovable statement, I think I had better end.

Lecture at the Tagore Conference of the Indian Council for Cultural Relations (ICCR), 10–12 October 2011 in New Delhi.

Bengal's Gifts to the World

There is a beautiful poem by Rabindranath Tagore in his book *Balākā* (1916), called *Dān* ('Gift'). It is a love poem in which the poet asks what gift he can possibly give which would be equal to his beloved:

O my love, what gift of mine
　Shall I give you this dawn?
　　　A morning song?
　But morning does not last long—
　　The heat of the sun
　　　Wilts it like a flower
　And songs that tire
　　　　Are done.[1]

He goes on to consider various other gifts—a lamp, flowers, jewels. But the only real gifts he can offer are 'fleeting': they are special moments of transcendence which lie beyond all material or physical expression. In the 2002, I published a book of my own poems which I called *Gifts*.[2] There is a poem in it called 'Adam's Gift', addressed to my wife and located in our home in Northumberland. Maybe I was subconsciously influenced by Tagore's poem, for I discard material gifts in favour of the non-material:

[1] *Selected Poems* (1985), p. 81.

[2] William Radice: *Gifts: Poems 1992–1999*. Grevatt & Grevatt, Newcastle upon Tyne 2002.

My gift today is the gift of tranquillity
Possessed by this house, which like our tongue,
Our Englishness, our daughters sprung

From us but with new lives of their own,
And our strange, combined selfhood grown
From twenty-one years of shared living,
Is not just ours for the making or giving.

In thinking today about Bengal's gifts to the world, her intangible, non-material gifts are those that I want to focus on. Of course there are material gifts or exports that I could talk about. One could easily devote a whole lecture to the textiles and embroideries that are such an important part of the Bengali cultural tradition, and which made Bengal so attractive to traders and conquerors in the early days of colonial expansion. That tradition was never quite killed off, even by the devastation wrought on hand-loom weavers by the import of cheap manufactured textiles under British rule. Textiles and garment-making are crucial to the economy of Bangladesh today, and their scope is not limited to low-cost clothing exports. I can recall more than one important exhibition in London in recent years of *kāñthā* embroideries, and the potential is surely there for growth in that area and the revival of Bengal as a creator of exquisite textiles. Another, by no means insignificant gift from Bengal to the wider world is the 'Indian' restaurant industry, which in Britain and in most other Western countries is dominated by cooks and restaurateurs from Sylhet. It is now as impossible to imagine urban life in the West without Bangladeshi-run restaurants as it is to imagine it without pizzerias or hamburger bars. But Bengal's material exports are not the focus of my talk today, for she has given things to the world that are more profound and beautiful than even the finest *kāñthā* or the most succulent chicken *tikka māsālā*.

First on my list would be the Bengali language. I have been learning it, reading it, teaching it, translating it, speaking it for nearly forty years now, and have never doubted that Bengali—Bangla—is a language of extraordinary intrinsic beauty. I don't think my pupils at SOAS have ever doubted this either, even those who never got beyond the beginner's stage. But to celebrate Bengali as Bengal's supreme gift to the world may immediately beg some questions. Although there are large numbers of Bengali speakers in many parts of the world, and in future decades their numbers may grow considerably, Bengali is not a language that has been exported or spread in the way that English or Spanish have been through colonial conquest. Very few non-Bengalis learn the language and university facilities for studying it to an advanced level are pitifully few. One should also be wary of ranking languages in terms of their beauty. All languages are miraculous: infinite in their potential and capable of expressing every nuance of thought or feeling. But some languages are grammatically more elegant than others, just as some mathematical theorems or some chess games are more elegant than others. Languages, like the wonderfully varied flora and fauna that fill our planet, are like works of art with no one creator. They have evolved over time, often in ways that defy that any rational or scientific explanation. Just why and how Bengali should have developed its perfectly integrated system of articles, pronouns and demonstratives; its smooth regularity of verb forms; the deliciously logical and concise way in which its sentences are constructed using participles or possessive case endings instead of cumbersome sub-clauses; these features, and many more, never cease to amaze me. I often feel that Bangla is like a perfectly honed and shaped pebble, with almost no flaws or roughness or sharp edges. Not many foreigners are able to hold that pebble in their hands, but its sheer existence adds to the world's stock of miracles, and thus plays a part in making our planet such an astonishing world in which to live.

Language may seem to be tangible enough. It is made out of physical sounds, or letters on the page. But the sounds or grammar of a language, although it is through them that meaning is expressed, can paradoxically have qualities that go beyond meaning. This is what Shamsur Rahman was getting at in his famous poem *Barnamālā, āmār duhkhini barnamālā.* Written in reaction to the outrageous suggestion that the Bengali language could only be 'integrated' into the Pakistani nation if it was written in Roman or Arabic script, the poem expresses the poet's intense sense of belonging to the language in which he has grown, and in which he feels and lives. 'You have been my companion from birth', he says, and his dreams, his aesthetic sense, his responses to the natural world have all been shaped by it. 'You are the pupil in my eyeball....If you are uprooted, what would I have left?'

Shamsur Rahman employs poetry—great poetry—to express his feelings about his native language. It will not surprise you to hear that for me, Bengal's second great gift to the world has to be poetry, its wonderful accumulation of poetry from the *padābalī* and *mangal-kābya* of the pre-modern period, to masterpieces by your greatest poets such as Michael Madhusudan Dutt, Rabindranath Tagore, Nazrul Islam, Jibanananda Das, and Shamsur Rahman, or the extremely vigorous poetic culture of the present day, which here in Bangladesh has, as always, enriched the month of February by sustaining the Bangla Academy Book Fair and the Ekushey commemorations of those who laid down their lives in their struggle for the Bengali language.

Poetry, like language, is a mysterious mixture of the tangible and intangible. At one level, poems are objects: their dimensions can be described, things said about their construction, their use of metre or rhyme, and so forth. But at another level a poem is defined and recognised by its transcendental qualities—by that in it which is not prose, which cannot be limited or restricted to every-day, material, physical reality. Of all the arts, poetry is the most non-material in its basic medium: it does not require performers, or elaborate facilities; it is essentially just words on the page or in the mind or the memory. When the great Russian poet Osip Mandelstam was cruelly sent to a Siberian camp by Stalin, his wife Nadezhda preserved his poems by memorising them. In the Indian subcontinent, vast amounts of poetry and literature were handed down through memorisation. In Islam, special status is given to those who can memorise the whole Quran. This non-materiality, the way in which poetry can exist solely in someone's brain cells, is for me one of its most precious and resilient features. Maybe here in Bengal, poetry has acquired a special significance because life in the climatic and environmental conditions of the delta has often been and will always be so perilous. The region of Bengal is agriculturally fertile, which is why it is able to support such a large population, and it is culturally rich; but material prosperity for all its people continues to elude it. Bengali poets have always been sensitive to the sufferings of their fellow men and women, and have used poetry as a means of expressing the co-existence of beauty and suffering. Nazrul Islam did this memorably in his poem *Dāridrya* ('Poverty'):

On every side, life seems to have sprung
Forth afresh. Unmindful of myself, I sing
A joyous song of welcome. My eyes,
For no reason, fill with tears.
Someone has tied a thread of faith
Between me and the earth.
With soiled blackened hands, Earth comes
To make flower offerings: she seems
To be my youngest, most darling
Daughter. But suddenly I wake, to a wailing
In the house; my child who has not eaten
Since yesterday weeps (cruel discipline)
All day in my house, hunger-torn.
I cannot, dear child of mine, give
You even two drops of milk. I have
No right to joy. Unbearable poverty
Has become both my wife and child, perpetually
Crying at my door…

I find myself thinking, too, of Shamsur Rahman's poem *Duhkha* ('Sorrow'), in which in a wonderful succession of images he finds that in all aspects of life—even the most beautiful and joyous—'Sorrow writes its name'. I am quoting my own translations, and again the question is begged: if poetry is one of Bengal's gifts to the world, and yet the communication of that gift depends on translation—there being so few non-Bengalis who can read the poems in the original—can one in that case call Bengali poetry a gift to the world? Is it not rather a gift by Bengalis to other Bengalis? But as with the intrinsic beauties of a language, I believe that the sheer existence of great poetry, even if not everyone has access to it, adds to the sum total of what makes our world special and life worth living. As a translator of Bengali poetry, I never feel that I am communicating a gift that would not be there were I not communicating it. My poem 'Adam's Gift', which I mentioned at the beginning, ends with the line 'When the gift I give is already there', and that is what I feel about poetic translation: it is merely a gift to others of something that is already there.

I think there are some specific reasons why, for me, the poetry of Bengal has always seemed to be 'already there'. It is not just because I have come to know it quite well over the years and have become familiar with Bengali culture and society through many visits to Bangladesh and West Bengal. Rather, it is because of its humanism, syncretism and openness. In studying the poetry and literature of another country, there is variation in the amount of prior knowledge or 'homework' that has to be done in order to understand it. If I want to understand, say, the poetry of Wales, I probably need to do a lot of work on the mythological and historical traditions of Wales, and develop an understanding of the rituals and expectations of their national poetic festival, the *Eisteddfod.* Of course there is quite a lot of knowledge that I have had to acquire in order to read and translate Bengali poetry. In order to translate Michael Madhusudan's great epic, *Meghnadbadh Kābya,* I have had to learn about the Sanskrit epic tradition and acquire a reasonable knowledge of Hindu mythology in order to understand the similes and allusions. To read Tagore I have had to learn about the Upanishads, Vaishnavism, or the classical Sanskrit poetry of Kalidasa.

But never have I felt that these traditions create barriers, erect walls round Bengali poets and writers. This has much to do with the very important Bengali tradition of religious syncretism. Any scholar of the poetry of the pre-modern period knows that it arose from a mingling of Hindu and Islamic, Sanskrit and Persian traditions, and that a spirit of syncretism has survived strongly in the folk traditions of Bengal, especially the songs of the Bauls, in which through their mixture of Tantrism and Sufism, and their pursuit of a spirituality that transcends any one religion, we have Bengali openness and tolerance at its best. This is a real gift to the world, and a necessary one. Although relations between Hindus and Muslims in Bengal have not always been easy, and divisions between the two communities led to the partition of Bengal in 1947, it has always seemed to me that the inter-cultural and syncretistic traditions of Bengal have survived here in Bangladesh. In a way, the failure of the Pakistan experiment and the emergence of an independent Bangladesh in 1971 showed the resilience of that tradition—its refusal to countenance a society defined by one religion or another. Bangladesh became, through her independence struggle, a homeland for free Bengalis, whatever their faith. I know that under an earlier, non-democratic government, Islam was declared the state religion of Bangladesh. But I do not feel that this has fundamentally affected the way in which Bengali society works, whether here or across the border in West Bengal. It certainly has not affected the way in which Bengali poetry works, for a desire to express a spirituality that is non-sectarian is fundamental to it, and a narrow or doctrinal outlook, has always been taboo. One hardly needs to say that this outlook is one that the world as a whole badly needs, and it would be a happier and more peaceful place if this particular gift of Bengal was universally received and applied.

It is a gift that has been fostered by many Bengali poets through the ages, but I do not think anyone will object if I give pride of place to Rabindranath Tagore for promoting it so tirelessly and memorably, not only in innumerable poems and songs but also in his educational endeavours at Santiniketan. When I heard about the aspirations of Bengali International[3] and your plans for a new university here in

[3] A cultural society registered in the UK.

Bangladesh,[4] I was particularly interested by the connections that were mentioned between these goals and the ideals and achievements of Visva-Bharati. Here in Bangladesh, Visva-Bharati might seem to be an Indian institution, and the name might appear to incorporate the word Bharat, which is the ancient name for Hindu India. But Bharati is also a name for Saraswati, the goddess of learning and the arts, and 'Visva' means universal.

Tagore was active in many fields, but he was more fully and naturally himself as a composer of songs than anything else. I would like to end these reflections on Bengal's gifts to the world by thinking about Tagore's songs, and about the musical traditions of Bengal generally. In Bengal, music primarily means song, and in Bengali songs the other gifts I have mentioned—Bengali language and poetry; Bengali humanism, syncretism and openness—are all combined and expressed. I said earlier that the non-materiality of poetry, its simplicity of physical means, is for me among its most precious attributes. Coming from the Western tradition as I do, music might seem to be a much more cumbersome affair: one thinks of our huge choirs, orchestras and opera houses: the whole network of music colleges and exams, of instrument makers and recording companies and festivals on which our musical life depends. In Bengal, by contrast, music can be something far simpler and more transferable than that. Tagore was fascinated by the Baul singers of Bengal because they could do so much with so little: they did not even need a drum or *tablā* to communicate rhythm, they could do that perfectly just by their skilful playing of the *ektārā* or *dotārā*.

As a translator, I found for many years that the songs of Tagore were beyond my powers: I didn't know how to translate them in a way that would convey their musical qualities and indicate straightaway to a reader that they are songs, not poems. In my new translation of *Gītāñjali* I believe that I have finally arrived at a translation method that captures the simplicity and musicality of Tagore's song texts. Here

[4] This lecture was held in Dhaka.

is one that I particularly like, which for some reason was left out of the published translation by Tagore himself in 1912 of the poems and songs of *Gītāñjali*. It is poem no. 28 in *Gitimālya* (1914), and Tagore's own translation of it—a very good one—is found at no. 58 in the manuscript in his *Gītāñjali* translation. Tagore's own translation reads:

> More life, my lord, yet more, to quench my thirst and fill me. More space, my lord, yet more, freely to unfurl my being.
> More light, my lord, yet more, to make my vision pure. More tunes, my lord, yet more, stirring the strings of my heart.
> More pain, my lord, yet more, to lead me to a deeper consciousness. More knocks, my lord, yet more, to break open my prison door.
> More love, my lord, yet more, to completely drown myself. More of thee, my lord, yet more, in thy sweetness of grace abounding.

In my own translation it reads:

Give me more, more, more life
My spirit filling, my thirst quenching
in your world, world
Give me more, more, more life
My spirit filling, my thirst quenching
in your world, world
Give me more, more, more space

More light, more light
lord, poured
into these eyes
More light, more light
lord, poured
into these eyes

Give me more, more, more music,
filling my flute with tunes

Give me more pain, more pain
Give me more consciousness
Tear open all doors, smash down all walls
Give me more pain, more pain
Give me more consciousness
Tear open all doors, smash down all walls
Give me more release, more release

More love, more love,
that the 'I' in me
may drown
More love, more love,
that the 'I' in me
may drown
Give me more, more, more streams
of nectar to drink
Give me more, more, more

What is extraordinary about Bengal—which makes me feel glad and privileged to have been involved with Bengali culture for so many years—is that I can read out a song like that, linking it by implication with the aspirations of Bengali International or Visva-Bharati, of Bangladesh or of West Bengal; read it out to an audience of Bengalis that might include Hindus or Muslims; read it out on an academic occasion, or a state occasion, or at some kind of national festival such as Ekushey and no one will think this strange. This kind of unity of poetic, moral, religious and personal feeling seems to me to be Bengal's greatest gift to the world. It is great, because it can so easily and effortlessly become universal too. I can think of many contexts and audiences in Britain where it might initially seem strange to read out such a poem, but such is the directness and simplicity of Tagore's utterance that I do not think it would take more than a few minutes for any audience to adjust to it and to find it meaningful and relevant.

Tagore's entire life and work was impelled, I believe, by a longing for *purnatā*, wholeness or completeness. We find in Tagore a constant spirit of convergence; a bringing together of different streams into one river as great as the rivers that debouch into the Bay of Bengal. That spirit of convergence, reflected in the great river systems of your country, is what I believe Bengal above all can and should give to the world. The fact that you have the sensibility to do this, and have accumulated such a wealth of poetry and music and culture to express it, has something to do with the fact that Bengalis are not a conquering race. The British famously categorised them as 'non-martial'. It is a rather dismal fact that those nations—from the Romans to the Spanish or the British—who have given a lot to the world in material or administrative or political terms, are also those who have been conquerors, and have therefore brought tyranny and arrogance and oppression quite as much as they have spawned politics or bureaucracy or educational advance. Bengalis have not been imperialists or conquerors, and that is precisely why their gifts to the world have been more intangible. But as the poetic examples I have given you today have shown, the most intangible gifts are actually the most profound.

Rabindranath Tagore
The Next Fifty Years

The name of this conference is 'Tagore: The Global Impact of the Writer in the Community', and my subject is, 'Rabindranath Tagore: The Next Fifty Years.' These are huge, sweeping topics, and I must admit that when I sat down to write this address I suddenly felt confused and overwhelmed. The numerous events that I have attended all over the world, ever since Tagore's 150th birth-anniversary celebrations began at the end of 2009, have emphatically shown what a truly gigantic figure Tagore was. He wrote so much, he did so much, he created so much. His career was truly global. There seems to be no place in the world where you can't find pieces of his legacy. You only have to glance through the programme that has been drawn up for this conference to see the enormous range and diversity of topics we are going to have to tackle. Where shall I start?

Because of the struggle I felt and still feel, this lecture is going to be punctuated by four interludes that I hope will both reconnect me with my subject and draw all of you in, too: the first at the beginning, two more in the course of it, and a fourth at the end. The relevance of these interludes to my argument may not be immediately apparent at the beginning, but I hope will be so by the end.

Bengalis say that for every mood, every experience they can find a song by Tagore that reflects it. So let me start with a song: one that reflected my own initial state of mind. It is a late song, written in 1937, one of a group of songs written for a *Barshāmangal* or Festival of the Rains held in Kolkata on 4–5 September that year:

Chinile nā āmāre ki, 'Did you not know me?' Here is a translation by the French musicologist, Alain Daniélou, one of his *Poèmes chantés*, his beautiful arrangements for voice and piano of eighteen songs by Tagore:

When you came to me in the night of storm and rain
How could you think me gone?

Lampless I waited alone
In the darkened corner, lost in dream I waited
And you went away finding no one
In that dark and silent house, waiting
You then went away

When you came to me in the night of storm and rain
How could you think me gone?

When you came so near me, how could you forget
That at a touch my door will open, at the lightest touch?

But this mischance changed my fate
The ship of love at that moment
Crashed upon the shore, helpless
How could you think me gone?

In the howling wind, all night
I waited counting the hours
In the storm how could I hear the sound of your wheel
In the storm how could I hear?
While the storm was raging and the thunder rolling,
Clasping my breast I lay weeping and trembling with fear
While the lightning in the bitter sky
Scrawled its curses again and again

When you came to me in the night of storm and rain
How could you think me gone?[1]

As with so many of Tagore's songs, you can read different things into it according to your mood or sensibility. I found an echo of my bewilderment, my sense of block and isolation. Others may find in it a reflection of some kind of rupture in a human relationship. For Tagore himself, the stress and foreboding in the song may have been a premonition of the serious illness that was to strike him unconscious for nearly 48 hours on 10 September 1937, soon after the *Barshāmangal*. What is undeniable, whatever your personal interpretation of the song, is its impact. As soon as you know the meaning of the words, it becomes both piercingly personal and achingly universal. We would not be here today, holding this conference, if Tagore had not had the power to achieve this kind of emotional impact—first in his native Bengal, and then internationally.

If I felt confused when I embarked on writing this lecture, then I can take some comfort not only in the fact that there are numerous songs and poems by Tagore that match the mood I felt, but also because Tagore himself, when he became internationally famous, also often felt deeply confused by the role that he was expected to play. In my reading recently of his letters to C. F. Andrews, I was struck by how recurrent his feelings of confusion were, how frequently he felt he had strayed into roles which, as a poet, he felt ill-equipped for, and which he felt did not suit him. He frequently pined for times when he had been more innocent and carefree, for a 'lost paradise of mind' when he could be 'fully what I am':

> And am I not a poet? What business have I to be anything else? But unfortunately I am like an inn, where the poet lodger has to

[1] 'Quand tu es venu'/'When you came to me', *Poèmes chantés/Song-poems*, transcription, traduction et adaptation pour voix et piano par Alain Daniélou. Éditions Michel de Maule, Paris 2005, p. 66.

> accommodate strange bedfellows by his side. Yet is it not high time for me to retire from this none too lucrative business of the innkeeper?[2]

That was from a letter written to Andrews from Santiniketan on 9 July 1917. Four years later, on 26 February 1921, during a highly successful tour of the United States, he wrote to Andrews in a similar vein, regretting that the 'Schoolmaster' in him had taken over from the poet:

> Why have I been made to carry this burden, I ask myself over and over again, shouting myself hoarse in this noisy world where everyone is crying up his own wares? Pushing the wheelbarrows of propaganda from continent to continent—is this going to be the climax of a poet's life? It seems to be like an evil dream, from which I occasionally wake up in the dead of night and grope about in the bed asking myself in consternation: 'Where is my music?'[3]

Five months later, on the voyage back, his anxiety about his prophetic role and peddling of messages was even greater:

> Who is there to save a poet from disaster? Can anyone give me back my good-for-nothingness? Can anyone restore me to the provision with which I began life's journey to the realm of inutility? One day I shall have to fight my way out of my reputation; for the call of my Padma river still comes to me through this huge and growing barrier. It says to me: 'Poet, where are you?' And all my heart and soul try to seek out that poet. It has become difficult to find him. For the great multitude of men have heaped honours on him, and he cannot be extricated from under them.[4]

These are heart-rending words. Let us keep this fundamental tension in mind, between the poet who wanted to be above all carefree, idle, 'good-for-nothing', and the man who felt obliged to preach, to

[2] Rabindranath Tagore: *Letters to a Friend.* Edited with two introductory essays by C. F. Andrews, George Allen & Unwin, London 1928, p. 75.

[3] Ibid., p. 126.

[4] Ibid., pp. 175–76 (5 July 1921).

spread a message, to try to do good in the world, as we now consider how Tagore's image has fared in the world over the years, what has been added to it during these past two years of birth-anniversary celebrations, and what changes and further developments we can expect in the future.

Poet or prophet? Creative artist or the 'sage of Santiniketan'? There is no doubt that during the first phase of Tagore's international reputation, the second of these two identities prevailed. The tone, the impression, the expectation was established right at the beginning at the famous soiree on the 7 July 1912 at William Rothenstein's house in Hampstead, North London, when Tagore was presented to a gathering of intellectuals, and his translations of *Gitanjali* were read out by W. B. Yeats. It was his sage-like demeanour and appearance, his air of mystic serenity that made the most abiding impression. For those who were there he 'made present for me forever the divine thing that I can only find by flashes and with an agonising uncertainty' (May Sinclair); he was 'a sweet creature beautiful to the eye in a silk turban…speaks very little but looks beneficent and intelligent' (Thomas Sturge Moore); he made it possible to 'imagine a powerful and gentle Christ, which I never could before' (Frances Cornford).[5] When Yeats wrote his introduction to *Gitanjali*, he consolidated this impression with similar language, quoting a Bengali doctor whom he met as saying of Tagore, 'He is the first among our saints who has not refused to live, but has spoken out of Life itself, and that is why we give him our love.'[6]

At all the Tagore conferences that I have attended over the last two years, there have been papers on Tagore's *Rezeptionsgeschichte*, the history of his reception in various lands. Though he experienced wide differences of social and political circumstance, and though his speeches on his extensive travels ranged through religion, education, aesthetics, nationalism, universalism and more, the story in these papers (in the Western world at least: in the Far East, in Persia and in India itself it

[5] For further details, see the Introduction to *Gitanjali* (2011).

[6] *Gitanjali* (2011), Appendix C, p. 166.

was rather more complex) has essentially been one of variations on a theme: that of the seer from the East, to whom people flocked not so much for his poetry but because he had wise and spiritual things to say. The only exceptions to the rule, perhaps, were Soviet Russia in 1930, where the spiritual message had to be suppressed in favour of his concern with rural reconstruction and the education of the poor, and Spain, which Tagore never visited, where the focus fell—and has continued to fall throughout the Spanish-speaking world to this day—on Tagore the poet, rather than Tagore the preacher.

This was because Tagore's translator into Spanish, the famous poet Juan Ramón Jiménez, working with his English-speaking wife Zenobia Cambrubí Aymar, replaced Yeats' introduction to *Gitanjali* with a prose poem which addressed Tagore very much as a fellow poet. Jiménez went on prefacing each book of Tagore that he and his wife translated with a poem of his own, and although his notions of Tagore as a poet were undoubtedly limited by what he was able to gain from Tagore's own English translations (he never had any personal contact with Bengalis or Indians), the focus on Tagore throughout the Hispanic world has remained unusually literary, much less devotional than it was elsewhere.

In the English-speaking world, the image of Tagore the prophet rather than Tagore the poet became entrenched and has proved very hard to shift. For a long time it seemed that only Unitarians or those with an abiding interest in his spiritual teaching were attracted to him. Edward Thompson tried heroically with his book *Rabindranath Tagore, Poet and Dramatist* of 1926 (revised and expanded in 1948 after Tagore had died), to show that Tagore was a poet of true originality and genius, but his work fell largely on deaf ears, partly perhaps because it lacked any critical assessment of Tagore's stories or novels. Just how entrenched attitudes to Tagore among the British literary establishment still are—negative, because they have tended to be anti-spiritual—was dismally shown in 2011 by articles in the *Guardian* by Ian Jack, who recommended that we should forget that Tagore was a poet at all, and by the Notebook column at the back of the *Times*

Literary Supplement (TLS), which began with the rhetorical question 'Who reads Rabindranath Tagore now? Not many, it is safe to say. Yet a century ago, Tagore, whose 150th anniversary falls this year, was all the rage.' (The *Guardian* has recently redeemed itself with an excellent leader on Tagore, published on 30 April 2012.)

Unknown to the writer of the TLS Notebook, however, a fight-back on behalf of Tagore the poet and writer has been unfolding, in Britain, in Germany, in India, and many other countries. It would have been difficult to organize this and many other conferences and events without the existence of this 'new wave' on which so many people with an interest in Tagore now ride, especially those who do not have access to the Bengali language. Many new translations have been done, direct from Bengali, and discussions of Tagore are by no means restricted now to his own translations or to the secondary translations thereof that were done in his lifetime. My *Selected Poems* of Tagore, first published in 1985, perhaps opened a door, but it was a door through which many other people have gone through—Ketaki Kushari Dyson here in Britain, Martin Kämpchen in Germany, Victor van Bijlert in Netherlands, and Hannele Pohjanmies in Finland. In India many new translations especially of Tagore's fiction and essays, published by Penguin India, and by Oxford University Press under the editorship of Sukanta Chaudhuri came out. Recently the massive compendium *The Essential Tagore*, edited by Fakrul Alam and Radha Chakravarty, was published by Harvard University Press and Visva-Bharati (2011).

Add to all the new translations critical studies such as *Rabindranath Tagore's the Home and the World: A Critical Companion*, edited by P. K. Dutta (2003), and the mainstream publication of Krishna Dutta and Andrew Robinson's biography *Rabindranath Tagore: The Myriad-Minded Man* (1995) and its companion volume of their *Selected Letters of Rabindranath Tagore*, published by Cambridge University Press (1997), and you had, when all the 150th birth-anniversary celebrations started, a situation in which Tagore the poet and writer had emerged sufficiently strongly for conferences and events to be able to give just as much emphasis to Tagore the writer as to Tagore the man with a message.

So where are we now, and what trends and challenges can we discern for the future?

That last question, so difficult to answer, gives me a lead into my second interlude: a poem from *Gitanjali*, no. 27 in the standard text of Tagore's translation, no. 49 in his manuscript. I will read it to you in my own new translation. In Bengali, this is the song *Kothāy alo, kothāy ore ālo!*

Where's the light, the light?
Ignite it with the fire of longing
    The lamp is there, but no flame
    What is this doom on my brow?
Death would be preferable
Light the lamp with the fire of longing

Pain's envoy sings, 'O breath of life,
    God stays awake for you'
Pain's envoy sings, 'O breath of life,
    God stays awake for you
Shrouded in the dark
He calls you to a tryst
Valuing you for your sorrow,
    God stays awake'

The sky is crammed with clouds
    Rain pours down
In the depth of this night for what
    Am I suddenly awake?
Why is my breath thus caught?
    Rain pours down

Lightning, flaming for an instant,
just makes the darkness thicker
Lightning, flaming for an instant,
just makes the darkness thicker
I do not know where, far away,
A song with a bleak tune
Drags my life down a path
where the dark thickens

Where's the light, the light?
Ignite it with the fire of longing
Clouds thunder, wind howls
Time passes, but this deep night,
Black as a whetstone, doesn't pass
Light love's lamp with my breath
Ignite it with the fire of longing[7]

The 'new wave' in Tagore appreciation began in the mid-1980s which has done a lot to make Tagore the poet and writer credible and present again on the international stage, counter-balancing the earlier image of him as a sage and a prophet. The earlier phase, that of Tagore's reputation in his own lifetime, certainly took care of the word 'global'; the second phase from 1985 to the beginnings of the 150th birth-anniversary phase has done a lot to confirm and substantiate the word 'writer'. But the reading I have just given you of that wonderful song from *Gitanjali* was a performance. And this signifies what has been added to Tagore's image by all the anniversary celebrations. It is the *performative* aspect: Tagore as a creative artist who operated not just with the written word, but with music, drama, and dance. Looking back through all the celebrations, it is extraordinary how rich they have been in highly creative performances, and it is all the

[7] *Gitanjali* (2011), pp. 67–68.

more remarkable to note that many of these took place in the context of conferences and academic gatherings at which one would never normally expect such things.

In December 2009, Reba Som, Director of the Indian Council for Cultural Relations' Tagore Centre in Kolkata, organised a remarkable festival, 'Tagore Beyond Frontiers', which was designed as a curtain-raiser for all the many world-wide celebrations to follow, but which also, in retrospect, set a distinctively innovative and creative tone. It included performances of his dance-drama *Natīr pūjā* and his famous play *Dākghar* ('The Post-Office'); it even included a fashion show of outfits for women in the nineteenth century on which the Tagore family had an influence.

But what I particularly and vividly remember from the festival was Tanushree Shankar's dance production based on Tagore's English poem 'The Child'. This was a wonderfully youthful and athletic display that was performed to an exhilarating sound-track that included Schubert's Ave Maria sung—at full volume—in Bengali. My friend Martin Kämpchen was there, and I remember that we agreed after the performance that this—though we couldn't at that point say exactly how—represented the future, the way that Tagore and his significance are likely to be carried forward.

As I cast my mind back through the last two years, and leaf through the pile of conference brochures and publications and anthologies that have accumulated, I find that the *performance*s are what emerge most strongly in my memory. Events such as Debashish and Rohini Raychaudhuri's performance of Rabindrasangit—without accompaniment!—at the Dartington Tagore Festival in May 2011; or Valerie Doulton's production of *The Post-Office* at the Nehru Centre and the British Library; or the *Liederabend* of western musical settings of Tagore by brilliant student musicians from the Musikhochschule in Stuttgart, that was part of the 'Rabindranath Tagore und Deutschland' event that Martin Kämpchen organised at Deutsche Literaturarchiv in Marbach back in March 2011; or the 'Waves of Joy' music and dance sequence put on by Sharmila Roy Pommot during the tribute to

Tagore held at the Smithsonian Institute in Washington DC; or 'Flying Man', the programme of poems for the twenty-first century with jazz improvisations by Zoe and Idris Rahman that I myself took part in at the British Library; or the reading I did from *Gitanjali* with songs from it sung by Reba Som at a small studio theatre in Lund, Sweden, where a Tagore song was also sung by a local choir trained by Bubu Eklund; or the stunning fusion of Tagorean dance, Rabindrasangit and flamenco that concluded the 'Tagore En España' Festival in Valladolid; or the dance and song performance on Tagore's songs of the monsoon and the autumn put on by the Netherlands Bengali community as part of the international Tagore seminar organised by the Friends of the Kern Institute in Leiden in September 2011; or Ash Mukherjee's wonderful 'Song of the City' ballet put on by Akademi: The Centre for South Asian Dance, in the uniquely chilly and spooky Southwark Vaults in London; or the exquisitely performed recording of arrangements of Rabindrasangit for string quartet that Partha Chatterjee played us at the 'My Tagore; why Tagore' seminar held in Ahmedabad in October 2011; or the performance in February 2012 before an audience of more than six hundred people in Kolkata of Tagore's play *Rājā* in English, directed by Debashish Raychaudhuri in which I was privileged to play the part of the invisible Raja; or the performance not so far away from us here in Hexham, Northumberland of Alain Daniélou's magical versions of Rabindrasangit for voice and piano, performed by two local musicians with readings and commentary from me in November 2011. I could go on and on, and each one of those memorable events would deserve a description as long as this lecture.

What all these performances and experiments show is that Tagore, in the twenty-first century, is taking on a profile and a significance akin to Shakespeare in the sense that it is simply impossible to separate the academic discussion of Tagore or the translation of Tagore or the teaching of Tagore from the *performance* of Tagore. This is hugely exciting, and I am personally proud of what I may have done to help some of these developments forward. They make me prepared to bet that, as the years go on this century, we will see Tagore being used more and more worldwide as an extraordinarily rich resource for the performing arts.

For my third interlude let me read you, in my new translation, another poem from *Gitanjali* that reflects his creative vitality, the spark he transmitted that is beginning to light such spectacular fires. It is a sonnet, originally published in Tagore's book *Naibedya* (1901), and I have translated it into English sonnet form. We live in an age of performance and visual transmission: a writer who becomes part of it becomes inseparable from life itself, and connects with 'community' in the title of this conference, because communities these days are not just local—they are connected electronically across national, political or cultural barriers.

The wave upon wave of life that night and day
Rushes through every vein of this body of mine
Is the great triumph of life that, in the same way,
Dances worldwide with marvellous rhythm and line—
Is the same life that soundlessly, joyously through
Every pore of the earth's skin upwardly pushes
Blades of grass in their billions, stimulates new
Flowers and leaves—year after year it gushes
And swings like tides of birth and death that grow
And ebb on the world-ocean endlessly.
I feel that those ceaseless waves of life now flow
In my limbs, a source of immense strength in me.
    That vast vibration, age after age advancing,
    Through all my veins today is dancing, dancing.[8]

A second feature of the current, anniversary phase of Tagore's reception is that Tagore the prophet, Tagore the thinker, is by no means dead. He has not been supplanted either by Tagore the poet/writer, or by Tagore in the performing arts. What we have seen at the

[8] *Gitanjali* (2011), p. 84.

more academic events that have been held is increasingly serious and sophisticated attention being given to his ideas, particularly in the fields of history, education, feminism, nationalism, universalism, and issues to do with rural development and the environment. This is not some kind of revival of the mindless admiration for the wise man of the East; it is a serious and scholarly appraisal of ideas that were complex and constantly changing in the light of experience and circumstances.

Amartya Sen, in his lecture on 'Why we still need Tagore' at the British Library, London, on 6 May, 2011, set the tone for this new kind of intellectual respect. Read Michael Collins' excellent book, *Empire, Nationalism and the Postcolonial World: Rabindranath Tagore's Writings on History, Politics and Society* (Routledge, 2011), or Sabyasachi Bhattacharya's brilliant new intellectual biography, *Rabindranath Tagore: An Interpretation* (Penguin Viking India, New Delhi, 2011), and you will find a Tagore who, in his day—and for our day too, through his writings—had all the characteristics of what we would nowadays call a 'public intellectual'. I am sure we will hear more about this intellectual side to Tagore and we shall also rightly hear about Tagore the activist—the campaigner (to use another present-day term) who strove to put his ideas into practical effect, at Shelidah, Santiniketan and Sriniketan, the early history of which has been expertly researched by Uma Das Gupta and Kathleen O'Connell.

A third aspect of Tagore that we have seen emerging very strongly during this birth-anniversary period, in addition to the performative, intellectual and activist aspects, is that of Tagore the painter. I haven't yet seen a compendium of the critical responses to the exhibitions of Tagore's paintings that have been held over the last year in Berlin, Paris, London, New York and Chicago, so it is too early for me to assess what impact they have had. In London, the exhibition suffered a bit from the rather cramped, shoebox-like room that was chosen for it at the Victoria & Albert Museum, and the lack of publicity even at the entrance of the museum. But in Chicago, where I recently gave a lecture connected with the Tagore exhibition at the Art Institute, the paintings seemed to me to have a stunning effect, because of the beauty and spaciousness of the hanging, the excellence of the commentary, and the proximity of the paintings to masterpieces in the museum to which Tagore seemed fully commensurate.

In a way, it is a shame that an exhibition as great as that has to be dismantled and be sent back home to India. What a difference it would make to Tagore's profile worldwide if there were substantial groups of his paintings on loan to major art galleries across the world. This is something that I hope the authorities in India will begin to think about, because it is far better that they should be displayed in that way than stored, out of sight, in a strong-room at Rabindra-Bhavan, Santiniketan.

For the fourth and last of my interludes I would like to show you, without any comment, a few of Tagore's paintings. We had a song at the beginning; two poems along the way; now we are going to see what he called his 'versification in line'. Common to all three genres is the uniquely Tagorean quality of *rhythm* which is what unites all his creations and activities into what he called *purnatā*—completeness, fullness, wholeness. Tagore wrote in his essay 'My Pictures':

> But one thing which is common to all arts is the principle of rhythm which transforms inert materials into living creations. My instinct for it and my training in its use led me to know that lines and colours in art are no carriers of information; they seek their rhythmic incarnation in pictures.[9]

The pictures were liberating for him—and are liberating for us today—because they expressed his rhythmic creativity in its purest, freest form, untrammelled by his moral preoccupations.

In a letter to Andrews from New York on 14 January 1921, speaking of the danger of narrowness and negativity in Gandhi's non-cooperation campaigns, Tagore wrote: 'The complete man must never be sacrificed to the patriotic man, or even to the merely moral man.'[10] What has

[9] *English Writings* (1996), vol. 3, p. 635.
[10] *Letters to a Friend* (1928), p. 115.

been so positive and exciting about this whole birth-anniversary period is that something in the worldwide perception of Tagore that was inert and not quite living has begun to take on new, real, rhythmic life, and the 'complete man' in him has started to dance.

Previously, during the prophetic phase of Tagore's reception, that rhythm and those dance-steps were barely perceived at all, because everything was communicated through English—through self-translations in which it was difficult for Tagore fully to express his voice—and through secondary translations of his English. In the second phase, what we might call the literary phase, the rhythm and the dance began to emerge in some translations. Certainly in my own translations I tried to capture the movement of the original; but it is only in this third, the birth-anniversary phase, that the rhythm of Tagore is actually starting to be heard, through performance, through exposure to the paintings, and also through close study of his intellectual writings, because, just as there is rhythm in his feelings and their artistic expression, so there is rhythm in his thoughts and his way of constructing an argument.

Before I end, let me briefly list a few areas where I think we need further attention and development, things that I hope will indeed be pursued during the next fifty years. In this, the new Scottish Centre of Tagore Studies, whose inauguration we celebrate today, and its co-partner the Centre for Literature and Writing at Edinburgh Napier University (ScoTs and CLAW—what splendid acronyms!)—will undoubtedly have a significant part to play.

1. We need to return to Tagore's *religious ideas*. His poetry and songs are never far away from them. People have been nervous of exploring them, because we have been living through a largely secular age, and because the focus on Tagore's spirituality during the first, prophetic phase of appreciation produced so much nonsense. But read Tagore's writings on religious and spiritual topics in Bengali—especially the beautiful sermons that he delivered at Santiniketan and which were collected into the two volumes called *Sāntiniketan*—and you will find every religious emotion from grief

and struggle to serenity and joy, expressed with precision and truth. Read many of his letters, his English letters too, for example to C. F. Andrews, and you will find the same qualities.

2. Rabindrasangit needs to be performed and transmitted worldwide with freedom from inappropriate accompaniments. In terms of probing and communicating the feelings of the songs, I think we can go a lot further. We need to go deeper and deeper into the songs of Tagore, and if this is done, they will take their place among the supremely great poetic and musical legacies of the world.
3. Tagore's *plays* need to be widely performed, in vigorous new translations and adaptations, with directors feeling as free and creative as Tagore himself encouraged his students and collaborators to be in performances in Santiniketan in his lifetime.
4. We need more *critical appreciation* of his literary works. Many of them are profoundly mysterious and bafflingly complex. Readers need help with them, just as they do with Dante or Shakespeare or Goethe or any great writer. They need to be able to connect his creative works with his life and ideas. It occurred to me recently that a book needs to be written which would simply take a number of major literary works by Tagore, and analyse them clearly and accessibly to the benefit of students and the general reader of today.
5. Finally, we sometimes need—though this may not be a tactful thing to say at the start of a conference—to stop talking about Tagore and to stand back and to simply *contemplate* him. This is after all what we do with all great artists. There is a place for scholarship, for analysis, for conferences, for discussion and all the rest. But at the end of the day, if Tagore is to continue to mean something to us in the twenty-first century we need to gaze, contemplate, listen, and wonder.

Keynote address of the conference *'Tagore: The Global Impact of the Writer in the Community',* Scottish Centre of Tagore Studies (Scots), Napier University, Edinburgh, 4 May 2012.

Photo Essay

By

Martin Kämpchen

Photo 1

William Radice's life is intimately interwoven with India. As he tells us in his essays, he visited India in his youth and then, impressed by this country and its culture, decided to learn Bengali in London. Extremely language-gifted, Radice began reading Bengali poetry and prose after only one year. He was deeply influenced by his mother, Betty Radice, who was a translator of Latin classics for Penguin Books. William began to translate India's Nobel Prize winning writer Rabindranath Tagore's poems. His translations transformed the way Tagore was appreciated and accepted outside Bengal and even in Bengal.

William Radice was a lecturer of Bengali at SOAS, University of London all his working life, but he was foremost a poet in English and, with the sensibilities of a poet, became a competent and inspired translator.

Photo 2

Photo 3

The Wayfaring Translator

William Radice's many visits to India and Bangladesh, to European countries and to the USA are connected to lectures, conferences, seminars and visiting professorships. From 2011 to 2013, India celebrated Rabindranath's 150th birth anniversary, the centenary of the publication of *Gitanjali* and the subsequent award of the Nobel Prize for Literature to Tagore. William Radice was invited to events in Asia, in Europe and in North America. There are few major events which he did not attend. Here we see William Radice addressing a seminar in Ahmedabad (photo 2) in October 2011, organized by Shailesh Patel, and participating at a seminar in Marbach (Germany) in March 2011 (photo 3), organized by the Deutsche Literaturarchiv. Radice delivered his speech in German. From left are Christian Weiss, Alokeranjan Dasgupta, Martin Kämpchen, William Radice, Rahul Peter Das and Marcel Lepper of the Deutsche Literaturarchiv.

Photo 4

Photo 5

Photo 6

After the seminars and conferences there was time for personal exchanges which are almost as important as the formal deliberations. Taking food together is always a way to come closer to scholarly colleagues and students still unknown. William Radice is a social person and loves to interact with colleagues and audiences.

We see (photo 5) from left Partha Ghosh, Elizabeth and William Radice, Debashish and Rohini Raychaudhuri in Ahmedabad. William is deeply interested in music, also in Rabindrasangit. His favourite singers, Debashish Raychaudhuri and his daughter Rohini, often accompanied William when they gave lecture-concerts together. William never forgets that he is an author. Wherever possible, his books are on sale and he loves to sign them, as every author does (photo 6).

Photo 7

Photo 8

William Radice often visited East Europe for lectures and seminars on Rabindranath. Here we see him in Sigisoara, Romania (photo7) and at Budapest, Hungary; photo 8 shows William (back row) together with other Tagore scholars.

Photo 9

Photo 10

Delhi and Santiniketan are the places, apart from Kolkata, that William Radice visited most often in India. Also he was always ready to travel to Dhaka in support of Tagore Studies. In Santiniketan he stayed for prolonged periods when he prepared his *Selected Poems* of Tagore and again in 2010 when he prepared his new Gitanjali translation. We see him with the Librarian of Rabindra-Bhavan in Santiniketan (photo 9) and sightseeing in Delhi (photo 10).

Photo 11

Photo 12

Photo 13

Photo 14

Photo 15

Memories

William Radice is associated with the Tagore Centre UK in London and its founder, Kalyan Kundu, from very early on (photo 11 of 1988). William travelled sometimes taking his family along. Here he poses with his wife Elizabeth and one daughter in front of old monuments in Delhi (photo 12 of 1998). William loves to play the piano and listen to music; he also cooks. For a while he found much-needed relaxation in knitting. We see him proudly displaying a self-knit pullover (photo 13 of 2009). Until recently the family lived in the village Riding Mill, Northumberland, in the north of England. There, one of his poems was unveiled as a plaque among friends and neighbours (photo 14 of 2012). While travelling, he is apt to make numerous friends, so with the cat Mina in Chittagong (photo 15 of 2012).

Photo 16

Retired and active

Now Elizabeth and William Radice lead a retired life in Cambridge, UK near one of their daughters' home. Here we see them sitting in the Botanical Garden near their home (photo of 2016).

PHOTO CREDITS:

Rabindra-Bhavan, Santiniketan 1, 9.

Shailesh Parekh, Ahmedabad 2, 5.

Deutsches Literaturarchiv, Marbach (Germany) 3.

Martin Kämpchen, Santiniketan 16.

Imre Bangha 7, 8.

Kalyan Kundu 11.

All other photos have been provided by Elizabeth and Helen Radice. We thank all of them for their assistance.